**Oryx Sourcebook Series
in Business and Management**

Women in Administration and Management
An Information Sourcebook

Oryx Sourcebook Series in Business and Management

Paul Wasserman, Series Editor

**Oryx Sourcebook Series
in Business and Management**

Women in Administration and Management

An Information Sourcebook

by Judith A. Leavitt
Supervisor, Rockwell International—Collins Division, Cedar Rapids
Information Center

Phoenix • New York
ORYX PRESS
1988

016.658
L 439w

The rare Arabian Oryx is believed to have inspired the myth of the unicorn. This desert antelope became virtually extinct in the early 1960s. At that time several groups of international conservationists arranged to have 9 animals sent to the Phoenix Zoo to be the nucleus of a captive breeding herd. Today the Oryx population is over 400 and herds have been returned to reserves in Israel, Jordan, and Oman.

1 0001 000 002 317

Copyright © 1988 by
The Oryx Press
2214 North Central at Encanto
Phoenix, Arizona 85004-1483
Published simultaneously in Canada

Printed and Bound in the United States of America

∞ The paper used in this publication meets the minimum requirements of American National Standard for Information Science—Permanence of Paper for Printed Library Materials, ANSI Z39.48, 1984.

Library of Congress Cataloging-in-Publication Data

Leavitt, Judith A.
   Women in administration and management : an information sourcebook / Judith A. Leavitt.
   p. cm. — (Oryx sourcebook series in business and management ; no. 7)
   Updated ed. of: Women in management. 1982.
   Includes indexes.
   ISBN 0-89774-379-2
   1. Women executives—United States—Bibliography.   I. Leavitt, Judith A. Women in management.   II. Title.   III. Series.
Z7963.E7L43   1988
[HD6054.4.U6]
016.658'0088042—dc19   87-23192

To my sisters
Susan, Jane, and Marsha

For there is no friend like a sister
In calm or stormy weather;
To cheer one on the tedious way,
To fetch one if one goes astray,
To lift one if one totters down,
To strengthen whilst one stands.
Christina Rossetti (1830–1894)

Contents

Introduction

LITERATURE—1981 to 1986

The literature on women in management from 1981 to 1986 addresses many of the same themes as the literature of the previous ten years: salaries, mentors, networking, management training, women as directors and bosses, comparisons of men and women managers, and the psychology of women in management. However, three new themes appear in the recent literature. Their development seems to be a direct result of the progress of women managers.

First, several observers write about the "glass ceiling," or the obstacles that keep women from progressing to top management. The authors of *Breaking the Glass Ceiling*[1] studied seventy-six "successful" women for three years. They concluded that the same barriers that kept women out of top management in the 1970s will continue to impede their progress into the twenty-first century: the pressures of combining career and family, lack of line management skills, little support from senior executives, male resentment of women's success, increased competition, and few female role models or mentors. These issues are covered in the chapter Progress and Status of Women in Management and the chapter entitled Obstacles.

Second, there is a large body of literature on the theme of entrepreneurship. With job satisfaction and the need to achieve as the prime motivators, women started small businesses at six times the rate of men from 1974 to 1984. By 1986, there were 3 million women-owned businesses in the United States, almost half of them in the service sector. A U.S. Small Business Administration spokeswoman comments on this phenomenon: "The 1970s was the decade of women entering management, and the 1980s is turning out to be the decade of the woman entrepreneur."[2]

Alex Taylor's August 18, 1986, article in *Fortune* magazine, "Why Women Managers Are Bailing Out," is a thoughtful review of

---

1. Ann M. Morrison, Randall P. White, and Ellen Van Velsor. *Breaking the Glass Ceiling: Can Women Reach the Top of America's Largest Corporations?* Reading, MA: Addison-Wesley, 1987.
2. Earl C. Gottschalk, Jr., "Distaff Owners: More Women Start up Their Own Businesses, with Major Successes." *Wall Street Journal* (May 17, 1983): 1.

what some observers call a new trend, i.e., the growing number of women managers who are leaving the corporate world to start their own businesses. According to Taylor, executive women leave corporations for a variety of reasons: they find it is harder for women than it is for men to get ahead, they believe they are not paid as well as their male colleagues, they feel stifled by organizational rigidity, and the demands of combining family and career and the strains in two-career families are too great. The stories of these corporate "drop-outs" are covered in the chapters entitled Women Business Owners and Women Entrepreneurs.

With the increase in the number of management women in the workplace, a third issue arose—the personal and work relationships of management men and women—thus, a chapter entitled Sex and Romance. Eliza Collins, senior editor of the *Harvard Business Review*, provoked a debate in the literature over the appropriate way to handle office romance in her September/October 1983 *Harvard Business Review* article "Managers and Lovers."

In the past five years alone (1981–1986), more than 800 new pieces of literature were identified, indicating an increasing interest in the topic of women in management in both the scholarly and popular literature.

STATUS OF WOMEN IN MANAGEMENT

What changes have occurred in the status of women in management in the past five years as reported in the literature? These statistics present a concise picture:

- The U.S. Department of Labor Statistics reports that women held 36 percent of all executive, managerial, and administrative positions in the United States in 1985. However, women are still only 5 percent of upper-level managers, according to the U.S. Department of Commerce, Bureau of the Census, as reported in *Money Income of Households, Families and Persons in the United States, Series,* P-60, No. 142, 1984.
- In ten years the number of women earning MBA degrees increased 344 percent, compared with 25 percent for men (1976 to 1986). Women were 26 percent of all MBA candidates in 1981. That figure had grown to 33 percent by 1986.
- A 1986 Equal Employment Opportunity Commission source shows that progress has been minimal for black women executives. From 1974 to 1984 the percent of black women officials and managers grew only slightly—from .7 percent of the total number of officials and managers in the United States to 1.7 percent.
- From 1970 to 1985, notes the U.S. Bureau of Labor Statistics, the number of couples in which both are managers,

professionals, or technical employees grew from 1.7 million to 3.5 million.

- Male views about women managers are changing. In a 1965 *Harvard Business Review* article, only 9 percent of the males surveyed held "strongly favorable" attitudes toward women managers. In a duplicate survey conducted twenty years later, 33 percent of the males indicated "strongly favorable" attitudes toward women executives.
- In a Columbia University study, Mary Anne Devanna found that female MBA graduates are paid the same starting salaries as male graduates with the same qualifications. Within ten years, however, the women are earning 20 percent less, regardless of company or position.
- Catalyst, a nonprofit organization that studies career and family issues and the needs of working women, reported in 1986 that 44 percent of the top 1,000 U.S. corporations have at least one woman board director, but within that group of companies, there is still only one woman chief executive officer (Katherine Graham of the *Washington Post*). Catalyst predicts that by 1990 women will represent 45.3 percent of the workforce.
- One percent of working women earned over $50,000 in 1986, compared with 9 percent of working men. In 1985 only 12 percent of all working women earned more than $20,000 a year.
- The number of self-employed women rose 43 percent from 1975 to 1985 according to U.S. Bureau of Labor Statistics figures. By 1984 women owned 25 percent of all small businesses in America, and women are starting small businesses at three times the rate of men.

THE FUTURE

The growing numbers of working women in the United States has been called the "subtle revolution." The increasing numbers of executive and management women has changed and will continue to change the attitudes and actions of American businesses. Corporate leaders would do well to heed this advice from Mary Cunningham, author of the article "Corporate Culture Determines Productivity."

> There are numerous direct costs associated with a corporate culture that does not include women as a normal part of organization activity, particularly at the highest levels of decision-making. The loss in productivity as a result of resentment or frustration is not obvious but it is nonetheless real. If such rejection ultimately causes the woman to leave, the time and money spent on her training are an obvious waste.
>
> In my opinion, people are our most underutilized resource in

America today. And to the extent that we continue to accept barriers which prevent certain talented individuals from achieving the most responsible levels of corporate power, we are wasting the intelligence, creativity, and judgment of our people. Can this country really afford to pay such a price for discrimination?[3]

Acknowledgements

Special thanks to Barry Buelow, Craig Martinson, and Dennis Sutherland for technical assistance. Their generosity is greatly appreciated.

To Coleen Beck, Debra Hawes, Julie Petersen, Marlene Sigwarth, and Kathy Visser, with gratitude. Their efficiency, professionalism, and teamwork make supervision a joy.

Most of all, a special thank you to David, Joe, and John for their love and support.

---

3. Mary Cunningham, "Corporate Culture Determines Productivity," *Industry Week* (May 4, 1981): 82–84, 86.

Progress and Status of
Women in Management

1. Baron, Alma S. "Women in Management: Another Look." *Personnel Administrator* 29 (August 1984): 14, 19.

Baron reports on a follow-up survey (1983) of 1978 research on women in management. While the number of women in professional and technical jobs grew 8.3 percent, and the number of women in managerial and administrative jobs grew 10 percent from 1979 to 1983, the women list, with few exceptions, the same problems reported in 1978. Time management was chosen by 22 percent of the women as the biggest problem in 1978—today poor top management is given as the most difficult management problem. In both 1978 and 1983, 16 percent of the women selected sexual discrimination as the biggest problem. The most significant change was in the area of career and family. In 1983, 7 percent more women are married, 14 percent more have children, and 43 percent indicate they would relocate for career advancement.

2. Bartlett, Robin L.; Poulton-Callahan, Charles; and Somers, Patricia. "What's Holding Women Back?" *Management World* 11 (November 1982): 8-10.

The authors chronicle the rise in women's labor force participation since the 1950s but point out that, while females accounted for 63 percent of all clerical workers in 1950, that number increased to 80 percent in 1980. Sex-role stereotypes, educational barriers, work experience, the hierarchical organization structure, lack of informal socializing, and lack of power keep women from attaining management positions in large numbers. In an insert, Janet Mason discusses the "feminine" characteristics women bring to management.

3. Bennett, Amanda. "Following the Leaders." *Wall Street Journal* (March 24, 1986): 10D-11D.

Unlike their predecessors of twenty years ago who started as secretaries, younger women are more likely to move into management positions directly after business school. Creative Research Associates interviewed women managers who have been working for ten or more years and earn $50,000 or more a year and full-time female MBA students. Findings indicate the younger women agonize more about career and family conflicts—their older colleagues often opted for one or the other. According to a recent Korn/Ferry study, 52 percent of successful women were divorced or unmarried, compared to only 5 percent of their male colleagues.

4. "Best Firms for Female Executives." *Duns Business Monthly* 124 (September 1984): 14, 19.

Management consultant and Yale University professor Rosabeth Moss Kanter compiled a list of the twelve best companies for women managers: AT & T, Atlantic Richfield, CBS, Control Data, General Electric Medical Systems Group, Hewlett-Packard, IBM, Merck & Co., Proctor & Gamble, Security Pacific Corp., Stop & Shop Cos., and U.S. West. The companies were selected for the number of women in top posts, the company attitude toward women's advancement, and the opportunities they provided women.

5. Blotnick, Srully. "Dangerous Times for Middle Managers." *Savvy* 7 (May 1986): 33-37.

Blotnick claims the corporate pyramid has turned into a diamond as the number of people who are stuck in middle management increases. He reviews how the management style of the 1970s became obsolete in the 1980s and describes for women managers in their twenties, thirties, and forties the appropriate and most effective management strategies.

6. Brophy, Beth, and Linnon, Nancy. "Why Women Execs Stop before the Top." *U.S. News and World Report* (January 5, 1987): 72-73.

A recent Korn/Ferry International survey of almost 1,400 senior executives found only twenty-nine women, and those female executives earned an average salary plus bonus of $116,810 compared to $215,000 for their male counterparts. Some of the barriers to women in top management include male managers' unease with women as peers, the pressures women executives encounter in balancing career and family, assumptions that women will refuse transfers, women choosing staff jobs rather than line jobs, and women's reluctance to negotiate salaries. More women are dropping out of the corporate world, because of the "glass ceiling," and companies must identify talented executive women and develop ways to move them into top management positions.

7. Brown, Linda Keller, and Kagan, Julia. "The Working Woman Survey: A Survey of Where Corporate Women Are Now and What They Want Next." *Working Woman* 7 (May 1982): 92-96.

Former director of the Cross-National Project on Women as Corporate Managers (Columbia University) and author of *The Woman Manager in the United States*, Brown coauthored this survey article on the corporate woman with *Working Woman* articles editor Julia Kagan. Data are from the July 1981 questionnaire answered by more than 1,500 readers. A picture of the executive woman emerges from the survey: a college graduate (6 percent have MBAs) with a median income of $21,900 who is isolated, because there are few, if any other, women at her level. Forty-seven percent of the respondents are married, and one-third have children. Inserts chart power profile, power industries, outside activities and memberships, what the women want, and satisfaction/optimism level.

8. Butcher, John. "Women in Management: The Government's Role."
Women in Management Review 1 (Winter 1986): 195-201.
Under Secretary of State at the Department of Trade and Industry
Butcher spoke at the Institute of Directors and *Working Woman* magazine conference on government's efforts on behalf of women and on the
work shadowing scheme. Butcher states that while women constitute 42
percent of the workforce, only 2 percent of all directors are women. He
reviews the obstacles to women, what measures can be taken to overcome those obstacles, and outlines steps the government is taking to
improve opportunities for women. Finally, he describes the work shadowing scheme, a program of the Institute of Directors. In work shadowing, sixth-form female students "shadow" women executives for a week
to learn first-hand about women's role in industry and management.

9. "Catalyst Honors Female Executives." *The Woman Engineer* 6
(Summer 1986): 12.
Catalyst, a nonprofit career and family organization, honored four top-
level American businesswomen for their overall leadership abilities at an
awards dinner attended by 800 people from the business community.
Catalyst predicts that by 1990 women will account for 45.3 percent of
the United States workforce and reports that 44 percent of the top 1,000
United States corporations have at least one women board director.
Other statistics: nine out of ten industrials have at least one woman
director; women now account for 45.4 percent of accounting degrees,
13.3 percent of engineering degrees, and 28.9 percent of MBA degrees.

10. Colwill, Nina L., and Erhart, Marilyn. "Have Women Changed the
Workplace?" *Business Quarterly* 50 (Spring 1985): 27-31.
Researchers interviewed fifteen men and fifteen women to ascertain
perceptions about the impact of women in the workplace over the past
twenty years. Only four of the thirty respondents felt that the women's
movement had had no effect on the workplace, and over half of those
surveyed believed that women have more chances to attain upper-level
and nontraditional jobs. Twenty-eight of the thirty respondents indicated
that women in the workplace have not affected the structure of their
organizations, and the majority said that women were more confident,
competent, and independent as a result of working. In response to a
question regarding their predictions about working women, most respondents believed that the number of women in the workforce would
continue to grow. Includes tables.

11. Cooper, Cary L. "Positive Action for Female Executives." *Women
in Management Review* 1 (Spring 1985): 15-18.
Forty percent of the graduates of management departments and business
schools in the United Kingdom are women, but they still have trouble
reaching middle- and senior-level management positions. Cooper challenges organizations to take positive action by setting annual goals,
targets, and deadlines for promoting women, to make these goals explicit
in the organization's annual report, to seriously consider parental leave,
and to consider career schemes that would allow women to manage the
demands of work and home. Finally, he suggests that women who work
part time be allowed prorated pensions and benefits.

12. Davidson, Marilyn J. "Women Managers: The Present and the Future." *Women in Management Review* 1 (Summer 1985): 91-94.

Although women are 30.5 percent of managers in the United States, 18.8 percent in the United Kingdom, 16 to 17 percent in Germany and France, and 11 to 15 percent in Scandinavia, European women are still managers in traditionally female occupations—retailing, catering, and personnel—and have limited educational and vocational training opportunities. The encouraging fact is that more women are entering male-dominated professions, and women now account for 40 percent of management or business degree students in the United Kingdom and 10 percent of MBA students. Includes tables and references.

13. "Documenting Women's Slow Moves into Management." *International Management* 40 (January 1985): 54.

Working Women—An International Survey by Marilyn J. Davidson and Cary L. Cooper documents the status of working women in ten Western countries and the Soviet Union. This article briefly describes the findings for the Soviet Union (where women account for 51 percent of the workforce), the United States, Britain, Ireland, Sweden, West Germany, The Netherlands, Finland, Greece, Italy, and Portugal.

14. Dugas, Christine. "Women Executives Emerge from Corporate Shadows." *Ad Forum* 4 (June 1983): 10-11, 63-64.

Dugas notes the rise in the number of female managers and MBA candidates and suggests that marketers tap this growing segment of the population. She reviews research about women managers and their career choices, then discusses areas for marketing to this special group: business travel, financial services, office equipment, information services, fashion, cars, liquor, perfume and lingerie, food, and household products. Includes statistics, photographs, and exhibits.

15. Dye, Thomas R., and Strickland, Julie. "Women at the Top: A Note on Institutional Leadership." *Social Science Quarterly* 63 (June 1982): 333-41.

Researchers examined twelve sectors of the United States' economy—industrial corporations; banks; utilities, transportation, and communication; insurance; law; investment firms; foundations; private universities; newspapers and television; civic and research and cultural associations; the federal government; and the military—to determine the numbers and roles of women in institutional leadership roles. Although women held only 4.1 percent of the top 7,783 institutional positions in 1980, that was more than double the number in 1970 (1.9 percent). Men and women leaders are compared in the following areas: education, age, leadership positions, career background, and marital status. Includes tables and references.

16. Ehrenreich, Barbara. "Strategies of Corporate Women." *New Republic* 194 (January 27, 1986): 28-31.

Ehrenreich claims that although women now constitute 30 percent of all managers and 40 percent of all MBA graduates, a "small but significant" number are leaving large corporations to return to the kitchen. Some possible reasons: biology is not compatible with business; sexism; the impersonal bureaucratic culture of the corporate world does not suit women; women wonder, after all, what is the point of striving to reach the top of the corporate ladder. She lists seven books that address the issues of women and success in the corporate world.

17. "Evaluating the Progress of Women Managers." *Management Review* 71 (September 1982): 4-5.

This two-page article discusses the book *Equal to the Task: How Working Women Are Managing in Corporate America* by Susan Easton, Joan M. Mills, and Diane Kramer Winokus. In their interviews of men and women managers, the authors learned that women's networks have become a powerful force, advertising still presents stereotypical views of women's roles, and women are more likely to be treated as equals in high technology occupations. One of the authors summarizes the book's message: "In terms of how women have developed their ambitions and strategies for achieving them, I'm very encouraged. In terms of 'the system's' reaction to women, I'm not."

18. Evans, Jane. "Will Women Lead?" *Management World* 12 (December 1983): 1, 7.

Executive Vice President of the Fashion Group of General Mills, Inc., Evans told the Women in Communications group that equality for women in the business world "is still a long way off." She cites the *Business Week* poll of forty-three leading United States companies that found only seven women in top leadership positions and lists some of the barriers to women in management.

19. Farnsworth, Steve. "Women Fill One-Third of Executive Posts." *Los Angeles Times* (April 11, 1984): p. 16, col. 1.

A just-released Census Bureau study shows that women held one of every three executive, administrative, and managerial positions in the United States in 1980 and the percent of women in law, architecture, and engineering nearly doubled from 1970 to 1980. However, women are still clustered in female ghettos—98 percent of all secretaries are female, and 75 percent of all elementary school teachers, bookkeepers, cashiers, waitresses, nurses, typists, maids, receptionists, and bank tellers are women. Representative Olympia Snowe (R.ME) told a Joint Economic Committee that pay equity is the most pressing issue for working women.

20. "Female Managers Now Well Received." *Management World* 11 (November 1982): 4.

A recent Louis Harris poll finds that 86 percent of 602 top executives believe women managers are doing a good job. However, in a *Business Week* survey, 41 percent of those polled claimed it was more difficult to promote women to high-level positions than they had anticipated.

21. Feuers, Stelle. "Women in Management: Two Points of View. Shortening the Odds." *Community and Junior College Journal* 52 (October 1981): 6, 10-12.

Feuers reminds readers that although more women have attained management positions, they still hold only 6 percent of middle management positions and one percent of top management posts. She tells women they must be willing to pay the price (extra hours, travel), build networks, take risks, develop a specialization, and get visibility in order to succeed in management.

22. Forbes, J. Benjamin, and Piercy, James E. "Rising to the Top: Executive Women in 1983 and Beyond." *Business Horizons* 26 (September/October 1983): 38-47.

Two management professors review the status of women in management and studied the listings in *Standard and Poor's Register of Corporations, Directors, and Executives* for data on female executives. They profile women managers based on background, birthplace, mobility, education by age group, region of employment, positions held, location by industry, and relationship between various categories. Top female executives are, for the most part, middle-aged or older, born in the United States, have an undergraduate degree (33 percent) or graduate degree (18 percent), and work in manufacturing firms (48 percent). Includes figures, tables, and references.

23. Fowler, Elizabeth M. "Women as Senior Executives." *New York Times* (November 10, 1982): sec. 4, p. 23, col. 1.

Korn/Ferry International conducted a survey of 300 top women executives. The findings indicate that most women succeed in fields like banking or consumer products rather than heavy industry; their average age is forty-six years; average salary is $92,000; they have worked for the same company thirteen years, work fifty-three hours a week, and travel out of town thirty-three days each year. Few of the women are active in community service. Thirty percent had a graduate degree, usually in business or law. Only 41 percent of the women were married. Most of the women executives had reached the top by one of three routes: marketing/sales, financial/accounting, or professional/technical.

24. Fraker, Susan. "Why Women Aren't Getting to the Top." *Fortune* 109 (April 16, 1984): 40-45.

Ten years after women started entering management in greater numbers, there is still only one woman CEO of a Fortune 500 company, Katherine Graham of the *Washington Post*. What holds them back? Some reasons given are blatant sexism, a lack of assertiveness, children, subtle barriers such as lack of constructive criticism, a lessening in government commitment to affirmative action, and lack of geographic mobility. Many executive women who are frustrated by their lack of progress in the corporate arena are leaving to start their own businesses. The number of women-owned businesses increased 33 percent from 1977 to 1980, compared to 11 percent for men. Includes photographs.

25. Fraser, Jill Andresky. "You Are Where You Live." *Savvy* 4 (October 1983): 38-43, 45-48.

The percentage of working women holding executive, managerial, or administrative positions in the United States is 7.4, but the percent varies from region to region. Fraser describes the best cities for women managers—New York, Chicago, San Jose, Minneapolis-St. Paul, San Diego, and Atlanta—and the worst—Tulsa, Cleveland, Baltimore, Birmingham, Detroit, Pittsburgh, and Boston. She gives honorable mention to Miami, Hartford, San Antonio, Wilmington, Phoenix, and Charlotte and characterizes Austin, Portland (Oregon), Portland (Maine), Salt Lake

City, and Santa Rosa as sleepers. Her choices are based on the percent of women in management positions in the city; the number of women in professional and management positions in the city's largest corporations; the number of women active in professional clubs and women's groups; chamber of commerce, and government in each city; quality of life in the city; and interviews with women living and working in these cities.

26. Galagan, Patricia. "A Most Important Development." *Training and Development Journal* 40 (May 1986): 4.

The editor of *Training and Development Journal* comments on the March *Wall Street Journal* supplement on the corporate woman and the "glass ceiling." She notes that although women experience difficulty making it beyond the first level of management, they are progressing in other areas. Labor Department statistics show that women now hold the majority of professional jobs in the United States and are starting their own businesses at five times the rate of men. Galagan concludes that perhaps women don't want a male-oriented equality and "the glass ceiling will prove to be irrelevant."

27. Geng, Veronica. "Petticoat Power." *The New Yorker* 59 (June 13, 1983): 42-44.

Geng writes tongue-in-cheek about the influx of women into the management ranks. She gives diagrams of the General Business Code, transmitted by breast-pocket-handkerchief semaphore, and describes the four types of mentors: inferential, insinuational, manifestational, and verbal.

28. Guido-DiBrito, Florence; Carpenter, D. Stanley; and DiBrito, William F. "Women in Leadership and Management: Review of the Literature, 1985 Update." *NASPA Journal* 23 (Winter 1986): 22-31.

Researchers review the literature from 1981 to 1984 on how four different managerial themes effect productivity, power, leader styles and behavior, and performance and promotion. They conclude with a discussion of patterns they discerned in the research literature. Includes tables and references.

29. Hellwig, Basia. "The Breakthrough Generation: 73 Women Ready to Run Corporate America." *Working Woman* 10 (April 1985): 98-101, 146, 148, 150.

Working Woman talked to forty-five top executive recruiting firms to determine whether there were any women ready for top corporate posts. The recruiters identified seventy-three executive women—of whom 36 percent have MBAs and an additional 24 percent have earned master's degrees. Their average age is thirty-nine, and 75 percent work in service industries. The seventy-three women and their companies are listed and inserts include tips on being a good manager, career paths, and career risks that pay off.

30. Hendrix, Kathleen. "Women Executives: Is It a Doll or Bear Market?" *Los Angeles Times* (September 14, 1984): sec. 5, p. 1, 18-20.

Hendrix interviewed Judith Hofer, forty-three year-old president and CEO of May Co. California, about women in the workplace and reviewed the status of women in management. The nation's largest executive search firm, Korn/Ferry International, claims that there are only 300 to 500 women in senior management positions in major corporations, and only fifteen of 6,500 public companies are headed by women, according to *Savvy* magazine. Although Lester Korn of Korn/Ferry feels it is only a matter of time before large numbers of women move into senior management, management consultant Rosabeth Moss Kanter says that some discrimination is unconscious, because it has to do with comfort levels, and male senior executives feel most comfortable with people they understand—generally other males. Felice Schwartz, president of Catalyst, finds that corporations are unsure of women's commitment.

31. "How Executives See Women in Management." *Business Week* (June 28, 1982): 10.

A Louis Harris poll of 600 corporate executives found that women executives are accepted and viewed with less prejudice than in the past. However, 41 percent agreed that it was more difficult to promote women to high-level jobs than they had anticipated. Insert shows the percent responses to seven questions from the poll, which was sponsored by *Business Week*.

32. Howard, Carole. "Moving into Senior Management (address, October 11, 1984)." *Vital Speeches of the Day* 51 (December 15, 1984): 148-50.

In a speech delivered to the Seventy-Fifth Anniversary Conference of Women in Communications Inc., Howard briefly reviews recent news stories on women's progress into management ranks. She concludes that gains were made in the 1960s and 1970s, but progress slows in the 1980s as women attempt to join men at the top of the corporate hierarchy. She lists ten observations on how women can break through the barrier to senior management.

33. Johnston, C. B. "Women in Transition." *Business Quarterly* 49 (Spring 1984): 100.

The dean of the School of Business Administration, University of Western Ontario, notes the changes that have occurred since the first thirteen women graduated from the Honors Business Administration and Masters of Business Administration programs in 1973. In 1984, 25.8 percent of the 403 students were women, and women were gold medal winners in both programs for the first time. Johnston believes that women graduates have more career opportunities than they did eleven years earlier.

34. Kagan, Julia. "Cracks in the Glass Ceiling." *Working Woman* 11 (October 1986): 107-09.

Kagan believes that recent articles about women's progress to top management are too pessimistic. She points out that the average age for senior executives is fifty-one and that while there are many women managers in the "pipeline," it will be some time before the women who began earning MBAs in the 1970s reach that level of maturity. Several women who were dubbed the Breakthrough Generation by *Working Woman* in 1985 comment on women's progress or lack of progress into top management positions.

35. Kanes, John, and Kanes, Martha. "You Oughta Be in Pictures." *Savvy* 3 (February 1982): 12-13.
The authors scanned recent issues of *Business Week, Forbes,* and *Fortune* magazines in their search for photos of women business executives. In a 222-page issue of *Business Week,* they found one picture of a woman business executive. A glance at ads found photos of women executives in airline, computer manufacturing, and banking advertisements.

36. Kanter, Rosabeth Moss. "Men and Women of the Corporation Revisited." *Management Review* 76 (March 1987): 14-16.
Kanter concludes that the premise of her 1977 book, *Men and Women of the Corporation,* still holds—i.e., productivity, motivation, and career success are determined largely by organizational structure. She describes six areas where she thinks companies are making progress toward improved productivity and quality by making opportunities available to women.

37. Larwood, Laurie, and Powell, Gary N. "Isn't It Time We Were Moving On?: Necessary Future Research on Women in Management." *Group and Organization Studies* 6 (March 1981): 65-72.
The authors critique recent research about women in management and recommend that the scope of future research be expanded. They note the importance of studies on women in management to policy decisions and both men's and women's organizational career development. Larwood and Powell examined ninety-nine studies in detail and categorized the research into three areas: organizational issues, societal issues, and issues concerning women. They urge researchers to expand the current knowledge on women in management by going beyond the topics of discrimination and socialization and concentrating on applied research or research with an action or use orientation. Includes references.

38. Lawson, Carol. "150 Women Are Invited to Dinner on Amex Floor." *New York Times* (October 1984), sec. 2, p. 8, col. 2.
One hundred fifty business and professional women, members of the Committee of 200 and the Women's Forum, attended a dinner on the floor of the American Stock Exchange. Arthur Levitt, Jr., chair of the exchange, commented on the status of women in business, noting the progress (women are the fastest-growing group of entrepreneurs, sole owners of 2.8 million small businesses, four times the number of five years ago and one-fourth of the United States' total), but pointed out that "they haven't really scratched the surface yet." Several of the attendees and their affiliations are mentioned.

39. Lublin, Joann S. "Women Executives Are in Demand as the Economy Recovers and Views Change." *Wall Street Journal* (November 29, 1983): p. 1, col. 5.
An executive recruiter notes the trend toward hiring women into top jobs as more women indicate a willingness to relocate. The trend extends beyond the traditional women's fields (retailing, financial services, consumer goods, and publishing) to other areas such as transportation, high technology, aerospace, mining, and durable goods manufacturing.

40. Machlowitz, Marilyn. "Leaving the Fast Lane." *Working Woman* 7 (August 1982): 77-78.

Business Week writes about women managers who are "topping out" or "leveling off"—content to remain in a position or at a level with which they are satisfied. One executive recruiter, however, advises women to go upward as soon as possible, claiming that "At this point, women have to move more."

41. Mailer, Chloe. "On the Way Up—How Women Are Gaining Footholds in Management." *Equal Opportunities International (UK)* 4 (1) (1985): 5-10.

The author, for five years an editor of a management magazine, reviews the progress of women managers since World War I. She emphasizes the work of Elizabeth Pepperell as assistant director of the Industrial Welfare Society, the first woman in that position. Mailer describes the Pepperell Development Course and results of a survey of 200 women who attended the course. Includes tables and references.

42. Marshall, Judi. "A Testing Time, Full of Potential." *Women in Management Review* 1 (Spring 1985): 5-14.

Marshall, lecturer in organizational behavior in the School of Management, University of Bath, interviewed thirty middle- to senior-level women managers in retailing and book publishing and concluded that women have reached a new stage of development. She describes four trends in this development and how they relate to women in management: a balancing of male and female values; training courses for women and women-only networks; women identifying and associating more with each other; dialog involving more women; and a need to improve speaking and listening skills to handle issues of power.

43. McKendrick, Joseph. "Viewpoint: Men versus Women." *Management World* 11 (November 1982): 11-13.

A survey of 172 Administrative Management Society members found that women account for less than 10 percent of all supervisory, middle management, and top management positions in the companies surveyed. Both males and females feel it is harder for women to advance in their organizations, and a majority of both sexes indicated they felt women were working to supplement family incomes. Ninety percent of the men had not heard of incidents of sexual harassment in their companies, while 60 percent of the women were unaware of sexual harassment incidents. Survey comments from males and females are found on page twelve.

44. Morrison, Ann M.; White, Randall P.; and Velsor, Ellen Van. "The Glass House Dilemma: Why Women Executives Dare Not Fail." *Working Woman* 11 (October 1986): 110-11, 146-47.

The authors, researchers at the Center for Creative Leadership, present advance findings from their study of seventy-six high-level women managers. The complete study, the Executive Women Project, will be documented in a book to be published by Addison Wesley in 1987. The women comment on risk taking and accepting occasional failure, citing the inability to sell an idea or project as the most common failure, and one in five failures were attributed to hiring the wrong subordinate.

45. Naffziger, Douglas W. "The Smooth Transition." *Training and Development Journal* 40 (April 1986): 63-65.

A professor of management at Western Illinois University, Naffziger points out that the number of women in management rose to almost 30 percent by 1983 and suggests that organizations need to address the issue of training to incorporate growing numbers of women into management. He advises starting with a need analysis, a careful plan of the contents and participants for on-going management training programs, and learning reinforcement after the course is completed. He concludes with a reminder to establish evaluation criteria, preferably including a cost/benefit analysis. Includes references.

46. "1985 NAFE Survey Results." *Executive Female* 8 (July/August 1985): 42-43.

NAFE (National Association for Female Executives) prints the results of a recent member survey. Among the forty-six areas covered are age, status, and salary; personal status; education; income; finances; and business travel. Forty-seven percent of the members are twenty-five to thirty years old; 50 percent are married or living with someone; 28 percent have completed college, and 20 percent have a graduate degree; 59 percent earn between $20,000 and $40,000 a year; 27 percent are managers, 19 percent are administrators, and 22 percent are professional/technicals; 47 percent have a savings plan; and 55 percent travel two to six times a year for business. Fifty-five percent are willing to relocate.

47. "The 1983 American Express Women in Management." *Equal Opportunities International (UK)* 2 (2) (1983): 34-36.

Baroness Young, Leader of the House of Lords, was the speaker at the first annual American Express "Women in Management" series of lectures. She commented on the history and progress of women in management and concluded with brief results of a report by the trade unions which called for more flexible working arrangements to facilitate women's progress as managers.

48. Oleatt, William A. "Women and Blacks in Management—A Slow but Steadily Upward Climb." *Office Administration and Automation* 46 (August 1985): 7.

In this editorial, Oleatt reviews the slow but steady progress of women and blacks in management. He cites statistics from Bette Stead's article on women in management in this issue and from a book, *Black Managers: The Case of the Banking Industry* by Edward D. Irons and Gilbert W. Moore. Oleatt lists these statistics as evidence for optimism about the future of women and blacks in management: more than half of all college students are female; more than half of all women in the United States now work outside the home; in the first quarter of 1985, full-time working women earned 66 percent of men's earnings.

49. O'Toole, Patricia. "The Outside Route to the Top." *Working Woman* 10 (November 1985): 130-32.

O'Toole chronicles the rise of women in management—from 15 percent of the nation's managers in 1970 to 34 percent in 1985. She points out, however, that of the 48 million American working women, less than one percent are upper-level managers, and women account for only 511 (4 percent) of the 12,000 directors of the nation's largest 1,000 corporations. Observers predict that Liz Claiborne will be the next woman to join Katherine Graham as CEO of a Fortune 500 company.

50. Pave, Irene. "A Woman's Place is at GE, Federal Express, P & G. . . ." *Business Week* (June 23, 1986): 75-76.
Women constitute 70 percent of all white-collar workers, but an Administrative Management Society survey found that only 10 percent of all managers are women. The fields that offer the most opportunities for women are packaged goods, retailing, banking and financial services, and computers and news. Women also look for companies that offer attractive working conditions—affirmative action, parental leaves, day-care, flextime, part-time work, and women's networks.

51. Price, Margaret. "Women: Reaching for the Top." *Industry Week* 217 (May 16, 1983): 38-42.
Price interviews several high-ranking women executives about their ambitions and the opportunity to become CEO of their companies. The head of a New York executive recruiting firm claims that "ten to twenty percent of the *Fortune* 1,000 companies will have women CEOs within the next ten years," but to date only one woman (Katherine Graham of the *Washington Post*) is chair of a major industrial company. Labor Department statistics indicate that women constitute 43 percent of the workforce but hold only 28 percent of all managerial positions and earned an average 55 percent as much as men in similar positions.

52. Rich, Spencer. "Census Reports Rise of Women Executives." *Washington Post* (April 11, 1984): A3.
The Census Bureau reported that the number of women managers, administrators, and executives rose from 18.5 percent to 30.5 percent from 1970 to 1980 due, in part, to improvements in women's educational qualifications. The gap between male and female full-time workers' salaries remains, however—women earned 62 percent as much as men in 1982. One expert testified to Congress that companies often placed young women in jobs with less growth potential.

53. Rogan, Helen. "Young Executive Women Advance Farther, Faster than Predecessors." *Wall Street Journal* (October 26, 1984): sec. 2, p. 33.
Younger management women have career plans and expectations much like those of men, unlike their predecessors, who frequently moved gradually into management positions as opportunities arose. This is one finding of a *Wall Street Journal*/Gallup organization survey of 722 female executives. The survey divided the women executives into six categories: top management; middle-level executives; young achievers; young, lower-level; senior, non-top; and late starters.

54. "Rumor or Innuendo: A Powerful Harassment." *U.S. News and World Report* 93 (November 29, 1982): 56-57.
Mary Cunningham, vice president of strategic planning for Joseph E. Seagram & Sons, answers these questions about women in business today: Are women making progress based on their abilities? Are career women getting help from men? Are women progressing faster in some

fields than in others? Are networks and mentors effective for women? What is she doing personally to advance women? She concludes with the comment that American businesses should be concerned about the economic consequences of prejudice against women managers.

55. Safran, Claire. "Corporate Women: Just How Far Have We Come?" *Working Woman* 9 (March 1984): 99-104.
Safran reviews the effect of twenty years of sex discrimination laws by charting the changes in three companies. In one company women are 5 percent of the managers, in another 8 percent, and in the third company, 16 percent.

56. Sanders, Doreen. "Here Come the Women—And It's about Time." *Business Quarterly* 49 (Spring 1984): 136+.
This article, a reprint of a 1973 *Financial Post* story, relates some of the attitudes and feelings of the thirteen women graduates of the fifty-year-old Western Ontario Business School. The average starting salary ($12,500) is described as "posh," and all of the women decline the rubric "women's libber."

57. Scholl, Jaye. "Corporations of the Year." *Savvy* 4 (June 1983): 30-37.
Savvy names eight companies where the "corporate culture" is most conducive to women's progress. All eight companies had these things in common: a constant increase in the number of women managers, affirmative action programs, open management styles, and companywide job postings. The article includes profiles and information on opportunities for women managers in these companies: CBS, Inc.; Citicorp; General Electric; Levi Strauss; Pacific Gas & Electric; Proctor & Gamble; Texas Instruments; and 3M.

58. Schwartz, Felice N. "From Getting in to Getting On." *Working Woman* 8 (September 1983): 131-33.
Schwartz, founder and president of Catalyst, claims the issue for women managers is no longer getting in, but advancing from entry-level to middle- and upper-level management. Some companies have specific programs for assimilating women into the corporation.

59. Smith, Adam. "The Myth, Fable, and Reality of the Working Woman." *Esquire* 101 (June 1984): 65-66, 68.
Smith reviews the current status of working women and asks, "Are women becoming more male as they move into traditionally male occupations, or is the workplace becoming more female?" He claims that the situation for women in Europe is different than in the United States, that change is occurring faster in the United States, and that Japan, Britain, and Germany will follow the United States' example in five or ten years. Smith wonders what things will be like when career women operate with women's sensibilities and leave behind the power suit, the masculine curriculum, and the masculine world.

60. Springer, Cecile M. "It's Time to Win with Women—Why and How." *Vital Speeches of the Day* 50 (July 15, 1984): 591-93.

Cecile Springer, director of corporate giving for Westinghouse Electric Corporation, cites facts and figures on women's advancement to the 1984 graduates of Seton Hill College, Greensburg, PA. She gives her formula for success—smart + education + hard work = independence— and claims that the timing is perfect for women to accept leadership positions in our society.

61. Stead, Bette Ann. "Women in Management—Some Progress, but More Is Needed." *Office Administration and Automation* 46 (August 1985): 24-27+.

The author of *Women in Management* (1978, 1985) and former chair of the Committee on the Status of Women for the Academy of Management, Bette Stead claims that although women have made some gains in management, progress has been slow. She cites statistics to prove her arguments and discusses four "old barriers"—women still do not have access to the informal community power structure, they are still stereotyped as emotional or illogical, there is still no Equal Rights Amendment, and women still find their identity through their husbands. She concludes by offering companies some advice on treatment of women managers.

62. Sutton, Charlotte Decker, and Moore, Kris K. "Executive Women—20 Years Later." *Harvard Business Review* 63 (September/ October 1985): 42-44, 48, 50, 52, 56, 58, 60, 62, 66.

Harvard Business Review surveyed 786 male and female executives to compare their attitudes toward women in business to the attitudes of *Harvard Business Review* readers in 1965. Only 9 percent of the men were strongly favorable toward women executives in 1965, compared to 33 percent in 1985. Based on responses to questions about how comfortable executives are working for a woman, how effective women managers are perceived to be, and whether or not women have to be exceptional to succeed in business, the researchers concluded that men's attitudes have changed more than women's. However, differences in salary between male and female executives continue, and there is still resistance to female managers. Includes tables and exhibits.

63. Taylor, Alex III. "Why Women Managers Are Bailing Out." *Fortune* 114 (August 18, 1986): 16-23.

Women now earn one in three MBA degrees, but a study of 1976 graduates of seventeen prestigious business schools shows that a significant number of women have left the management ranks for a variety of reasons: (1) they believe it is more difficult for them to advance than it is for their male colleagues; (2) they are not paid as much as their male colleagues; (3) they dislike the "organizational rigidity" of corporations; (4) they are restricted to stereotypically female functions such as personnel, purchasing, and public relations; (5) demands of raising a family are very high; (6) they want to start their own businesses; (7) the two-career couple have difficulty balancing the demands of child care, travel, and relocation. Taylor concludes that corporations must adapt to the needs of businesswomen in order to retain them. He describes such efforts at nine major companies.

64. Trost, Cathy. "Women Advance in Management, but They Still Feel Resistance." *Wall Street Journal* (October 29, 1985): p. 1, col. 5.

A *Harvard Business Review* survey shows progress for women managers (male executives with negative attitudes toward female executives fell from 41 percent in 1965 to 5 percent in 1985), but pay differentials are still substantial—half of the men in the survey earned $100,000, while only 10 percent of the women earned that much. An Administrative Management Society poll of 200 managers indicated that 69 percent said there was an increase in the number of female managers in the last five years, but women managers claim stereotypes and corporate politics make it more difficult for them to advance. Finally, a Pace University study found that women MBA graduates are less likely to be married or have children than are their male counterparts.

65. Van Fleet, David D., and Saurage, Julie G. "Recent Research on Women in Management." *Akron Business and Economic Review* (Summer 1984): 24.

The authors review the recent research on women in management, grouping the studies into three categories: effects of sex and attractiveness on hiring, attitudes toward female managers, and perceptions about female leadership abilities. The research supports these conclusions: women are discriminated against in hiring decisions, women have more favorable attitudes toward women managers than do males, and higher educated men and women have more favorable attitudes than those with less education. Finally, women were considered as effective as men in real work situations. Van Fleet and Saurage call on organizations to reduce sex discrimination by improving their hiring programs, increasing management's awareness of discrimination, and reviewing employee evaluation and promotion procedures. Includes table (Composite of Research Reviewed) and extensive (83-item) bibliography.

66. Von Seldeneck, Judith M. "A Time to Recharge: Women in Management Have a Rough Fight Ahead." *Management World* 11 (November 1982): 1, 6.

The author notes the slowdown of women's progress into management during the Reagan administration. The Women Employed Institute in Chicago reports that female managers and administrators account for only 7 percent of the female workforce, and fewer than one percent of working women are directors or on boards. Von Seldeneck believes that the Committee of 200, a network of female corporate executives who run or own companies with $5 million annual sales or manage corporate divisions of that size, will help women in management.

67. Wente, Margaret. "The Woman Who Never Was." *Canadian Business* 58 (June 1985): 253-54, 256, 259.

The pipeline argument is used to explain why there are no female chief executives of the Top 500 companies, i.e., women have only been in the pipeline for about fifteen years, so it will be some time before they qualify for top positions. The last census shows that only 3,175 of the 5 million Canadian women in the labor force hold senior management jobs. Wente believes women are stuck in the pipeline at the valve between middle and senior management, in part, because men tend to promote those who resemble them in actions, looks, and thought—other men. She offers three tongue-in-cheek suggestions for reaching the top: marry the major shareholder and wait for him to drop dead, wait for the old guard to drop dead, and have a sex-change operation.

68. Westoff, Leslie Aldridge. "Women's Work." *A New Republic* 194 (February 24, 1986): 6.

Westoff writes a letter to the editor to contradict statements made by Barbara Ehrenreich in her January 27 article, "Strategies of Corporate Women." She disagrees with Ehrenreich that the small number of women leaving corporate life to return to the home indicates a trend, citing statistics that show the opposite trend: 70 percent of all women between the ages of twenty-five to fifty-four are working, and the United States Department of Labor projects the figure will be 80 percent by 1995. At the same time, the percent of women managers is rising, and the number of self-employed women rose 22 percent in the last four years.

69. "Why Women Get the Jobs." *The Economist* 300 (August 23, 1986): 13-14.

Women have captured 73 percent of all new jobs created in the United States since 1979. Many of these were part-time positions, but economists predict that women will instead be employers, entrepreneurs, bankers, and politicians in the next ten years. They offer as proof the fact that American women now own a quarter of all small businesses, Canadian women a third, and their French counterparts a fifth. Women are more likely to hold senior management positions in the following fields: information (public relations, computer services, and the press), financial services, tourism, and design.

70. "Woman's Work." *America* 150 (April 14, 1984): 271.

An International Labor Organization study reports that Japanese women factory workers earn only 43 percent as much as their male counterparts, the worst for any industrialized nation, and a decline from 46.5 percent in 1973. *Fortune* magazine reports that no women head any of the companies in the Fortune 500; only one company, the Washington Post, has a woman CEO; and only four of the 154 people enrolled in Harvard Business Schools' Advanced Management Program are women.

71. "Women Held 30.5% of Management Jobs in America in 1980. . . ." *Wall Street Journal* (April 11, 1984): p. 1, col. 3.

That figure compares to 18.5 percent a decade earlier. Women have increased their share of many male-dominated professions—they accounted for 17.1 percent of the nation's judges in 1980, up from 6.1 percent in 1970.

72. "Women Managers: Low in Numbers." *Management World* 11 (March 1982): 24.

Women represent 5 percent of middle managers and one percent of top management. Dr. Linda Keller Brown writes in *The Woman Manager in the United States* that the number of women managers increased only one percent since 1947. Brown's research and a study by Natasha Josefowitz indicate that male and female managers have much in common.

73. "You've Come a Long Way Baby—But Not as Far as You Thought." *Business Week* (October 1, 1984): 126+.

Polled by *Business Week*, women managers across the United States say that, although overt discrimination is gone, it is difficult for women to get beyond lower- and middle-level management. Some believe that males over forty-five still retain stereotypical attitudes toward women managers, and that women will not be promoted to top positions in large numbers until that generation of male executives retires.

74. Zeitz, Baila. "The Crisis in Middle Management." *Working Woman* 8 (September 1983): 133-36.

One senior research associate at the Conference Board says women are moving up in management, but a second Conference Board senior research associate claims few are advancing to upper-level management. A third observer, a former Conference Board research associate who is currently a professor of accounting at Southern Methodist University in Dallas, estimated in 1977 that it would take women thirty years to achieve parity at all levels of management.

Salaries

75. Arrington, Christine Rigby. "The Pampered Princesses." *Savvy* 2 (July 1981): 32-37.

The baby-boom generation of executive women often discovers that high salaries still don't seem sufficient to cover lifestyle expectations. The "psychology of entitlement" causes babyboomers to expect things others regard as privileges. Frequently, nonexecutive women pay more than they can afford for an executive lifestyle. The author advises investing in educational expenses to improve skills, rather than investing in $350 suits.

76. Bartlett, Robin L., and Miller, Timothy I. "Executive Compensation: Female Executives and Networking." *American Economic Review* 75 (May 1985): 266-70.

Professors of economics at Denison University, Granville, OH, studied 132 top female executives to determine the effect of networking on their success. Their data show that executive salary is determined by the size of the company and the number of hours worked per week and also strongly support their theory that "who you know" affects compensation. They concluded that. . ."women who 'plugged in' to networks, as measured either by memberships in private clubs or on corporate boards, profited substantially by these additional contacts and information." Includes one table ("Determinants on Female Executive Compensation") and references.

77. Conway, John A., ed. "The Working Woman." *Forbes* (November 5, 1984): 8.

The Conference Board reports that although women constitute 50 percent of all college students, earn 30 percent of all law degrees, and 23 percent of all medical degrees, less than 10 percent of women with college degrees occupy managerial positions—whereas 25 percent of college-educated men hold management jobs. In addition, female managers earn only 50 percent as much as their male counterparts.

78. "A Female Variety of Bracket Creeping." *Industry Week* (October 15, 1984): 13.

The Conference Board notes that 53 percent of all women work outside the home, and in households with annual incomes of $40,000 to $50,000, 70 percent of the wives work. Women managers and administrators still earn only half as much as their male counterparts.

79. Harragan, Betty Lehan. "Are You Really a Manager?" *Savvy* 3 (July 1982): 19-20.

Harragan, a well-known business consultant, defines exempt and nonexempt job classifications and clarifies the responsibilities of four exempt job categories: executive, administrative, professional, and outside sales people. "Exempt" and "nonexempt" were terms established by the Fair Labor Standards Act of 1938, and the booklet *Regulations, 541: Determining Executive, Administrative, Professional, and Outside Sales Exemptions* gives additional information on the four exempt categories.

80. Hazelton, Lynette. "A Salary with Fringe on Top." *Essence* 14 (May 1983): 26.

Because fringe benefits can be equal to 30 or 40 percent of your salary, it is important to negotiate them wisely. Some companies offer tuition reimbursement, incentive bonuses, stock options, profit sharing, health benefits, severance pay, travel, or organizational memberships. Negotiate for fringe benefits before you take a job and during a good performance review, when you have saved the company money, or when you have accepted additional responsibilities.

81. Koretz, Gene. "An Earning Chasm Separates Female Managers from Males." *Business Week* (March 19, 1984): 16.

Research coordinator of Columbia Business School's Center for Research in Career Development, Mary Anne Devanna has completed a study, *Male/Female Careers: The First Decade.* She studied the careers of forty-five men and women MBAs and found that after ten years women MBA grads earned almost $10,000 less than their male colleagues. The biggest salary differentials were in manufacturing.

82. McCarthy, Michael J. "Women's Salaries Reflect Disparities in Executive Suites." *Wall Street Journal* (December 1, 1986): sec. 2, p. 31.

A recent Heidrick and Struggles survey indicates that executive women (vice-president and up) have made gains, but still only earn 50 percent as much as their male colleagues—$124,623 compared to $213,000 for the men. The typical female executive in the survey is forty-four years old, white, Protestant, and childless. "Forty-one percent of the women are unmarried, compared with only 7.5 percent of the men." The women generally work a fifty-five-hour week, and 42 percent believe there should be a national parental leave policy.

83. O'Toole, Patricia. "Hers." *New York Times* (May 21, 1981): sec. 3, p. 2, col. 1.

A writer who advises executive women on personal financial matters learns that while women earn sixty-five cents for every dollar that men earn, top executive women earn only thirty-seven cents for every dollar earned by top male executives. The chief executive search firm, Heidrick and Struggles, surveyed 1,300 of the country's largest corporations and found that the majority of top executive women are corporate secretaries or assistant corporate secretaries and earn $50,000 a year or less, while males are senior officers and earn $134,000 a year. The salary discrepancy applies not only to older women (in their fifties and sixties) who have reached the top, but also to young women. A 1978 Stanford

University study shows that five years out of business school, men earn an average of $38,000, women an average $30,000.

84. "The Pay Gap Fails to Narrow Much between Female and Male Managers." *Wall Street Journal* (August 4, 1981): p. 1.
Although the number of women managers doubled from 1969 to 1980 (to 2.9 million), women managers still earn only 54 percent as much as male managers, according to the United States Labor Department.

85. Priestland, Sue C. "Women Move into Executive Slots but Salaries Lag Behind." *Association Management* 35 (August 1983): 65-67+.
Priestland summarizes the results of the "1983 Association Executive Compensation Study," a survey of 4,600 representatives of 1,200 United States associations. Results show that the number of women in executive positions in associations increased from 23 percent in 1981 to 36 percent in 1983, but in every category (chief paid executive, communication director, research director, personnel director, etc.), women made less money than men. Comparisons of 1980 and 1981 surveys indicate a steady increase in compensation for association executives. Chief staff officers of associations may order a copy of the study from ASAE Publications, 1575 Eye St. N.W., Washington, DC 20005. Price is $50 (members), $100 (nonmembers).

86. Samuelson, Robert J. "Frustration Deepens for Working Women." *Washington Post* (July 19, 1983): D7-D8.
Although 60 percent of all married women now work outside the home, full-time working women still earn only 59 percent as much as males; in part because women still hold major responsibility for child rearing and household tasks and thus feel dual pressures. A recent survey of senior women executives found that only 50 percent were married compared to 95 percent of their male counterparts.

87. Trost, Cathy. "The New Majorities." *Wall Street Journal* (March 24, 1986): 15D.
Observers worry that as women move into male-dominated occupations, salaries and status in these fields will suffer. A recent National Academy of Science report claims that as the percent of females in occupations increased, pay decreased. From 1970 to 1980 women assumed a majority in these fields: insurance adjusters and examiners, computer operators, and typesetters and compositors.

88. Wills, Kendall J. "Losing the Salary Game." *New York Times* (February 20, 1983): sec. 3, p. 27, col. 1.
The research director at Columbia's Center for Research and Career Development studied 200 men and women Columbia MBA graduates. The study shows that although women MBA graduates started with the same salaries as the men MBA grads, within ten years there was a pay gap among men and women with equal training and credentials. Women earned only 81 percent as much as the men. After ten years, women in manufacturing earned an average of $41,818 while men in manufacturing earned $59,733. The researcher concluded that marriage, motherhood, theories of motivation, and occupational choice did not explain the

difference in the pay gap, but that promotion may often be based on potential rather than merit.

89. "Wives Are Bringing Home More of the Bacon." *Business Week* (June 23, 1986): 30-31.

In 1983 5 million wives, or 20 percent of those wives in dual-earner marriages, earned more than their husbands. Most of those women work full-time, are college graduates, and hold professional, administrative or managerial positions.

90. "Women and Money—And the Job Ladder. Studies: Lagging in Financial Savvy. . . . And in Scramble for Executive Rooms." *Des Moines Register* (October 12, 1986): 2A.

Money magazine's profile of Americans shows that women do not understand many financial and investment terms. The sixteenth annual University of Michigan survey of top officers of United States companies finds that fewer women are being promoted to vice-president.

91. "Women MBA Grads from Some Leading Business Schools Earn Less than Men." *Wall Street Journal* (June 2, 1981): p. 1.

In spite of a dramatic increase in the number of women MBAs, women graduates with the same or more work experience as men earn $1,300 to $2,000 less. An Indiana University spokesperson says women do not believe they have the same range of options as their male colleagues, and some schools claim that the women's lack of assertiveness, not sex bias, accounts for the differences in salary.

92. "Women Receiving MBAs This Year from Carnegie-Mellon University. . . . " *Wall Street Journal* (September 13, 1983): p. 1, col. 5.

According to this brief item in the Labor Letter, women MBA graduates from Carnegie-Mellon University in 1983 averaged a starting pay of $32,675, just 2.3 percent below the average starting salary for male MBA graduates. In 1982 the gap was 4 percent.

93. "Women's Salaries Still Low." *Dun's Business Monthly* 123 (November 1983): 14.

Although women now constitute 45 percent of the workforce compared to 30 percent in the early 1970s, they still earn only 60 percent as much as men and hold only 27 percent of all managerial positions in white-collar jobs.

Mentors and Networking

94. Anderson, Susan Heller, and Dunlap, David W. "A Woman's Coalition." *New York Times* (January 31, 1985): sec. 2, p. 3, col. 4.

Muriel Siebert, first woman member of the New York Stock Exchange and candidate for the United States Senate in 1982, called together thirty-five women who head New York women's organizations. Her intent was to start a coalition to lobby for day-care, child support, and more female government appointees.

95. Berry, Patricia. "Mentors for Women Managers: Fast-Track to Corporate Success?" *Supervisory Management* 28 (August 1983): 36-40.

Mentors may be valuable assets to women who want to move up in management. Berry asks the questions, "What's a mentor?" and "Why have a mentor?" She briefly tells how to find a mentor and then lists potential problems: a woman may choose the wrong mentor, she may become too dependent on her mentor, or she may become romantically involved with a male mentor. A mentor can assist the woman manager in the art of corporate politics.

96. "Blacks Need Mentors to Get Ahead: AKA Leader." *Jet* 66 (August 20, 1984): 14.

Freddie Groomes, assistant for human affairs to Florida State University's president and national coordinator for Alpha Kappa Alpha sorority, claims having a mentor is the only sure way to get ahead. She started a mentor program for sorority members and says, "Mentors assist with career planning, interviews, and internships and give personal counseling."

97. Boeker, Warren, et al. "Are the Expectations of Women Managers Being Met?" *California Management Review* 27 (Spring 1985): 148-57.

The authors collected data from the San Francisco Network, the Bay Area Women's Forum, and the Peninsula Women's Network (networks for middle-management women) to evaluate programs designed to recruit, encourage, and improve the performance of women in management. The women answered questions about twenty-two policies and programs intended to provide equal employment opportunities for women. Only five of the twenty-two items (maternity leave, women in management workshops, an affirmative action officer, a written affirmative action policy, and flexible working hours) were available to most of the women. Programs the women would prefer are ones that would benefit them economically: cafeteria-style fringe benefits, career placement for a spouse, pension funding, and day-care. Includes tables and references.

98. Bowen, Donald D. "Were Men Meant to Mentor Women?" *Training and Development Journal* 39 (February 1985): 30-34.
Bowen gives a "working" definition of mentoring and describes a study of thirty-two mentor/protégé pairs in a wide variety of fields. He reviews the results of the study, indicates problems and benefits of mentoring, and concludes with suggestions to corporations for legitimizing the mentoring process. Includes tables.

99. Clarity, James F., and Weaver, Warren, Jr. "For Women Only." *New York Times* (September 7, 1983): sec. 2, p. 8, col. 2.
Female executives in Washington, DC, decried the lack of a business club where they could network. One-hundred fifty women executives and government officials have given $200,000 in dues to found the all-woman Executive Club.

100. Clawson, James G., and Kram, Kathy E. "Managing Cross Gender Mentoring." *Business Horizons* 27 (May 6, 1984): 22-32.
The authors advise men and women managers on how to deal with close developmental (mentor/protégé) cross-gender relationships. They begin by discussing the characteristics of effective developmental relationships, then tell how to manage intimacy or the perception of intimacy, and conclude by stating that extremes of intimacy or distance make relationships less productive. Includes figures and notes.

101. Colwill, Nina L. "Mentors and Protégés, Women and Men." *Business Quarterly* 49 (Summer 1984): 19-21.
The author of *The New Partnership: Women and Men in Organizations*, Colwill encourages a broader view of mentoring and cross-sex mentoring. She defines mentors, sponsors, guides, and peer pals and reviews the sex-role traps in mentoring: sexual alliances, father-daughter relationships or over-parenting, the "assistant-to," and the token protégé. For women who do not have upper-level female role models in their organizations, one writer suggests alternatives: negative role models, multiple role models, partial role models, role models from other occupations and organizations, cross-sex role models, and nonreciprocated mentorship.

102. "Corporate Women's Groups Operating at 50 U.S. Corporations . . . ." *Wall Street Journal* (June 3, 1986): p. 1, col. 5.
Catalyst, the New York-based research group, will link fifty United States corporate women's groups as the Corporate Women's Group Resource. One Catalyst official said the group will "enable us to increase our knowledge about women in corporate America today."

103. Cox, Meg. "Clearer Connections." *Wall Street Journal* (March 24, 1986): 20D.
Many of the women's networks of the 1970s have changed focus—from nurturing to professional contacts and financial benefits. Betty Lehan Harragan, author of *Games Mother Never Taught You*, claims women's networks are becoming more realistic. Carol Kleiman says there were 1,400 women's networks when she wrote *Women's Networks* five years

ago; now there are 5,000, of which the Committee of 200 is the most prestigious and powerful.

104. DeWine, Sue, and Casbolt, Diane. "Networking: External Communication Systems for Female Organizational Members." *Journal of Business Communication* 20 (Spring 1983): 57-67.

The authors describe the focus and intent of women's networks and review a case study that evaluated the effectiveness and usefulness of career-oriented women's networks. Women joined a women's network primarily to gain information. Other objectives listed were job opportunities to promote business/self, to give information, to recruit women for jobs, to meet women, to attend educational programs, and for career guidance. Findings of the study of middle- and low-level management women indicated that active women "networkers" are not likely to join formal networks. Includes tables and notes.

105. Dullea, Georgia. "On Ladder to the Top, a Mentor Is Key Step." *New York Times* (January 26, 1981): sec. 2, p. 6, col. 2.

Young women in business are frequently advised to find a mentor who can help them in their climb up the corporate ladder. Three successful businesswomen describe their mentor-protégé experiences: Geraldine Stutz of Bendels, Kathryn Eichhoff of the consulting company Townsend-Greenspan, and Nan Talese of Simon and Schuster. Rena Bartos, senior vice-president at J. Walter Thompson, warns that the mentor-protégé relationship may be "another fairy tale."

106. Hume, Ellen. "Women Swap Tips on How to Succeed at Bipartisan Meet." *Wall Street Journal* (April 28, 1986): sec. 1, p. 14.

For four days female politicians and businesswomen voyaged up the Mississippi River on a steamboat, sharing advice and experiences during the first "New Partnerships" conference. Attendees included 1984 Democratic vice presidential candidate Geraldine Ferraro; Judith Calders, vice president of Ziegler Securities in Chicago; and Representative Lindy Boggs, Democrat, Louisiana, a founder of the Congresswomen's Caucus.

107. Jacobs, Sanford L. "Women Chief Executives Help Each Other with Frank Advice." *Wall Street Journal* (July 2, 1984): sec. 2, p. 21.

The Chief Executive Roundtable is open to women who own and operate New York-area companies with annual sales of $1 million to $10 million. Members meet monthly and share advice on a wide variety of problems, often expressing their opinions in "brutally frank" fashion. A major advantage of the group is the chance to be open about company problems without compromising confidentiality.

108. Kelly, Louise. "On the Job (Mentors and Women)." *Working Woman* 7 (May 1982): 40.

Although the media, business school classes, and books tell young women they must have a mentor or corporate sponsor, Kelly claims that what women managers really need is flexibility. Success, she says, is a result of hard work, timing, talent, and luck, not because of working with a mentor, usually male.

109. Klemesrud, Judy. "Special Relationship of Women and Their Mentors." *New York Times* (April 11, 1983): sec. 1, p. 22, col. 2.

Nancy Collins, assistant to the president of the Palo Alto Medical Foundation, surveyed 400 professional women for her book, *Professional Women and Their Mentors.* Two-hundred twenty-five of the women said that mentors made a "very valuable" contribution to their careers. Ms. Collins, who has had three male mentors herself, found in her study that most women (299 of the 400) believe a mentor should be someone other than one's boss. Only seventy-five of the women in the study chose their mentors. Most women (236) just "fell into it." Collins believes the Queen Bee syndrome is less of a problem than it used to be—that many women in high management positions are now willing to serve as mentors for other women.

110. Konrad, Walecia. "Influence Brokers for Women in the Corporation." *Working Woman* 11 (October 1986): 112-13, 115.

Corporate women's networks actively work to help women develop their skills and to encourage management to change corporate policies on nondiscrimination, maternity leave, and child care. Catalyst has located forty-five corporate women's networks in the United States. Konrad describes the ups and downs of the Association of Women in Management at Eastern Airlines. The Honeywell Women's Council started in 1978 and had a full-time administration from 1982 to 1985. The budget was cut in half in 1986 when the company scaled back. The Women's Advisory Council (WAC) is thirteen years old and counts as one of its achievements a companywide maternity and paternity policy.

111. Loden, Marilyn. "Networking: It Can Change Your Life (address, May 27, 1981)." *Vital Speeches of the Day* 47 (August 1, 1981): 613-16.

A district staff manager for New York Telephone, Marilyn Loden delivered the speech on networking to the Women in Management network at Michigan Bell Telephone. She reviewed the rise of women into middle- and upper-level management and told how networking can be used to relieve the special stresses encountered by women in management. The advantages are a chance to explore common concerns, to test reality, and to build support.

112. "Managing the Male Mentor-Female Protégé Interface." *Management Review* 73 (November 1984): 7-8.

The number of male-female mentor-protégé relationships is increasing, and business writers warn both sexes to define the limits of the relationship. A relationship that is too intimate may result in guilt, loss of self-confidence, loss of reputation among co-workers, loss of career opportunities, or lawsuits, and disrupted careers. One result of such relationships is the reinforcement of biases against working women.

113. Nazario, Sonia L. "Gentlemen of the Club." *Wall Street Journal* (March 24, 1986): 19D.

There are still a large number of exclusive, all-male private clubs that have voted to exclude women or only allow women access to certain areas or on certain special occasions. A 1984 New York City law requires clubs with over 400 members to make membership available to women. The article lists clubs that exclude women, clubs that exclude men, and men's clubs that have opened to women and the year they opened.

114. "'Old Girls' Networks: Self-Help Groups Spring up for Female Managers." *Wall Street Journal* (August 4, 1981): 1.
Female managers have launched numerous career or "old-girl" networks featuring newsletters, business contacts, job banks, and speakers. However, Geraldine Dreffs, treasurer at *Newsweek*, advises women to join men's trade groups instead.

115. Reich, Murray H. "The Mentor Connection." *Personnel* 63 (February 1986): 50-56.
The author surveyed male and female executives and compared their mentor experiences to determine the importance of mentoring to their career progress. Most of the women (90 percent) were mentors to other women, while less than 5 percent of the men selected female protégés. Women cited these benefits of having a mentor: assignment to special projects, creation of new positions, autonomy on difficult tasks, career guidance and counseling on company politics, greater self-confidence, and feedback about weaknesses. For women, mentor relationships often developed into close friendships.

116. Rogan, Helen. "Take My Mentor—Please." *Harper's* 267 (October 1983): 6, 8.
A backlash is building against mentorism which has been touted, along with networking and dressing for success, as essential tools for the woman who desires a management position. Rogan says we may be entering what social critics call "the third stage of feminism," an attitude that calls for equality at the same time that we appreciate the differences between the sexes. As a result, women should be changing the "male" system, not just adopting its strategies—i.e., networking and mentors. She calls for more down-to-earth advice.

117. "Role Models: Women Executives Begin Serving as Others' Mentors." *Wall Street Journal* (August 4, 1981): 1.
Eighty percent of female senior executives are mentors for lower-level women, according to a Korn/Ferry International poll. Some female managers, however, feel "overstressed" as mentors and some refuse, preferring to be "left alone to do their jobs."

118. Salmans, Sandra. "Pittsburgh's Top Brass All Love the Duquesne Club." *New York Times* (August 9, 1981): sec. 6f, p. 17, col. 1.
Three women were admitted as members to the exclusive Duquesne Club in 1980. The three women—Alberta Arthurs, president of Chatham College; Paula Hughes, first vice president of Thomson McKinnon Securities and a trustee of Carnegie-Mellon University; and Sister Jane Scully, president of Carlow College and a director of Gulf Oil—join 2,500 men in the 100-year-old club but are still not allowed access to the gym, the tap room, and the grill.

119. Stamell, Marcia. "50 Ways to Leave Your Mentor." *Savvy* 4 (September 1983): 20, 22.

A survey of 440 professional women determined that women find it more difficult than men to end associations with their mentors. They also have fewer mentors than men. Nancy Collins, author of *Professional Women and Their Mentors*, believes that women often lose sight that mentor-protégé relationships should be temporary, that the relationship ends when you stop learning from your mentor.

120. Still, Leonie V., and Guerin, Cecily. "Networking Practices of Men and Women Managers Compared." *Women in Management Review* 2 (Summer 1986): 103-09.

Australian men and women executives, directors, and managers answered questions about their business, social, and professional networking practices. Women executives were more likely than men to seek advice from a wide range of contacts, but both groups preferred same-sex contacts. The researchers conclude that women used networks for establishing relationships, rather than for career purposes. References include information on WAM (Women in Management), founded in Sydney, New South Wales, in 1979.

121. Stuart, Reginald. "Businesswomen of Atlanta Finally Have a Home." *New York Times* (August 19, 1981): p. 12, col. 1.

A private dining club for businesswomen, the Women's Commerce Club, opened in Atlanta. The 200 members pay a $500 initial membership fee and $30 a month. The Atlanta Club, like the Blaisdell Place Club in Minneapolis, has its own building. Other business women's clubs will open soon in New York, Washington, San Francisco, and Los Angeles. Some clubs, including the 11,000 member Women's Economic Club of Detroit, do not plan to invest in their own building, and as one Atlanta retail store owner said, "I don't need a club to tell me I've arrived."

Management Training for Women

122. Ames, Michael D., and Deide, Dorothy. "Training and Developing Women Managers: Are They Really a Special Case?" *Personnel Administrator* 27 (November 1982): 19-20, 22, 24-26.

Ames and Deide ask, "Should women be allowed to be groomed for middle- and top-level management positions?" and review recent research on women managers. Writers claim that effective managers must perform well in four areas: a favorable attitude toward work, psychological and social preparedness for work, technical and administrative skills, and understanding organizational dynamics. The authors call for a two-phase training program for women in management: phase one provides training in technical/administrative skills and understanding of organizational politics, and phase two, which should include male colleagues and supervisors, covers favorable attitude and psychological and social preparedness. Includes figures and references.

123. Berryman-Fink, Cynthia, and Fink, Charles B. "Optimal Training for Opposite-Sex Managers." *Training and Development Journal* 39 (February 1985): 26-29.

The problem with women-only management training programs is that they teach women a masculine management style. The authors offer a model for androgynous management training—a combination of male (task-oriented) and female (people-oriented) styles. The androgynous training follows these steps: conduct needs assessment, formulate objectives, conduct training, and evaluate. Includes references.

124. Cook, Michael H. "Women in Management—Separate but Equal." *Training and Development Journal* 36 (February 1982): 4-5.

Cook wonders whether the women-only management education programs of the 1960s and 1970s are passé for the 1980s. He agrees that ideally there should be one type of management education for both women and men, but practically, the need for unique management training programs for women will continue through the 1980s. Alma Baron, professor of management at the University of Wisconsin-Extension, notes that since 1973 the number of women attending the Management Institute's women-only seminars has more than doubled.

125. Cornwall, Deborah J. "Managing Women for Success." *Supervisory Management* (January 1985): 34-39.

Cornwall uses case studies of four women to illustrate how male managers can coach women in management. The cases discuss overcompensation, equal pay for equal work, stereotypes, distractions from career goals, and the use of politics. Cornwall reminds male managers not to assume that women's goals are different from men's.

126. Doole, Isobel. "Women in Business—Is a Different Advisory Approach Necessary?" *Equal Opportunities International (UK)* 4 (3) (1985): 34-36.

Doole is owner of a marketing research agency and the organizer for management development for women programs conducted by the Yorkshire and Humberside Regional Management Centre. She claims that women business owners do not seek help from small business counseling programs, because the courses are not relevant to the women's needs. Doole concludes by calling for courses that recognize women's unique strengths and approaches to problems. Includes references.

127. Dorrell, Jean. "'Women in Business' as a Special Topics Course in the Collegiate Business School." *Journal of Business Education* 58 (April 1983): 254-57.

Lamar University offered an experimental Women in Business class in the summer of 1982. Ninety-three students attended the two-week course, using Norma Carr-Ruffino's *The Promotable Woman* as a textbook. Twenty outstanding women in the community shared their experiences with the class.

128. Fitzgerald, Louise F., and Shullman, Sandra L. "The Myths and Realities of Women in Organizations." *Training and Development Journal* 38 (April 1984): 65-70.

The authors review the myths and assumptions about women as managers that block their progress and list an eleven-point plan to help trainers and organizations provide career development for women managers: (1) conduct realistic recruitment efforts, (2) begin career development efforts immediately, (3) use assessment centers for selection, promotion, and development, (4) develop women's management skills through project teams and project management assignments, (5) monitor efforts to develop women managers, (6) include women in the organization's career planning efforts, (7) offer career development programs for women, (8) make women a part of the organization's image, (9) make organizational information available to all employees, (10) publicize openings throughout the organization, and (11) create multiple job paths. Includes references.

129. Glucklich, Pauline. "Women's Management Training in a Ghetto?" *Personnel Management* 17 (September 1985): 39-43.

The author reviews the status of women's management development training in Britain and describes in some detail single-sex management training for women in the Civil Service. She concludes with a list of nine steps personnel directors can take to improve equal opportunity for women. Includes references.

130. Harragan, Betty Lehan. "Management Training for Women." *Working Woman* 9 (February 1984): 38.

The author of *Games Mother Never Taught You* and *Knowing the Score* responds to a question about women-only management courses. She notes that funding for women's management development and career seminars has lessened since 1981, but argues that general business courses are still not bias free. Harragan claims there is a continuing need for specialized management training programs for women.

131. Hayden, Virginia, and Knowles, Wilf. "Innovation and Positive Action in Management Education." *Women in Management Review* 2 (Spring 1986): 12-17.

The authors describe the executive MBA program of the IMCB (International Management Centre in Buckingham). Participants are sponsored by their organizations for the eighteen-month program—a two-week introduction followed by weekly evening sessions and six residential weekends. IMCB intends to implement two Positive Action MBA programs for women in 1986/1987—one in London and one in Yorkshire. Up to a dozen women will participate in each. Includes references.

132. "Helping Women Managers Succeed." *Personnel Journal* 60 (July 1981): 522, 524-25.

An assistant professor and academic coordinator for continuing education for the College of Business Administration, Pennsylvania State University, advises organizations on ways to remove organizational barriers to women managers: (1) place women together with men on corporate taskforces, (2) hold after-hours work meetings in places where women are accepted as professionals, (3) put two or three women in each work group, (4) encourage women managers to meet other women managers within and outside their organizations, (5) decrease the power of the "old boy's network," and (6) formalize the mentor or sponsor relationship.

133. Hymowitz, Carol. "Tradition-Bound Alcoa Develops Training to Challenge Concerns Old-Boy Network." *Wall Street Journal* (November 15, 1983): sec. 2, p. 29.

The Aluminum Company of America instituted training programs for male and female employees that include information on motivation, problem solving, and teamwork. Charles W. Parry, Alcoa's chair, heads the company's equal-employment opportunity committee. Company spokespersons claim the number of women managers and professionals tripled in the past eight years.

134. Jaffe, Betty. "A Forced Fit." *Training and Development Journal* 39 (September 1985): 82-83.

Jaffe, the president of New York-based Career Continuum, says present career and management development programs are not helpful to most women managers, because their careers do not match the career/life stage theories of those programs. She offers an outline for redesigning human resource development programs. Includes Transition Resource Matrix (Table I) to aid individuals in assessing their coping strategies and expand their use of resources, and references.

135. Kurtz, Margaret A. "Internship: A Key in Management Training for Women." *Journal of Career Education* 10 (September 1983): 32-39.
Kurtz, professor and chairperson, Department of Business, Colby-Sawyer College, NH, describes the twelve-week internship program for women studying for the bachelor of science in Business Administration. She reviews strengths and weaknesses of internships and writes that students make an hour-long presentation on their internship experience at a two-week seminar following the internship. From 1973 to 1983 the enrollment in Colby-Sawyer College's Business Administration program grew from thirteen to over 100.

136. Lee, Chris. "Training for Women: Where Do We Go from Here?" *Training* 23 (December 1986): 26-27, 29-32, 34, 39-40.
Lee reviews the status of women in management, citing a recent *Wall Street Journal* report that says only 2 percent of top executives in a survey by Korn/Ferry International were women. The *Wall Street Journal* claims invisible barriers—the glass ceiling—keep women from middle- and upper-level management positions. The author asks what role training should play in alleviating this problem. Several organizations claim that the time for single-sex management development training is past. Now corporations such as DuPont and GTE are instituting classes designed to improve communication between men and women and classes that address the issues of barriers to women in management.

137. Linscott, Judy. "How to Keep Good People When You Can't Promote Them All." *Working Woman* 20 (February 1985): 24-25.
By 1995 there will be five candidates for every middle management job. Companies need to devise ways of challenging management employees who have plateaued. Some suggestions: lateral transfers, education, career planning, job rotation, self-management, and mentoring.

138. Lyles, Marjorie A. "Strategies for Helping Woman Managers—Or Anyone." *Personnel* 60 (January/February 1983): 67-77.
Lyles describes how socialization, lack of political awareness, and tokenism serve as barriers to women's management development, then tells how organizations can use the resources of information, social contacts, and power to help eliminate these barriers. She provides a decision-tree (Figure 1) for analyzing helping strategies. Includes figure.

139. Macdonald, Eleanor. "The Need for Training and Development." *Women in Management Review* 1 (Spring 1985): 40-44.
Macdonald, a founder of the Women in Management Association, began all-women management courses in 1969 to give women a place to develop confidence. In addition, women now have many informal groups where they can acquire speaking, negotiating, and team skills.

140. Millard, Richard J. "Reaching New Student Markets: A Women in Management Course." *Teaching of Psychology* 10 (October 1983): 169-70.
Millard describes a discussion-oriented Women in Management course developed for students at Creighton University, NE. Thirty females and four males registered for the night class—fourteen psychology majors, eleven business or communication majors, and nine students from the

community. *Women in Management* (Stead, 1978) and *The Managerial Woman* (Hennig and Jardim, 1977) served as textbooks, and the course covered five topics: stereotypes of women managers, sex-role socialization, leadership theories and differences in male-female management styles, mentors and support networks, and equal employment opportunity. The author concludes with a discussion of course requirements and an evaluation.

141. Novarra, Virginia. "Management Education: A Case for Women's Studies?" *Women's Studies International Forum* 5 (1982): 69-74.
An experienced manager in both the public and private sectors and author of *Women's Work—Men's Work—The Ambivalence of Equality*, Novarra questions why the women's movement has not addressed the issue of women in management. She reviews the status of management training for women, women's studies and management education, and describes the Anglican Regional Management Centre seminar on management training for women held in 1980. Novarra concludes that there should be coalitions between women's studies, the women's movement, and women executives.

142. Pedler, Mike, and Fritchie, Rennie. "Training Men to Work with Women." *Women in Management Review* 1 (Summer 1985): 75-84.
Because men relate to women as mothers, wives, or lovers, they may have difficulty finding comfortable and productive ways to work with women. The authors make a case for women-only management development, claiming that separate-sex training is a means of raising consciousness and women's confidence, before women work with men in situations where men hold the organizational power. Includes references and appendix that lists benefits and costs of having more women in management.

143. Rothwell, Sheila. "Cost-Effective Approaches to Women's Career Development." *Women in Management Review* 1 (Spring 1985): 30-39.
Rothwell proposes a strategic planning model designed to improve career development for women. The first step is an organizational audit to determine the numbers of women managers in various departments, what percent of all management positions that represents, and where women are blocked from management positions. Organizations might then set targets for increasing the percent of women managers and implement personnel policies of recruitment, training, development, promotion, and retention. She calls for continual monitoring, evaluation, and adjustment of the equal opportunity strategy. Includes diagrams and brief references.

144. Rothwell, Sheila. "Management Courses and Women." *Ergonomics* 27 (May 1984): 547-56.
Organizations use management development programs especially for women to increase the number of women in managerial positions. Rothwell explains the Henley Women's Scholarship Scheme, designed to prepare women for high-level management jobs. Ten women accepted scholarships to attend Henley's General Management Courses, and all were rated highly for their abilities and hard work as chairpersons and secretaries of their study groups. After completing their studies the

women returned to the same positions they held before, and none were promoted. Rothwell reviews the status of women in management courses and concludes with an appendix, "Opportunities for Women in Management Education (1982)," listing institution, course title, and a description of the courses. Includes references.

145. Schmidt, Peggy J. "Management-Development Courses." *Working Woman* 7 (August 1982): 16, 20, 22, 24.

Schmidt, the author of *Making It on Your First Job*, lists twenty management development courses, some specifically for women. She includes information on the sponsor, dates, location, length of course, cost, intended audience, subject areas, teachers, participants, credit, and date the course was established, followed by a general description of the course and a name to contact for further information.

146. Scriven, Jeannie. "Women in Management." *Equal Opportunities International (UK)* 2 (4) (1983): 21.

Scriven, who attended Henley Management College on a scholarship, describes the nine-and-a-half-week training course in general management. The students work in "syndicates", groups of eight who work together throughout the course. She illustrates the subtle differences in the way female students are treated and tells what women can learn from the course.

147. Spruell, Geraldine Romano. "Making It Big Time—Is It Really Tougher for Women?" *Training and Development Journal* 39 (July 1985): 30-33.

Although many women have earned middle-management positions, 59 percent of the Fortune 1,000 corporations had no female directors by 1985. These reasons are given for the lack of women in top management positions: women do not have enough experience for top management positions, discrimination continues, companies do not put women on visible projects, and women are not as ambitious as men. Organizations can actively help women by providing women-only training programs, but many women discourage separatist training, believing it perpetuates the myth of the weaker sex and the need for special training.

148. "Support from the Top Is Hard to Get, According to 1,600 Women in Management." *Wall Street Journal* (January 29, 1985): p. 1, col. 5.

Alma Baron, University of Wisconsin, polled women managers to see if they received adequate training and guidance from top management. Over 50 percent felt they did not. Seventy percent of the women agreed it is possible to have both a career and a family.

149. Watson, Eileen D., and Hodgson, Richard C. "Women in Management: Reducing the Price of Success." *Business Quarterly* 49 (Spring 1984): 137-43.

The authors, members of the Organizational Behavior area of Western's School of Business, claim that women managers pay a different price for success than do their male colleagues, as they encounter unique situations in their working relationships with men. Watson and Hodgson propose a five-part framework for developing women managers and reducing the need for each woman manager to learn "by experience."

150. "Where Industry Gains from Self-Confident Women." *Management Today* (January 1985): 13.

Julia Cleverdon leads the Pepperell unit of the Industrial Society. The Pepperell development course for women is a four-day course designed to increase women's motivation and to help them determine career goals. Cleverdon's goal is to "maximize the talents and energy of working women." She claims women's main problem is lack of confidence.

Sex-Role Stereotypes

151. Andrew, John. "Woman Accuses a Chinatown Bank of Nurturing Old Sexist Customs." *Wall Street Journal* (May 26, 1982): 33.
Peggy Joslyn, a former executive at General Bank of Commerce, filed a $6 million sexual harassment suit against the bank after repeated offensive remarks from Oriental businessmen. Mrs. Joslyn, born in Taiwan, received critical phone calls from other Chinese as a result of her lawsuit, but she believes it is time to speak up for Asian women.

152. Arkkelin, Daniel, and Simmons, Rosemary. "The 'Good Manager': Sex-Typed, Androgynous, or Likable?" *Sex Roles* 12 (June 1985): 1187-98.
Thirty-two psychology students rated sixteen managerial profiles for masculine, feminine, or a combination of masculine and feminine traits. Consistent with other research, the students rated masculine characteristics as more desirable than feminine characteristics for managers. However, the respondents rated androgynous (masculine-feminine) characteristics as equally desirable as masculine characteristics. Includes tables and references.

153. Baron, Alma S. "What Men Are Saying about Women in Business." *Business Horizons* 25 (January/February 1982): 10-14.
Professor of management at the University of Wisconsin Extension-Madison, Alma Baron questioned 8,000 men who attended executive development programs about their attitudes toward women in management. Baron found that half of the men accepted women in managerial roles, and men with higher levels of education were more accepting of women managers, as were men who work for women managers. Eighty-seven percent of the men surveyed disagreed with the statement "Generally women become top executives by using sexual favors."

154. Brenner, O. C., and Bromer, John A. "Sex Stereotypes and Leaders' Behavior as Measured by the Agreement Scale for Leadership Behavior." *Psychological Reports* 48 (June 1981): 960-62.
Sixty-six male and sixty-six female graduate business students responded to the twenty-item Agreement Scale for Leadership Behavior to determine the similarity or difference in their behavior when confronted with a specific leadership situation in the business environment. Results indicated that both male and female managers prefer stereotypically male

leadership behaviors, reinforcing Schein's (1976) "think manager—think male" theory. Includes tables and references.

155. Cash, Thomas F., and Kilcullen, Robert N. "The Aye of the Beholder: Susceptibility to Sexism and Beautyism in the Evaluation of Managerial Applicants." *Journal of Applied Social Psychology* 15 (1985): 591-605.

Sixteen male sex-typed subjects, sixteen female sex-typed subjects, sixteen androgynous males, and sixteen androgynous females, all college students enrolled in an introductory psychology class, reviewed resumes with photographs and rated applicants for a managerial position. The researchers found that sex-typed raters gave higher recommendations to attractive applicants than did androgynous raters. Includes table and references.

156. Chonko, Lawrence B. "Machiavellianism: Sex Differences in the Profession of Purchasing Management." *Psychological Reports* 51 (October 1982): 645-46.

Ninety-eight male and twenty-four female purchasing managers completed a Machiavellian personality orientation questionnaire, the Mach IV Scale. The respondents were higher in Machiavellian orientation than most other groups, and females scored significantly higher than males, which is not consistent with the findings of other studies. Chonko suggests that, because purchasing has been a male-dominated profession, female purchasing managers may feel they have to prove something by being more assertive or aggressive. Includes references.

157. Fortino, Denise. "The Office Family." *Working Woman* 7 (April 1982): 98-101.

Employees may relate to co-workers, bosses, or subordinates as if they were family members. Women managers may not fit the family stereotype of the nurturer, mother, or sister and may be viewed as the "bad" mother or witch. Christine Mosca-Miehalec, director of a Westport, CT, seminar company, advises women managers to come to terms with their authority, not to relinquish or camouflage it.

158. Izraeli, Dafna N., and Izraeli, Dove. "Sex Effects in Evaluating Leaders: A Replication Study." *Journal of Applied Psychology* 70 (August 1985): 540-46.

Researchers at Bar-Ilan University and Tel Aviv University replicate a 1976 study by Bartol and Butterfield to test the hypothesis that sex-role stereotypes bias the performance evaluation of managers. Their research differed in four variables—respondents, culture, timing, and instrument—and their findings differed in that no sex of leader effects were found. Includes tables and references.

159. Jabes, Jak. "Causal Attributions and Sex-Role Stereotypes in the Perceptions of Women Managers." *Canadian Journal of Behavioral Sciences* 12 (January 1980): 52-63.

One-hundred forty-four female managers in the Ottawa area participated in an experiment to determine the extent of sex-role stereotyping of male and female managers. Respondents' answers indicated a positive bias toward women managers and acceptance of an active rather than passive role for women managers. Includes table and references.

160. Kanes, John, and Kanes, Martha. "The Girls in the Executive Suite." *Savvy* (July 1983): 11.

Although *Business Week* and *Fortune* magazines have revised their formats, their coverage of women in business remains patronizing and stereotypical. A case in point is an April 1983 issue of *Fortune*, where Olive Ann Beech, honored for her induction into the Hall of Fame for U.S. Business, is described by her late husband Walter as having "pretty good-looking legs."

161. "Male Bias Just Won't Quit." *Management Review* 72 (August 1983): 54.

University researchers surveyed 162 male and 113 female business college students about their attitudes toward women. In 99 percent of the cases, the men retained more traditional views of woman's role. Their biases were strongest in six areas: leadership, breadwinner, social behavior, parent-spouse, female sex role, and male courtesy role. The women, on the other hand, expressed increasingly liberal views about their roles.

162. Mason, Janet. "Opportunities for Women." *Management World* 14 (October 1985): 16-17.

Sixty-nine percent of the women responding to a recent Administrative Management Society survey believe it is harder for women than men to advance in their companies. Both sexes agreed that sex stereotypes held by male managers is the number one problem for women managers. Women also cited lack of mentors, lack of visibility, and lack of "knowledge of the game" as barriers to advancement. Insert highlights men's advice to women and women's advice to women.

163. "Nonverbal Communication: A Threat to Women Managers?" *Management Review* 72 (May 1983): 56.

A Fordham University professor believes that women managers may be limiting their potential because of their nonverbal communication style. They may exhibit "courting" or "quasi-courting" nonverbal cues in body movements, facial expressions, gestures, use of space, and eye contact. These behaviors, according to the researcher, indicate powerlessness and subordinate status. Women must learn to recognize these nonverbal behavior patterns and seek to change them.

164. Parlee, Mary Brown. "Getting a Word in Sex-Wise." *Across the Board* 21 (September 1984): 7-10.

The former director of City University of New York's Center for the Study of Women and Society claims that the way women talk is a disadvantage in the corporate world. Women generally have high-pitched voices, use more inflections, speak faster, and use more qualifiers and questioning intonations—"it seems," "don't you think?" Women also tend to smile frequently when speaking, nod often, and maintain eye contact while speaking. Executive women often try to avoid these feminine speaking patterns by talking "more slowly, more evenly, more loudly" to appear more businesslike.

165. Pearson, Dick. "Perceptions about Women Managers." *Supervisory Management* 29 (October 1984): 29-34.

Employers are often reluctant to promote women to management, because of inaccurate perceptions about women's ability to make difficult decisions, the feeling that woman's place is in the home, and the belief that a working woman deprives a man of a job. Pearson lists the true barriers to women executives: the biological fact that women have children and management's concern that mothers will leave the workforce to be full-time mothers.

166. Peters, Lawrence H., et al. "Sex Bias and Managerial Evaluations: A Replication and Extension." *Journal of Applied Psychology* 69 (May 1984): 349-52.

Researchers replicate previous work on sex bias in performance appraisals, focusing on supervisory ratings of managers in the same job in the same organization. They conluded that sex bias did not appear to be a major force in performance appraisal ratings. Includes table and references.

167. Trotsky, Judith. "Must Women Executives Be Such Barracudas?" *Wall Street Journal* (November 9, 1981): 28.

From personal experience and conversations with others, the author concludes that many upper-level women executives are intent on achieving their goals regardless of means. This attitude may be more prevalent among older women, says Maryanne Vanderhelde, president of a New York consulting firm, due to the abuse and frustration these women have experienced in their careers. Other factors may be training, pressures, and the perception that what is viewed as assertive behavior in men is seen as aggressive behavior in women.

168. Van Hulsteyn, Peggy. "Look before You Weep: Getting Ahead at the Office." *Cosmopolitan* 199 (September 1985): 112, 117-18.

To counteract the stereotype of the "overemotional" executive women, follow this author's advice. It is important that co-workers respect you, but they do not all have to like you; accept criticism and learn from it; after apologizing to your boss for a mistake, ask for information on how you might have handled the situation; learn to work wih people you do not like. The author also offers six ways to avoid crying at the office.

169. Wiley, Mary Glenn, and Eskilson, Arlene. "Coping in the Corporation: Sex Role Constraints." *Journal of Applied Social Psychology* 12 (January/February 1982): 1-11.

Ninety-six middle managers (82 percent male) read one-page scripts, "Interaction in a Corporate Setting," and responded to a questionnaire to study reactions to several influence techniques. Researchers varied sex of the actor, sex of the other, and the influence technique used by the actor in the scripts. Respondents viewed influential males as more powerful and higher in corporate position than females who were given identical descriptions in the scripts. Includes tables and references.

170. Williams, Mary. "Something as Simple as a Smile May Make or Break a Female Manager." *Wall Street Journal* (February 16, 1984): p. 37, col. 2.

According to the findings of a study of men and women working together, "Women smile more, and women are perceived (by their peers) to be less effective managers." Carl Camden, communications professor at Cleveland State University, and Carol Kennedy, nursing professor at Ohio State, performed a second study—this time the subjects were nurses in management positions. Preliminary findings indicate that people prefer working for the more nurturant, "feminine style" managers as opposed to those managers with a male, "task-oriented" style.

171. "Women as Managers." *Personnel Journal* 60 (November 1981): 828.

Virginia L. Carter, former president of the Los Angeles chapter of the National Organizaton for Women, tells businesses that by excluding women from top management they have eliminated a large pool of prospective managers, since half the population is female. Speaking to the Personnel and Industrial Relations Association in Los Angeles, Carter described three difficulties corporate women still face: stereotypes, insecurities, and discrimination. Carter tells women to get into as many jobs as quickly as possible rather than to focus on affirmative action and equal employment opportunity.

Black Women Managers and Business Owners

172. "Barbara Proctor: I Made It Because I'm Black and a Woman."
Ebony 37 (August 1982): 142-44.

Barbara Proctor is president of Chicago's Proctor and Gardner Advertising Inc., the second largest black-owned advertising agency in the United States. An illegitimate child who grew up in rural Black Mountain, SC, Proctor will earn $15 million this year. She credits her grandmother's advice and the necessity to provide for her son as impetus for her success. Includes photographs.

173. "Black Women College Presidents." *Ebony* 41 (February 1986): 108-10, 115.

An American Council on Education's Office of Women in Higher Education study shows that black women are only fourteen of the 286 women college presidents in this country, and most of the minority women college presidents (9 percent of the number of women college presidents) were appointed since 1980. Frequently the black woman college president is the first of her sex, as well as the first black person, in that position. Includes photographs and profiles of the fourteen women.

174. Campbell, Bebe Moore. "To Be Black, Gifted, and Alone." *Savvy* 5 (December 1984): 66-70, 73-74.

The Bureau of Labor Statistics reported in 1984 that only 1,474,000 black women held executive, administrative, managerial, or professional positions compared to 22,250,000 white women. Black women in corporate America experience the stress of racism, sexism, and professional competition and, in addition, feel they must make the whites they work with feel comfortable. The higher black women move up the corporate ladder, the more they are isolated from other blacks.

175. Clarke, Richard V. "Playing to Win." *Essence* 11 (March 1981): 45, 47, 50.

More blacks have now entered management, but they are still clustered in lower-level management positions. To advance, Clarke recommends planning and setting career goals with deadlines, obtaining advanced degrees, gaining broad experiences, "flying the flag" (letting people know who you are and what you can do), and job switching, if necessary. Clarke advises businesswomen to be their own best advocates.

176. "Ebony/Jet Heiress Linda Johnson Rice Surveys Her Empire." *Chicago* 35 (April 1986): 16.
Linda Johnson Rice (twenty-eight years old) is vice-president and assistant to the publisher of *Ebony, Jet,* and *EM* magazines; three radio stations; and a cosmetics company. When she completes her master's degree at Northwestern University, she will succeed her father as president and the only black in the *Forbes* Four Hundred. Johnson Rice is not involved in politics, claiming that black achievement is highlighted in her publications.

177. Edwards, Audrey. "Managing the Game." *Essence* 13 (March 1983): 70-72, 136, 140.
Edwards describes a forty-year-old black woman regional manager of a large bank, a twenty-eight-year-old product-information officer for a food company, and a thirty-three-year-old sales manager for a Houston telecommunications firm, their corporate experiences, lifestyle, and advice on being a black woman manager in sometimes hostile environments. Insert gives "affirmative action" tips: be realistic, affirm yourself, set priorities, delegate responsibilities, take risks, know that you are good.

178. Noel, Pamela. "Corporate Conquerors: Black Women on the Rise." *Ebony* 40 (November 1984): 76-78, 80, 82.
Noel profiles thirteen black women managers who work in Fortune 500 companies. Figures for black women managers remain low, however—1.6 percent of "officals and managers" compared to 2.7 percent for black males and 18.8 percent for white women, according to the Equal Employment Opportunity Commission (1982). The article includes photographs and brief biographies of the thirteen women.

179. Pattner, Emily, and Paris-Chitanvis, J. "Making a Statement." *Working Woman* 7 (July 1982): 64-67.
In 1981 black women accounted for 5.7 percent of the women managers in the United States, according to the Women's Bureau of the United States Department of Labor. Fashion experts say black women executives can express their individual style in the corporate world while presenting a professional image.

180. Steptoe, Sonja. "Strangers in a Strange Land." *Wall Street Journal* (March 24, 1986): 21D.
The Equal Employment Opportunity Commission claims that black women are less than 2 percent of all corporate managers, and there are fewer than twenty black women corporate officers in the Fortune 1,000. It is often difficult for black women managers to get line experience, and they frequently feel isolated and lonely.

181. Weathers, Diane. "Winning under the Double Whammy." *Savvy* 2 (April 1981): 34-40.
The black woman executive, sometimes termed the "two-fer" (scoring a point for being black and a point for being female), still accounts for a very small percent of corporate executives. Figures from the 1978 EEOC (Equal Employment Opportunity Commission) show that minority women were only 1.8 percent of all white-collar officials and managers. Interviews with several black women managers uncovered some common

threads: most of them had mothers, aunts, and grandmothers who worked outside the home; all were told there was nothing they could not do; and many, disillusioned with the lack of opportunity in the corporate environment, find they prefer the entrepreneurial style.

182. White, Frank, III. "Widows Who Run the Family Business." *Ebony* 39 (November 1983): 87-88, 90, 92.
Ebony features five women who assumed management of family businesses after the deaths of their husbands: Jolyn Robichaux, Baldwin Ice Cream Co., Chicago; Laverda Allen, Bay Cities Beauty Supply Co., Oakland, CA; Lou Nelle Sutton, Sutton-Sutton Mortuary, San Antonio, TX; Elma Summers, Summers Hotel, Jackson, MS; and Thelma Cash, Ray's Sausage Co., Cleveland, OH. Robichaux's company is one of the twenty largest black-owned businesses in Chicago.

183. White, Paula S. "On Top and in Charge." *Essence* 15 (March 1985): 88-93.
White outlines the careers and clothing styles for three black women executives: Kathleen Wyer Lane, director of sales and marketing for a corporate communications company; Phyllis Tucker, vice president of children's programs at NBC; and Gwendolyn England, skin-care specialist for Flori Roberts Cosmetics. Includes photographs and brand names and prices for clothing.

184. "Women at the Top." *Ebony* 37 (August 1982): 146-48.
Ebony profiles seven black women who have reached the top in their professions or careers: Margaret Bush Wilson, chair, National Board of NAACP; Dorothy I. Height, president, National Council of Negro Women; Coretta Scott King, president, Martin Luther King Jr. Center for Nonviolent Social Change; Dr. Ruth Love, general superintendent of schools, Chicago; Lenora Carter, publisher, *Houston Forward Times*; Dr. Lenora Cole-Alexander, director, Women's Bureau, United States Department of Labor; and Dr. Rosalyn Sterling, cardiovascular surgeon in Houston, TX. Includes photographs.

185. "Women with Clout in City Government." *Ebony* 39 (October 1984): 88, 90, 92, 94.
Ebony features fourteen black women who hold high-level positions in city government. Includes photographs.

186. Wright, Roosevelt; King, Shirley W.; and Berg, William E. "Job Satisfaction in the Workplace: A Study of Black Females in Management Positions." *Journal of Social Service Research* 8 (Spring 1985): 65-79.
Researchers studied differences in job satisfaction among black female managers in human service agencies. They found, among other things, that single or never-married females indicated greater job satisfaction. Includes tables and references.

MBAs

187. Anderson, Susan Heller, and Carroll, Maurice. "Striking It Rich." *New York Times* (February 20, 1984): sec. 2, p. 3, col. 2.

Alumnae and seventy-five women students of the Columbia Business School gathered for the fifth annual "Striking It Rich" conference. The women discussed sexual discrimination, office love affairs, and negotiating for raises and promotions. Almost 50 percent of those enrolled in Columbia Business School are women.

188. Bennett, Amanda. "A Road Already Traveled." *Wall Street Journal* (March 24, 1986): 11D.

Recent women MBA graduates expect to reach the top, but may be in for a rude shock, say their older female colleagues. Female MBAs in 1985 earned an average starting salary of $40,045. The younger women anticipate that corporations will accommodate their career and family concerns, as the women become increasingly valuable to the corporation.

189. "Boosting the Careers of B-School Grads." *Business Week* (October 11, 1982): 72.

A Stanford University study found that after graduation women MBAs earn an average $4,000 less than male MBA graduates. Several colleges have addressed this inequality by initiating programs to help businesswomen advance up the corporate ladder. Examples of such programs include the Wharton Women Alumnae Conference, the Women in Business Committee at Wayne State, the Women in Management group at Southern Methodist University, and the mentor program for women students at the University of Southern California at Los Angeles.

190. Feather, Frank. "De-Sexing of Management." *Industry Week* 211 (October 5, 1981): 15.

A cofounder and president of Global Futures network reminds readers that women now account for over half the students enrolled in American graduate schools of business. He points out that by the year 2000 these graduates will be heading most United States corporations and suggests there may be major societal transformations as male and female managers adjust their management styles.

191. Flanagan, William G. "What Makes Suzanne Run?" *Forbes* 136 (October 7, 1985): 152.

Flanagan reviews *Women Like Us* by Liz Roman Gallese. The book is subtitled, "What Is Happening to the Women of the Harvard Business School, Class of '75—The Women Who Had the First Chance to Make It to the Top." The reviewer claims that Gallese deals more with her subjects' personal lives than with their corporate careers and concludes that the book might be more helpful to the men who will compete with and marry them.

192. Gallese, Liz Roman. "Women Like Us (I)." *Working Woman* 10 (January 1985): 82-84, 104, 106-07.

The first installment in a three-part series from Gallese's book, *Women Like Us*, starts with an explanation of her motivation for writing this story of the women of the class of 1975 at Harvard Business School. Readers are introduced to two of the six women that Gallese profiles in the book.

193. Gallese, Liz Roman. "Women Like Us (II)." *Working Woman* 10 (February 1985): 113-14, 116, 118, 120.

In the second excerpt from Gallese's book *Women Like Us,* marriage and family are the issues. Readers meet Martha Davis who is concerned about relocation and Holly Lane Pfeiffer, mother of three who is trying to "do it all."

194. Gallese, Liz Roman. "Women Like Us (III)." *Working Woman* 10 (March 1985): 164, 166, 168, 172.

In excerpt number three from *Women Like Us*, Gallese introduces readers to Mary Pat Horner who had difficulty fitting in the business world and Tess Beckett, a woman who got control of her life at the expense of her marriage. One common thread in the stories of the women Gallese interviewed was the issue of compromise.

195. Johnson, Sharon. "Women and Long Workdays." *New York Times* (June 25, 1984): sec. 2, p. 9.

A professor in the Graduate School of Business, University of Texas, studied 1,500 women and men who had earned MBAs from the University of Texas from 1920–1980. She found that women workaholics—those who worked more than fifty hours a week—were more likely than their male workaholic colleagues to be single, divorced, or married several times. The male workaholics earned 30 percent more than other men who worked less than fifty hours a week, but female workaholics were more concerned than males about combining work with a family and said they found their careers more pleasurable than leisure or family activities. They also viewed themselves as less successful than the male workaholics in the survey.

196. Krasny, Robin. "Storming Harvard Business School: Diary of the First Year." *Savvy* 2 (June 1981): 32-38.

A *cum laude* Princeton graduate reveals the fears, failures, and fun of her first semester at Harvard Business School. Diary entries cover September 1979 to March 1980, when Krasny ended the first semester with grades in her three classes—Managerial Economics, Control, and Organizational Behavior. She received one fail, one satisfactory, and one excellent.

197. Mikalachki, Dorothy Martin, and Mikalachki, Alexander. "MBA Women: The New Pioneers." *Business Quarterly* 49 (Spring 1984): 110-14.

Seventy-one women graduates of the MBA program at the University of Western Ontario give advice to women entering the MBA program. Most graduates stressed having a career plan. Other issues discussed were problems of combining motherhood and a career, relocation for dual-career couples, politics and conditioning, and entrepreneurs. Women cited men's attitudes and women's lack of understanding of business politics as two obstacles that women in business encounter. Management political skills to be learned include team work, differentiating among colleagues, competition, self-interest, and planned movement to the top. Includes one table.

198. O'Toole, Patricia. "The Truth about the Value of an MBA." *Savvy* 2 (July 1981): 14-18.

In 1981, 54,000 MBAs graduated, 30 percent of them women. Initial job offers to MBAs are substantially higher than for other graduates, but after some time, salaries even out between MBAs and non-MBAs "doing equally good work." The best combination appears to be an undergraduate technical degree plus an MBA, especially for women. Women's salaries still fall well below those of their male counterparts. The median salary for male MBAs five years after graduation is $38,300, for women $30,000.

199. Rowan, Roy. "How Harvard's Women MBAs Are Managing." *Fortune* 108 (July 11, 1983): 58-60, 64, 68, 72.

Thirty-four women graduated from Harvard Business School in 1973—the first class to have been 5 percent female. Ten years after graduation, thirty-three of the women are working (all but one full time), eighteen are married, and fourteen have children. Their median salary is $57,000—lower than the average salary of their male classmates. By 1983 women made up 25 percent of the graduating business school class, and most of them had some business experience before attending Harvard.

200. "Survey Shows Women Leaving Manager Jobs." *Cedar Rapids (Iowa) Gazette* (July 31, 1986): 6C.

Sixty-nine percent of the men and women who received MBAs from the country's best business schools in 1976 chose jobs in large corporations, but ten years later 30 percent of the women were self-employed or unemployed compared to 21 percent of the men. Details of a survey were published in the August 18 issue of *Fortune*.

201. Weiss, Elaine F. "To B-School or Not to B-School?" *Savvy* 4 (December 1983): 36-39, 41.

As a "cult of adoration" developed about the MBA degree, the number of women MBAs increased ten times, from 1,500 in 1973 to 15,000 in 1983. An MBA degree may be more or less valuable depending on the rating of the business school—only 204 of the 550 MBA programs are accredited by the American Assembly of Collegiate Schools of Business.

One school, the Graduate School of Management at Simmons College (Boston), is for the woman reentering the workforce or changing professions. Although an MBA might guarantee a woman an entry-level position, studies show that women MBAs are frequently paid less than their male counterparts with comparable credentials and work experience.

Profiles of Women Managers

202. "Back in Harness." *Forbes* (July 1, 1985): 118.
Muriel Siebert has again picked up the reins at her discount brokerage firm, Muriel Siebert & Co., after a five-year stint as superintendent of the New York State banking system and an unsuccessful try at the Republican nomination for United States Senator from New York. Siebert says her firm lost its position in the industry while it was in a blind trust during her tenure in government.

203. Bartocci, Barbara. "I Had Money and Success, but Something Was Wrong." *Glamour* 81 (August 1983): 108, 110, 113.
The former president and owner of a successful ad agency, Bartocci has written a novel about adolescent problems. The Kansas City Hyatt Regency Hotel tragedy caused her to reassess her personal and career goals, and she chronicles her decision to sell her business and leave a $50,000 yearly income to return to creative writing. Two-thirds of the way through her first year as a full-time writer she had completed several short stories and two novels.

204. Beauchamp, Marc. "Report Card." *Forbes* 137 (June 30, 1986): 130.
Sandra Kurtzig, founder of ASK Computer Systems, Inc., retains her title as chair of the company but no longer serves as chief executive. She chose, instead, to study French Impressionist painting at Stanford, to travel, and to spend more time with her two children. Happy with her new lifestyle, Kurtzig says, "ASK was wonderful, but I never got wrapped up in the power trip of it all."

205. Beller, Miles. "Making Motown's Movies." *Harper's Bazaar* 118 (September 1985): 288, 292, 341.
Since 1981 Suzanne de Passe has been president of Motown Productions. At age thirty-nine, she earns a six-figure salary and manages a $10 million budget. To do it de Passe admits she had to sacrifice a social life and claims that power is the ability to move people.

206. Bettner, Jill. "After the Centerfold." *Forbes* (March 26, 1984): 43–44.
Christie Hefner, company president of Playboy Enterprises, owns 67 percent of the stock. The company reported a twelve cents-a-share profit, the first profit in two years.

207. Blank, Sally J. "Real Estate Tycoon: Wendy Luscombe at Full Gallop." *Management Review* 75 (November 1986): 14–15.
Wendy Luscombe, president of Pan American Properties and Buckingham Holdings since 1981, has a staff of twenty-five and responsibility for $1 billion in real estate and pension funds. Luscombe travels a great deal, acquiring properties in "second-tier towns" (Tampa, Seattle, Tulsa, etc.), and describes her new style as right-brained and more relaxed than the usual management style in the United Kingdom.

208. Braham, James. "Women at the Top." *Industry Week* 224 (March 4, 1985): 106–08, 110, 112–14.
Industry Week compiled a list of eighty-five top American female executives and divided them into "Corporate Climbers" and "Entrepreneurs." The list includes thirty-one women at the chair or CEO level and seventeen presidents. Both lists are divided by category: industrial, retailing, financial, or communications. The article includes photographs and brief descriptions of each woman.

209. Buckvar, Felice. "Scarsdale Woman Shares Her Success." *New York Times* (February 27, 1983): sec. 22, p. 4, col. 3.
Patricia Duncanson is chair of the Governor's Advisory Council on Minority Business Enterprises and president of Duncanson Electric Company, employer of thirty to fifty people. She was one of thirty women who participated in a year's training sponsored by the AWED (American Woman's Economic Development) Corporation, a nonprofit organization which counsels and trains women in business management techniques. AWED is open to any woman for a nominal fee. The toll-free number is 800-442-AWED.

210. Burstein, Patricia. "Carrying On." *Savvy* 5 (July 1984): 52–55, 57.
Savvy profiles two widows who took over family businesses after the deaths of their husbands. Gertrude Crain, secretary/treasurer at Crain Communications for thirty-two years, became chair of the board in 1973 and revenues have increased over 700 percent since 1970. Fran Muncey turned Bill Muncey Industries, a hydroplane manufacturer, from near bankruptcy three years before to a $70,000 profit in 1984.

211. Cohen, Jerry. "Woman Executive at 51: Come Back in a Few Years." *Los Angeles Times* (June 9, 1983): sec. 1, p. 1, 23–24.
As part of a series on growing older in twentieth-century America, Patricia Lindh, a fifty-one-year-old vice president at the Bank of America in Los Angeles, shares her views on middle age. She says her life is more sedentary, she is more irritable and less tolerant than she used to be, less inclined to smalltalk. She feels no threat from younger women, claiming women's rights was her reason for serving as White House liaison on women's organizations for President Gerald R. Ford from 1974 to 1977.

212. "A Company without Offices." *Harvard Business Review* 64 (January/February 1986): 127–36.
Eliza G. C. Collins, *Harvard Business Review* senior editor, interviews Steve Shirley, owner of F International, a computer consulting company that earned $10 million in sales in 1985. Shirley started her company in 1962 and now boasts 1,000 freelance employees in the United Kingdom,

The Netherlands, and Denmark. She says that her company works through flexibility and teamwork. Forty-nine percent of F International employees have children under the age of six, and 16 percent of the company's employees are male.

213. Cunningham, Mary. "What I Learned from Being a Woman in a Man's World." *Glamour* 82 (May 1984): 84, 87–88, 92.

In excerpts from *Powerplay: What Really Happened at Bendix*, Cunningham tells about the lessons she learned from her ordeal at Bendix Corporation. She believes that, in the end, both she and Bill Agee have become stronger and happier.

214. Davis, Peter. "The $100,000 a Year Woman." *Esquire* 101 (June 1984): 70–74, 76, 78, 81–82, 84, 86, 88, 90–92.

Davis chose Lisa Wolfson, who earns over $100,000 a year in a private investment firm, as the epitome of the latest American success story. He chronicles a typical day in Wolfson's career.

215. Donovan, Carrie. "Meeting Estée Lauder." *New York Times Magazine* (October 13, 1985): sec. 6, p. 86.

Two new books, an autobiography and a biography, chronicle the history of the Estée Lauder cosmetics company. *Estée: A Success Story* is Estée Lauder's own version of hard work and rewards. *Estée Lauder: Beyond the Magic* is an unauthorized biography painting a less sympathetic portrait of the cosmetics company founder and her rise to the top.

216. Dullea, Georgia. "'Enough Is Enough' for Ex-Superwoman." *New York Times* (November 15, 1985): sec. 1, p. 20, col. 2.

Thirty-seven-year-old San Franciscan Carol Orsborn founded Superwomen Anonymous, a group dedicated to "a life style of downward mobility." The organization of 200 Type E women, "high-achieving women who try to be everything to everybody," has no meetings and no officers, and the motto is "Enough Is Enough." For additional information write Superwomen Anonymous, Orsborn Group Public Relations, 1275 Columbus Avenue, San Francisco, CA 94133.

217. Ellis, James E.; Fabrikant, Geraldine; and Ames, Elizabeth. "Now Even Playboy Is Bracing for a Midlife Crisis." *Business Week* (April 15, 1985): 66, 68.

Christie Hefner, thirty-two years old and employed by Playboy Enterprises, Inc., since 1975, has plans for making the company smaller. As president she wants to change programming on the Playboy Channel, update the image of the Playboy clubs, and revise the magazine style.

218. "A Female CEO on the Right Lines." *International Management* (December 1982): 23–24.

After a stint as president of Olivetti's United States subsidiary, Marisa Bellisario was named head of Italtel, the state-owned Italian telecommunications company. After reducing the number of employees by 4,000, turnover was up 40 percent and the operating margin rose from minus $27 million to plus $20 million.

219. Fraser, Jill Andresky. "In Full Career." *Vogue* 174 (November 1984): 179.

Fraser profiles Sandra Kurtzig, founder of ASK Computer Systems, Inc., a software-development corporation with $65 million annual sales. She cites Bureau of Labor statistics showing that women accounted for 31.9 percent of managers in 1982 compared to 19.6 percent in 1972 but indicates that women managers are still found in traditionally female occupations: office management, health administration, banking, sales, education. She advises women to ask for flexible compensation packages, to guard against professional jealousy between colleagues, and to push for greater corporate support for child care.

220. Goodwin, Betty. "10 Distinguished Women Honored." *Los Angeles Times* (December 4, 1984): sec. 5, p. 4.

The Women in Business network honored ten "Distinguished Women of the Decade" at its tenth anniversary celebration. The honorees included a corporate president, an artist, a state chief justice, a college president, a playwright, a city council president, and a cosmetics company founder. In their three-minute acceptance speeches, the women spoke of the progress of women in business and the professions.

221. Graham, Pauline. "Mary Parker Follett (1868–1933): The Philosopher of Management." *Women in Management Review* 1 (Summer 1985): 85–90.

The author reviews Follett's life and work and her philosophy of management. She tells how *Dynamic Administration—The Collected Papers of Mary Parker Follett* helps her handle questions of responsibility, power, conflict, control, and authority. Graham claims that Follett's philosophy is relevant today and applauds her "rediscovery."

222. Green, Constance M. "High-Heeled Power: The Push for Success in the Corporate Arena." *Black Enterprise* 16 (August 1985): 104, 106–07.

Suzanne de Passe, thirty-five years old and president of Motown Productions, is the highest-ranking black woman in the entertainment industry; and Brenda Neal, a forty-two-year-old investment executive with Drexel Burnham Lambert, was the first black woman in the President's Club, an elite group of Drexel's highest-producing managers. Neal and de Passe are exceptions, however—there are only 764,000 black female managers, only 8 percent of the total number of female managers in the United States, according to a Bureau of Labor Statistics report. Many of those women are the only black managers in a division or company, and they believe that racism and sexism keep them from advancing to top posts.

223. Gross, Jane. "Against the Odds: A Woman's Ascent on Wall Street." *New York Times* (January 6, 1985): sec. 6, p. 16, col. 1.

According to industry experts, women fill one-third of entry-level investment banking jobs and earn about $50,000 a year. Karen Valenstein, thirty-eight-year-old first vice president at E. F. Hutton, earns more than a quarter-million dollars a year and is described by her peers, superiors, and clients as competitive, aggressive, persuasive, "a real scrapper," tenacious, and skillful at negotiating. Includes photographs.

224. Hendrix, Kathleen. "Eight Women Who Have Succeeded in the Highly Competitive Workplace." *Los Angeles Times* (September 16, 1984): sec. 6, p. 1, 14–16.

Hendrix profiles eight successful women in business and the professions: Virginia Oaxaca of Arco Petroleum Products; Sylvia Drew Ivie, attorney for the National Health Law Program; Gail Winslow, stockbroker at Ferris & Co., Washington, DC; Adrienne Hall, cofounder of an advertising agency; Barbara Casey, owner of a public relations firm in Malibu; Donna Shalala, president of New York City's Hunter College; Shirley Hufstedler, attorney and member of the board of Hewlett-Packard and US West; and Jane Evans, president and CEO of Monet Jewelers. Includes quotes and photographs.

225. Horovitz, Bruce. "50 Rising Stars for the Future." *Industry Week* (February 21, 1983): 48–49, 52–53, 56, 58, 60.

From names supplied by two-dozen executive search firms, *Industry Week* compiled a list of fifty "rising stars" for the 1980s. Eighteen of the candidates work in high-technology areas, thirteen in finance or service industries, seven in basic industries, six in consumer products, five in industrial equipment, and one in natural resources. The ten women named are Virginia Blackford, Patricia Cook, Jane Evans, Ursula Farrell Fairbairn, Julie H. Goodrich, Lynne E. O'Shea, Robyn Smith, Lisa Wachner, Lynne Stauffer, and Kendra A. Vandermeulen.

226. "How Five Executive Women Entertain in the Boardroom and at Home." *House Beautiful* 124 (November 1982): 28.

Five executive women share the secrets of their personal entertainment styles: Judy Hendren Mello, president of the First Women's Bank, entertains in the bank's dining room; Kitty D'Alessio, president of Chanel, serves lunch in the boardroom overlooking Central Park; Inger McCabe Elliot, president of China Seas, prefers family parties with colorful candles and napkins; JoAnn Barwick, *House Beautiful* editor, serves buffet style by the pool; and Colombe Nicholas, president of Christian Dior, enjoys after-theater dinners for two.

227. "In Conversation." *Women in Management Review* 1 (Spring 1985): 45–54.

Jackie Holman interviews Pauline Graham, lecturer, writer, and former merchandising director. Graham tells what motivated her to pursue a management career, why women managers do not have to emulate men, how she feels about her children's resentment of her job, how to determine whether to relocate, and why it is difficult to ask others—male or female—for help.

228. "The Joys of Big Money." *Harper's Bazaar* 118 (January 1985): 32.

Harper's Bazaar tells the story of Betsey Johnson, a 1960s fashion star who became president of her own manufacturing operation and chain of retail stores in the 1980s. Johnson claims that craziness is an asset in owning your own business and that her instinct substitutes for strategy.

229. "Karen N. Horn Will Become the First Woman President and Chief Executive of a Federal Reserve Bank May 1, When She Assumes the Job in Cleveland." *Wall Street Journal* (March 30, 1982): 37.
At thirty-eight, Karen N. Horn, an officer of Bell Telephone Co. of Pennsylvania, became the first woman president and CEO of a Federal Reserve Bank on May 1, 1982. After earning a doctorate in economics from Johns Hopkins University in 1971, Horn served as senior economist at the Federal Reserve System in Washington, economist and vice president for the First National Bank of Boston, and as treasurer of Bell.

230. Kaufman, Jacqueline. "Carol Taber, Working Woman." *Management Review* 75 (October 1986): 60–61.
Carol Taber became publisher of *Working Woman* magazine in 1983. Since then, circulation is up over 600,000, ad revenues up, and the magazine is worth $40 million compared to $500,000 in 1983. Taber expects circulation to go over one million and claims that the magazine "has done more to advance the status of working women than any other magazine has ever attempted." Twenty percent of the magazine's readership is male.

231. Konrad, Walecia. "How Bold Decisions Help a Business Beat the Odds." *Working Woman* 10 (November 1985): 47–49.
Theresa Wilborn started La Feminique Construction company in Cleveland against the advice of friends and associates, and after six years her company has projected revenues of $2.5 million. Wilborn's twenty-five-year-old daughter is the company treasurer.

232. Krementz, Jill. "Shirley Young." *Savvy* 6 (October 1985): 57–61.
This photo essay profiles Shirley Young, president of Grey Strategic Marketing, Inc., a subsidiary of New York-based Grey Advertising. A Phi Beta Kappa from Wellesley College, Young is a founding member of the Committee of 200 and a recipient of the Catalyst award for outstanding corporate director.

233. "Life at the Top." *Vogue* 173 (August 1983): 282–85, 375–77.
Twenty-one successful women answer *Vogue*'s questions: (1) Is it still a man's world? and (2) What keeps you looking your best? Respondents include Dianne Sawyer, Muriel Fox, Barbara S. Thomas, Denise Scott Brown, Dianne Feinstein, Lenore R. Zohman, Randall Forsberg, Jewell Jackson McCabe, Anne Meara, Carol Bellamy, Jane Bryant Quinn, Lois Korey, Susan B. Perricone, Florence Knoll Bassett, Faye Wattleton, Pam Hill, Patricia Nettleship, Nancy R. Newhouse, Maryann N. Keller, Ruth Clark, and Amy Hirsh. The women hold such diverse positions as news anchor, public relations executive, SEC commissioner, architect, mayor, doctor, comedienne, advertising agency partner, computer consultant, and presidents of government agencies, nonprofit organizations, and corporations.

234. Lloyd, Kate Rand. "The Working Woman Hall of Fame." *Working Woman* 11 (November 1986): 157–60, 162.
Working Woman established the "Working Woman Hall of Fame" in honor of the magazine's tenth anniversary. The article includes brief biographies and interviews of the first six honorees: Muriel Siebert, chair

and president of Muriel Siebert & Co., a discount brokerage firm; Lillian Katz, CEO of Lillian Vernon mail-order catalog business; Rosabeth Moss Kanter, chair, Goodmeasure consulting firm; Joan Ganz Cooney, founder and president, Children's Television Workshop; Dorothy Brunson, president, Brunson Communications; and Lucille Ball, cofounder and former CEO, Desilu Productions.

235. "Max Factor's Wachner Resigns as President of the Beatrice Unit." *Wall Street Journal* (August 31, 1984): 10.
After an unsuccessful leveraged buyout attempt, Linda Wachner resigned as president and director of Max Factor and Co. Max Factor was recently acquired by Beatrice.

236. McFadden, Maureen. "The Guru of the Corporation." *Working Woman* 11 (September 1986): 60–61, 64, 66.
Rosabeth Moss Kanter graduated *magna cum laude* from Bryn Mawr College in 1964 with a degree in sociology. Her 1977 book, *Men and Women of the Corporation*, has become a classic study in corporate structure and was followed in 1983 by *Change Masters*, a best-seller on corporate innovation. Kanter now teaches at Harvard Business School, earns $15,000 for a speaking engagement, and is writing a new book, *The Great Corporate Balancing Act*. With husband Barry Stein, she manages a forty-five employee consulting firm, Goodmeasure, that took in about $5 million in 1986. Explaining her personal vision, Kanter says, "There are things to be done in this world, and I want to be among the people doing them."

237. Nelton, Sharon. "Pushing Health and Women in Business." *Nation's Business* 73 (February 1985): 68.
Thirty-eight-year-old Kay Smith, the founder and owner of Accents on Health, calls herself a workaholic. She has a daily nutrition program on a Kansas City radio station and is president-elect of the Mid-America chapter of the National Association of Women Business Owners. Smith planned to open the "Women's Entrepreneur Center" in Kansas City in mid-1985.

238. Nemy, Enid. "The Woman Who's Arrived May Travel on a Bike." *New York Times* (August 29, 1982): 62.
Three female executives, Franchellie Cadwell of Cadwell Davis advertising agency; Carole Hyatt, head of Hyatt-Esserman Research Associates; and Edmee Slocum, executive director of the Musicians Emergency Fund, bicycle to work in business attire and in all kinds of weather. They like the freedom and the relaxation but agree there are hazards.

239. Nielsen, John. "After a Woman Is Scorned, a Publishing Family Cashes Out." *Fortune* (January 5, 1987): 93.
Forty-nine-year-old Sallie Bingham, novelist and playwright, was forced off the board of the family-owned media corporation by her brother, Barry Bingham, Jr. She claimed the men ran the business, expecting the women to remain in the background. With the sale of the publishing empire to Gannett, Sallie gave $10 million to establish the Kentucky Foundation for Women. The purpose is to support women artists who advance women's rights through their work.

240. Parker, L. D. "Control in Organizational Life: The Contribution of Mary Parker Follett." *Academy of Management Review* 9 (October 1984): 736–45.

Parker gives a biographical sketch of Follett and tells how her concepts of control in organizations reflected her personal philosophy. Her behavioral model of control includes self-control, power-sharing control, and group control. Parker believes that Follett's concepts of control anticipated the behavioral and systems concepts of control of the 1960s and 1970s.

241. Powell, Jim. "Cashing In." *Savvy* (April 1983): 88, 90–93.

In 1969, Evelyn Berezin formed Redaction, a word-processing company and sold the company to Burroughs for $35 million in 1976. This article includes eight tips to entrepreneurs on selling their companies.

242. "Reviving a Company." *Nation's Business* 73 (July 1985): 49–50.

Nation's Business profiles Frances Shaine, who took over as chair of SPM Manufacturing Corporation in 1980 when the family-owned company was losing market share in the photo-album business. By 1985 SPM employed 50 percent more workers, had installed new production equipment, and became an industry leader. Shaine says the art of communication is critical for business executives, and she maintains an open-door policy in her company.

243. Rowland, Mary. "Rebel of Wall Street." *Working Woman* 11 (April 1986): 64–65, 68, 70.

Rowland chronicles Muriel Siebert's progress from $65 a week research analyst to the first woman member of the New York Stock Exchange. Siebert, who also spent five years as New York's first female superintendent of banks, tells why she never married and why she uses strong language.

244. Schmerken, I. "Female Managers Stand by Their Records." *Pensions and Investment Age* 11 (December 12, 1983): 1, 61.

Schmerken profiles and quotes several women who have started their own investment firms. The problems are the same as those encountered by men—raising money and getting clients. Most of the women began their investment careers as research assistants in brokerage firms.

245. Simpson, Peggy. "Washington's Prime Mover." *Harper's Bazaar* 118 (September 1985): 270, 468.

Secretary of Transportation Elizabeth Hanford Dole supervises 102,000 employees and is responsible for a $28 billion budget. She started an organization called Executive Women in Government ten years ago and initiated an effort in the Transportation Department by which 600 women workers have been trained for higher-paying jobs.

246. Smith, Sarah P. "The Fortune that Pat Built." *Essence* 14 (February 1984): 29.

Patricia Smith Crawford left a part-time real estate job to start her own real estate development firm. After six years, the divorced mother of two was worth more than a million dollars. She lives according to fourteen personal laws. One of the laws is "Expect to pay the price."

247. Span, Paula. "Breathless." *Savvy* 6 (February 1985): 73–77.
Span profiles fashion mogul Diane von Furstenberg, the owner of the $300 million in sales Diane von Furstenberg Studio. Von Furstenberg started her career as a designer in 1971 with $30,000. Her trademark was the printed-jersey wrap dress, which she is updating for the 1980s.

248. Sweeney, Joan. "Executive's Success Evolved through Decades of Effort (Lorna Mills)." *Los Angeles Times* (September 17, 1984): 13.
Lorna Mills, vice chair of Laguna Federal Savings and Loan, has been with the firm since 1936. She claims that she always put the association ahead of her own life and has been loyal to the firm, although she has had many offers from other associations. Mills says she has never had a problem with sex discrimination, adding that her father told her she had a good brain. She believes that. . ."too many women are too aggressive now. I don't like it, because I don't think it's necessary."

249. Sweeney, Joan. "At 27, Banker Has Future Carefully Mapped." *Los Angeles Times* (September 17, 1984): 12.
Cathy T. Yosuda has an MBA from UCLA and works as a corporate banking specialist for First Interstate Bank of California. She is confident that she can balance career, marriage, and motherhood. She plans to spend some time in investment banking, and her long-range goal is to start a limited partnership to finance motion pictures. She credits the women's movement with making options available to her.

250. Taylor, Alex III. "New Outfit for a Queen of Beauty." *Fortune* (January 5, 1987): 56.
Forty-year-old Linda Wachner became president of Warnaco after a successful leveraged buyout. She immediately reorganized the company and has increased operating earnings 35 percent. Wachner, who earns $500,000 a year, is one of a handful of women who head Fortune 500 companies.

251. Tight, Mary Ann. "A Delicate Balance." *Savvy* 5 (April 1984): 87–89.
Lois Wyse, author of *The Six Figure Woman* and forty-five other books, owns Wyse Advertising, a $64 million advertising company with 190 employees. Winner of the prestigious Clio and Andy advertising awards, Wyse discusses the company's early years, the difficulties in combining career and children, and her writing.

252. "Top Earners: Washington Post Chairman Katharine Graham's $361,000 Earnings in 1980 Make Her the Highest-Paid Female Executive at a Publicly Held Firm." *Wall Street Journal* (August 4, 1981): 1.
According to executive recruitment firm Heidrick & Struggles, Golden West financial president Marion Sandler is second, earning $211,633 annually.

253. Tully, Shawn. "Playboy Makes the Boss's Daughter Boss." *Fortune* 106 (August 23, 1982): 105, 108, 113–14, 116, 118.
At twenty-nine, Christie Hefner, who graduated *summa cum laude* from Brandeis University in 1974, was named president of Playboy Enterprises by her father, Hugh Hefner. She cut overhead, gave her managers

more freedom, and hoped to make $10 million in pretax income in fiscal 1983.

254. "Twenty at the Top: *Savvy's* 1983 Roster of Outstanding Women Executives." *Savvy* 4 (April 1983): 38-47.
With assistance from organizations such as the Conference Board, Catalyst, Goodmeasure, Inc., and the Business Roundtable, *Savvy* selected the twenty American businesswomen most likely to become CEOs of Forbes 500 corporations. Almost all are corporate directors, their average age is forty, and eight belong to the Committee of 200. Most advocate a player-coach management style and a willingness to take risks. Includes photographs and profiles of the twenty women executives.

255. Van Benthuysen, Patricia. "Champions and Challenge." *Savvy* 5 (February 1985): 44-47, 50-57.
Savvy presents the nation's top twelve women executives of not-for-profit organizations with budgets from $1 million to $100 million. Includes stories and photographs of the women, among them Frances Hesselbein, national executive director of the Girl Scouts of the USA; Faye Wattleton, president of Planned Parenthood Federation of America, Inc.; and Joan Ganz Cooney, president of Children's Television Workshop.

256. "The Way We Live Now." *Ladies Home Journal* 102 (May 1985): 127-29, 203-04, 206, 208, 210, 212.
Ladies Home Journal profiles four women to point out the variety in women's lifestyles today: a New York city schoolteacher, an Illinois secretary, a California day-care provider, and a Baltimore executive. Nancy Roberts, at thirty-one, heads the Baltimore Citizens' Planning and Housing Association, a job she has held for six years. She has been called "A Woman to Watch in the 80s" by the *Baltimore* magazine and wants new career challenges, not material possessions.

257. Weiss, Elaine F. "Women of the Year." *Savvy* 5 (March 1984): 34-41.
Savvy gives "special recognition" to nine women from the corporate, professional, or entrepreneurial ranks for their accomplishments in 1983. The nine are Sue Joyce, president of Collet Ventures; Roslyn L. Baltimore, president, R. L. Baltimore Co.; Patti McVay, president, Fifth Season Travel; Carole Lewis Anderson, managing editor, Blyth Eastman Paine Webber; Heather H. Evans, president and designer, Heather Evans, Inc.; Susan G. Fisher, senior vice president, Marine Midland Bank; Sandra L. Kurtzig, president and CEO, ASK Computer Systems; Marjorie K. Balazs, president and chair of the board, Balazs Analytical Laboratory; Ellen Sills-Levy, executive vice-president and partner, Bernard Englehard and Associates, Inc. Includes photographs.

258. "When the Speaker Is a Woman." *New York Times* (September 11, 1983): sec. 3, p. 15.
As many as a dozen women are now big names on the "corporate lecture circuit." Some of the women who receive $5,000 or more per lecture are Juanita Kreps, former Secretary of Commerce; Mary Cunningham, vice president at Seagram & Sons; Jane Cahill Pfeiffer, former president of NBC; Rosabeth Moss Kanter, consultant and sociologist. More women

speakers are found in the $1,500-$2,000 range. A few women—Barbara Walters, Beverly Sills, and Ann Landers—earn more than $10,000 per appearance. Ross Associates represents women speakers and estimated they would book 155 women in 1983, with two-thirds of those women speaking on business subjects.

259. Wiley, Kim Wright. "Cold Cream and Hard Cash." *Savvy* 6 (June 1985): 36-41.
Wiley profiles Mary Kay Ash and her style of rewarding top sales people with pink Cadillacs, jewels, fur coats, and trips. Includes inserts, "Listening" and "Stretching" from *Mary Kay on People Management* (Warner Books, 1984).

260. Wilkinson, Stephan. "The Maestro of Merchandise." *Working Woman* 11 (June 1986): 62-64, 66.
Lillian Katz, founder and owner of the Lillian Vernon (catalog) Corporation, parlayed a $2,000 investment into a $119 million business. Katz is described as egotistical, but she once told a newspaper interviewer, "Our company is totally devoted to women. If I'm not gonna give them a chance, who is?"

261. "Women as Business Leaders: An Interview with Felice Schwartz." *Human Ecology Forum* 13 (1983): 21-23.
Felice Schwartz, president and founder of Catalyst and the first woman board member of the Business Council of New York, answers questions about women in management in the corporate world. According to Schwartz, female socialization is the greatest barrier to women's upward mobility, but some companies are working to eliminate such barriers. She describes a course developed by Catalyst to make college students aware of career and family issues.

Career and Family

262. Alsop, Ronald. "Prisoners of the Past." *Wall Street Journal* (March 24, 1986): 16D-17D.
Now that 54 percent of all women in the United States work and contribute almost 40 percent of family income, advertisers are beginning to revise their marketing techniques. Some ads that use the superwoman image to sell their products, however, do not appeal to working women.

263. Banbury-Masland, Brooke, and Brass, Daniel J. "Careers, Marriage and Children: Are Women Changing Their Minds?" *Business Horizons* 28 (May/June 1985): 81-86.
The authors surveyed ninety-four female MBA graduates five years after graduation. While the results indicated the women were still as career-oriented as when they were students, marriage and children had increased in importance. As these women move into executive positions, it will be more difficult for their companies to replace them if they decide to start a family and leave the workplace. Corporations will need to adopt arrangements such as flextime, child care, and work-at-home to help retain these valuable employees.

264. Baron, Alma Spann. "Career and Family: Can They Mix?" *Business Quarterly* 49 (Spring 1984): 128-32.
Baron, a professor of management at the Management Institute, University of Wisconsin-Extension, Madison, repeated parts of a 1978 study of women managers in research conducted in 1983. She noted positive changes in the attitudes about combining career and motherhood, claiming "the happiest, most fulfilled women in America today are those who combine a challenging career with family, including husband and children." She cites statistics documenting the increase in the number of women in the labor force, the number of women in management, and the number of women entrepreneurs. Includes references.

265. Bistline, Susan Mitchell. "Make Room for Baby." *Association Management* 37 (May 1985): 96-98.
Coworkers' perceptions of new mothers may cause more problems than organizations' maternity policies. Although they may be seen as less committed to their work, many working mothers feel they work more efficiently and have a broader point of view. Catalyst, the nonprofit career and family organization, offers a manual for use in planning

parental-leave policies. To order the manual, write Catalyst, 14 E. 60th St., New York, NY 10022.

266. Chapman, Fern Schumer. "Executive Guilt: Who's Taking Care of the Children?" *Fortune* 115 (February 16, 1987): 30-37.

In a recent Heidrick & Struggles survey, female corporate officers said that quality time with their children was the main personal sacrifice made for their careers. A *Fortune* survey of 400 working men and women with children under age twelve examines the relationship between child care problems and productivity. The main finding of the *Fortune* survey, conducted by New York's Bank Street College of Education and the Gallup Organization, was that child care problems are the most significant predictors of absenteeism and unproductive work time. Additional information on productivity costs can be found in a new book *Childcare and Corporate Productivity* by John P. Fernandez, a personnel services manager at A T & T. Includes table.

267. Coke, K. C. "Hers." *New York Times* (November 26, 1981): sec. 3, p. 2, col. 1.

A corporate wife with a career of her own relates how her husband's career moves have disrupted their family life. She makes a plea for corporations to recognize that corporate wives make valuable contributions to their husband's success and should be treated accordingly.

268. "Companies Start to Meet Executive Mothers Halfway." *Business Week* (October 17, 1983): 191, 195.

While most executive mothers return to work full time after the birth of their children, some women are able to make flexible work arrangements with their employers. A *Business Week* survey in twelve cities failed to turn up one company with a personnel policy regarding special arrangements for mothers, but many companies have instituted part-time arrangements to retain valued employees. Many women managers admit their careers plateau or suffer because of part-time work.

269. Conant, Jennet. "The New Pocketbook Issue." *Newsweek* (December 1, 1986): 72.

Almost 20 percent of working wives earn more than their husbands. A University of Chicago economist says studies indicate marriages are more likely to end in divorce when the wife earns more than her husband, but many men say they learn to adjust to their wives' larger paychecks and the resultant higher standard of living.

270. Davidson, Sara. "Having It All." *Esquire* 101 (June 1984): 54-56, 58, 60.

After fifteen years of feminist theory and action, Davidson asks, "How does a woman coordinate the roles of professional, wife, and mother?" She interviewed three young female Yale graduates who face this dilemma, and when asked the question, "If you had to choose between having a family and having a career, which would you choose?" they answered in unison, "family." Davidson chronicles her own career and family experiences and those of her friends and concludes that it's worth working to have it all—career and family—but the best option may be to do it sequentially—to emphasize career and marriage/children at different stages.

271. Fasciani, Barbara, and Sawyer, Susan G. "On the Front Lines of the New Family." *Executive Female* 5 (September/October 1982): 14, 16-17.

Louis Harris and Associates reported in "Families at Work" that 70 percent of the executive women in a nationwide survey would continue to work full or part time even if they had enough money to live as they liked. The executive mothers interviewed by Fasciani and Sawyer all mentioned guilt about their work, citing the lack of adequate child care facilities. Experts say executive mothers feel ambivalence and conflict, but if they decide they want careers, they must become comfortable with that decision. A career woman happy with herself and her marriage will be a better mother than a frustrated stay-at-home mother.

272. Feurey, Claudia P. "Kids Plus Careers Needn't Keep Mom in Arrears." *Wall Street Journal* (June 4, 1984): p. 26, col. 3.

Feurey refers to a September *Wall Street Journal* article about the difficulties management women experience when trying to combine family and career. She counsels executive women to use their managerial skills to organize and manage their home lives and suggests a three-step management approach: (1) conduct a feasibility study, (2) make your decision and set your priorities, and (3) implement your plans.

273. Gallese, Liz Roman. "Women with Demanding Careers and Children." *Wall Street Journal* (December 14, 1981): 30.

Studies of women graduates of the Columbia Business School and fifty women MBAs from another top business school show that 65 to 70 percent of the women are married and/or have children. Although the women spend a great deal of time away from their children, they have made arrangements for quality child care and many have full-time housekeepers. The author concludes that managerial women with children work long hours but spend most of their leisure time in family pursuits.

274. Gomez, Francine. "Why Women Must Make a Choice between Business and Home Life." *International Management* (July 1985): 52.

The chair of Waterman S.A. in Paris, Gomez warns professional women that, ultimately, they have to make a choice between family and career. She advises women to adapt two male techniques: career is priority number one, and suppress or control emotion. Finally, Gomez tells ambitious women to look upon colleagues as humans with specific functions, not as men or women.

275. Gottschalk, Earl C. Jr. "Maternity Leave: Firms Are Disrupted by Wave of Pregnancy at the Manager Level." *Wall Street Journal* 198 (July 20, 1981): 1.

The number of married women executives over thirty who are choosing to start a family is on the rise. This has created problems for businesses where many women in their thirties have moved up to management positions. Many of these executive mothers resume their jobs after childbirth, but more now choose shorter hours or leave the business world altogether until their children are older. Gottschalk profiles several executive women whose pregnancies had serious consequences for their employers. Includes direct quotes from the women—a television newscaster, a lawyer, bank directors, a management consultant, a personnel manager, an actress, a computer consultant, and a White House correspondent.

276. Harris, Jessica B. "Executive Singles: Lonely at the Top." *Black Enterprise* 14 (February 1984): 107-08, 115.
This article is subtitled "A Guide to Social Networking for Unmarried Professionals" and describes the need for black male and female executives working in nonblack companies to find groups of blacks with similar interests. Organizations that may help blacks survive the loneliness of corporate life incude fraternal organizations, churches, political parties, professional groups, Greek letter organizations, civic organizations, and alumni associations.

277. Henley, F. Milene. "Why Being a Mother Made Me a Better Manager." *Working Woman* 11 (November 1986): 268, 271.
A former manufacturing manager for IBM tells how becoming a mother helped her career. She gained patience, the ability to delegate, and self-confidence. Skills mentioned by other manager-mothers include ability to prioritize work, increased sensitivity, and a sense of independence.

278. Holmes, Kay. "Working Wife and House Husband; When Roles Are Reversed." *Parents* 56 (February 1981): 47- 51.
Mary McGovern and husband Rob Gutowski have reversed traditional roles—Mary is deputy director of Planned Parenthood International Division and travels abroad four months a year, while Rob has primary care for their son and their home, and works as a junior high school art teacher. See page 51 for an inset, "Eight Ways of Working at Role Reversal." Includes photographs.

279. Johnson, Catherine. "The Christmas Executive." *Working Woman* 11 (December 1986): 90-92.
Johnson tells how executive women cope with Christmas shopping, cards, gifts for bosses and subordinates, children's school vacations, the company party, and guilt about having more than their employees. The most difficult part of the season may be the return home, where even female executives are still somebody's daughter or sister.

280. Johnson, Sharon. "Working Families in Sweden and U.S." *New York Times* (May 25, 1984): sec. 1, p. 20, col. 5.
Eighty percent of Swedish mothers with children under age six are in the workforce, compared to 60 percent of American women. At a conference "The Working Family: Perspectives and Prospects in the United States and Sweden," a research fellow at the Conference Board states that Sweden has made greater progress toward aiding dual-career families, adopting liberal policies on maternity and paternity leaves, sick child care, state-supported child care, and six-hour working days for parents if desired. One speaker indicated that there were more American women in management positions, because they have broader opportunities in an expanded range of industries than their Swedish counterparts.

281. Lublin, Joann S. "Courting the Couple." *Wall Street Journal* (March 24, 1986): 24D, 26D.

The 27 million dual-earner couples in the United States are forcing corporations to reevaluate transfer policies, offer child care assistance, and provide other flexible work arrangements. By 1985 there were over 3.5 million couples in which both are managers, professionals, or technical employees, according to the U. S. Bureau of Labor Statistics.

282. Mansfield, Stephanie. "Hittin' It Big and Kissin' It Goodbye." *Washington Post* (February 26, 1985): C1.

Although a recent American Management Association survey found that 60 percent of the women they interviewed get the most satisfaction from their careers (compared to 37 percent of the men), some highly motivated and well-educated women are becoming disenchanted with the corporate life. The women cite as reasons for their decision the necessity to choose between career and motherhood, fatigue, and rebellion at having to "look, smell and talk like our fathers." Some of the dropouts call themselves "women at home" or "leisure persons."

284. Milite, George A. "A Catalyst for Change." *Management Review* 74 (January 1985): 34-36.

Now that almost half of the United States' labor force is female, major corporations are reevaluating their parental leave policies. To protect their investment in female executives, companies are offering work-at-home arrangements or "telecommuting," child care, and paternity leave. More than one-third of the companies in a recent Catalyst survey made paternity leave available to new fathers, but men are often reluctant to take advantage of this benefit because of the negative stereotype.

285. Mitchell, Constance. "Parental Leave: Women's Ranks Break on Issue." *Wall Street Journal* (September 24, 1986): sec. 2, p. 33.

The 2,700-member National Association of Women Business Owners opposes government-mandated workplace benefits, including parental-leave legislation. One spokesperson claims it would be an "enormous burden" on small companies. Another says it might mean hiring fewer women.

286. Mott, Gordon. "Following a Wife's Move." *New York Times Magazine* (April 14, 1985): 58.

A freelance journalist talks about his decision to leave a seven-year job in Mexico City and follow his wife to France where she has received a promotion in her company's Paris office. He discusses his own psychological reactions, career concerns, and reactions of colleagues. The advantages he foresees are a chance to travel and an opportunity to improve his French, the strengthening of his marriage, and a chance to test his commitment to women's rights.

287. "My Successful Business Was Ruining My Marriage." *Good Housekeeping* 201 (September 1985): 34, 41-42.

A former housewife who turned a small housecleaning venture into a thriving business with five employees, tells how she dealt with her husband's resentment. She sought his advice on several projects, he gradually became involved in her work, and the House Expert business continued to be a success.

288. Nelson-Horchler, Joani. "Babies Plus Boardrooms." *Industry Week* 228 (January 20, 1986): 29-30.
Professional women who reduce their hours after having children soon find they are off the "fast track." A few companies have instituted special programs of flextime or parental leave to accommodate the needs of their executive mothers. Eight companies use part-time professionals, according to the authors of a new book, *Part-Time Professional*: Merck & Co., Control Data Corp., Orkland Corp., AmeriTrust Corp., Travelers Insurance Cos., Cooper & Lybrand, Kaiser-Permanente, and Northern Natural Gas Co. Diane S. Rothberg, a coauthor of the book, says there are 2.3 million men and women working as part-time professionals.

289. Nelson-Horchler, Joani. "Executive Supermoms: Mixing Business Careers and Motherhood." *Industry Week* (February 3, 1986): 32-36.
Now that 60 percent of all married women with children under six years of age are in the workforce, employers need to provide flexible work arrangements to suit their needs. The Employee Benefit Research Institute claims that only 1,800 of 6 million United States employers make some form of child care available to their employees. The stress and conflict of balancing career and family are most difficult for lower- and middle-level women managers. According to a Korn/Ferry study of women managers, in addition to demanding careers, executive mothers generally still have primary responsibility in their families for child care and housework.

290. Nemy, Enid. "How Men Change When a Female Executive Marries." *New York Times* (August 25, 1982): sec. 3, p. 12.
Executive women comment on subtle changes in the attitude of their male colleagues after the women married in midcareer. The women felt they were seen as more stable, more responsible, and more professional after marriage. Marriage seemed to assure males that the women were serious co-workers, not swinging singles.

291. Roback, Jennifer. "Torn between Family and Career? Give Birth to a Business." *Wall Street Journal* (November 14, 1983): p. 30, col. 3.
The author responds to a September *Wall Street Journal* article on professional women who want more time for maternity leave and flexible work hours. One solution may be for more women to start their own freelance businesses. "Part-time freelancing" allows these women to continue the investment in their careers. Roback comments: "Liberation is not an obligation to catch up with men in the rat race, but the freedom to live on one's own terms".

292. Rogan, Helen. "Executive Women Find It Difficult to Balance Demands of Job, Home." *Wall Street Journal* (October 30, 1984): sec. 2, p. 33, 45.
According to a *Wall Street Journal*/Gallup organization survey of 722 women executives, women managers find it difficult to balance work/home conflicts. Half of the women felt that they had made personal sacrifices in favor of their careers. The sacrifices include lack of personal

time, difficulty sustaining romantic relationships, and the decision to remain childless. Fifty-eight percent of these executive women earn more than their husbands, but only 5 percent of the husbands assume major responsibility for child care.

293. Rogan, Helen. "A Generally Satisfied Group." *Wall Street Journal* (October 30, 1984): sec. 2, p. 33.
Eighty-two percent of the 722 executive women in a *Wall Street Journal*/Gallup organization survey are highly satisfied with their careers, and 78 percent are highly satisfied with their personal lives. Married women in the survey are more satisfied than their unmarried counterparts. The least satisfied women executives are unmarried and under age forty-five.

294. Rosen, Marcia. "Money or Men? When Push Comes to Shove." *Harper's Bazaar* 118 (September 1985): 264, 266, 474.
Corporate women can answer Rosen's twenty-five-point quiz to determine whether they define success in turns of money or a fulfilling relationship. Readers are asked to respond to questions about job opportunities, finances, personal relationships, work style, leisure activities, and other issues.

295. Stautberg, Susan Schiffer. "Bringing Career Skills to Bear on Your Pregnancy." *Wall Street Journal* (June 17, 1985): p. 20, col. 3.
The author of *Pregnancy Nine to Five* gives clues to managing your pregnancy and professional life. Some of the tips are investigate your maternity benefits, do not announce your pregnancy during the first trimester, watch out for power plays for your job, looking good is a must, and implement your career plans in the second and third trimesters.

296. Toman, Barbara. "Maternity Costs: Parenthood and Career Overtax Some Women Despite Best Intentions." *Wall Street Journal* (September 7, 1983): p. 1, col. 1.
Many young women who earned law and business degrees in the 1970s suffer fatigue, anxiety, and lower productivity after becoming a parent. When they choose to leave the workforce, employers lose valuable employees, and if the trend continues, women may lose some of the ground gained in the workplace in the last decade. Some women choose part-time or self-employment after the birth of a child. Barbara Kech, once a division manager for a manufacturing company, started her own firm and now employs twenty other women on a part-time basis. She says, "Industry is losing some valuable resources by remaining inflexible and not responding to society's changes. A part-time alternative is very important."

297. Tutelian, Louise. "Love and Remarriage." *Savvy* 7 (May 1986): 54-56, 58.
Executive women whose first marriages fail because their careers came first are finding happiness in second marriages. It may be an advantage in the second marriage to have a serious career focus, and sometimes executive women find a partner in the second marriage who acts as a career mentor. In an insert the author profiles five successful women whose remarriages have helped, not hindered, their careers.

298. Walsh, Mary Williams. "Career Women Rely on Day Care, Nannies to Meet Child Care Needs." *Wall Street Journal* (September 25, 1984): p. 31, col. 4.

Professional women are more likely to leave their children with day care centers or nannies, rather than relatives or friends. Finding either is a time-consuming, costly process. There are only about 200 companies that currently offer employees full-fledged day care.

299. Watkins, Linda M. "Executive Fathers Start Preparing Their Daughters for Corporate Life." *Wall Street Journal* (October 28, 1985): p. 25, col. 4.

Many male corporate executives are grooming their daughters for management positions, realizing that even if their daughters marry and have children they will probably work outside the home for twenty-five years. Executives start training their daughters for the business world by discussing business with them, allowing them to sit in on business meetings, training them to manage money, and counseling them on careers. A study of Twin Cities businesses shows, however, that daughters in family-owned businesses receive less help and encouragement than daughters of corporate executives.

300. Westheimer, Ruth. "Talk about Making It." *Mademoiselle* 91 (May 1985): 202-203, 256, 258, 260.

Dr. Ruth Westheimer interviews seven executive women about the personal costs and rewards of their success. Some of the women are married or married with children, and two of the women are single. The women, ranging in age from twenty-nine to forty-two, talk about work, sex, children, business travel, housework, and men.

301. "When the Mother-to-Be Is an Executive." *Business Week* (April 11, 1983): 128, 132.

A growing number of executive women discover that their pregnancies do not pose problems for their employers and do not hinder their careers. Most companies offer maternity leaves and let women work up to the birth if they choose. Executive women frequently wait until their thirties to start a family and then plan their pregnancies around their work schedules. According to one professor of gynecology, the number one problem for the pregnant manager is the negative attitude of older males. Pregnant executives themselves say locating business-like maternity clothes is a difficult problem.

302. "Working around Motherhood." *Business Week* (May 24, 1982): 188.

Because of growing numbers of managers who are also mothers, corporations are offering maternity leaves, part-time work, flextime, employer-sponsored child care, and other arrangements designed to accommodate the women's needs. Two-hundred forty employers now make child care facilities available, a 100 percent increase since 1978, according to The National Employer-Supported Child Care Project.

Women as Directors

303. "According to a Recruiting Firm, More Women Executives Are Being Sought." *Wall Street Journal* (January 22, 1985): p. 1., col. 5.
Spencer Stuart & Associates claims that more women are being sought for outside directorships. The executive search firm is seeking directors for eleven corporate boards—seven of those companies are specifically looking for qualified women.

304. Ansberry, Clare. "Board Games." *Wall Street Journal* (March 24, 1986): 8D-9D.
The number of top corporations with female board members jumped to 41 percent in 1985, up from 13 percent ten years ago. However, women still hold only 3 to 4 percent of all directorships in Fortune 1,000 companies. Some women directors use their position to advance the status of women although others say they "leave their gender outside the board room."

305. "Beyond Tokenism on Corporate Boards." *Management Review* 70 (December 1981): 46-47.
Three University of Texas researchers cite the gains made in women's appointments to corporate boards. Women still account for only 3 percent of major directorships, however, and over 88 percent of the corporations in this study had only one female director.

306. Byrne, Harlan S. "Firms Are Adding Female Directors More Slowly than during the 1970s." *Wall Street Journal* (April 7, 1982): 35.
Although one management consultant predicts that corporate boards will one day be composed equally of men and women, women currently hold only one percent of the board seats at public corporations. A Korn/Ferry study found that only 39 percent of 500 companies that responded to a survey had female directors, an increase of only 3 percent in two years. Lack of financial experience handicaps many women directors and some report feeling isolated and intimidated.

307. "Catalyst's Fab Four." *Savvy* 5 (May 1984): 98.
Catalyst, the nonprofit organization promoting women in business and the professions, says there are 250 senior management women qualified to serve on corporate boards. Four of the women were honored at a $300-a-plate awards dinner: Caryl S. Bernstein, executive vice president, general counsel, and secretary, Federal National Mortgage Association;

Cathleen Black, president of *USA Today*; Carol B. Einiger, managing director of the First Boston Corporation; and Dawn Mello, president of Bergdorf Goodman.

308. Daly, Stephen. "Women in the Boardroom: Coming up from the Ranks." *New York Times* (September 1, 1983): sec. 4, p. 1.
In contrast to their predecessors who were philanthropists or relatives, current women appointees to corporate boards are executives themselves. A recent study conducted by Heidrick Partners executive search firm shows that 70 percent of women elected as outside directors in the first half of 1983 were first-time board appointees and 90 percent held corporate positions. Although women are still only 4 to 5 percent of all outside directors, progress has been made, according to Catalyst—from forty-six directors in the nation's 1,000 largest corporations in 1969 to 527 in 1983.

309. Elgart, Lloyd D. "Women on Fortune 500 Boards." *California Management Review* 25 (Summer 1983): 121-27.
Figures show that the largest corporations in the Fortune 500 are more likely to have women directors than the lower-ranking companies, and certain industries—food, paper and related products, publishing, motor vehicles, aerospace, metal manufacturing, metal products, farm equipment, and electronic appliances—have more companies with female directors. However, women still hold only 2.8 percent of Fortune 500 directorships. Includes tables and references.

310. "Finding Top Women for Company Boards Can Be Difficult." *Wall Street Journal* (February 7, 1984): p. 1, col. 5.
The Association of Executive Search Consultants claims there are not enough women executives for corporate boards. Some highly visible and qualified women executives are already on boards and turn down several other offers each year, while others do not have time or see some offers as conflicts of interest.

311. Konrad, Walecia. "How Executives Get on Boards." *Working Woman* 10 (August 1985): 26.
Women still hold only 4 percent of the 12,000 directorships in the top United States' corporations. Eleanor Raynolds, of the executive search firm Boyden Associates, tells women how to prepare themselves for a corporate board position: (1) get involved in visible projects inside and outside the corporation, and (2) volunteer for local not-for-profit boards.

312. Lewin, Tamar. "Women in Board Rooms Are Still the Exception." *New York Times* (July 5, 1984): sec. 2, p. 1, col. 1.
Although the number of women on corporate boards increased in the late 1970s, 64 percent of the largest United States' corporations still have no women directors. According to a Catalyst study, there are 455 women on the boards of the top 1,000 United States' corporations, or three of the 14,000 directorships. The small number of women board directors parallels their numbers in top-level management. Felice Schwartz, president of Catalyst, says there are about 250 women who are prime candidates for corporate directorships, but it is difficult to get corporations to consider women who are not well known, regardless of credentials.

313. Lublin, Joann. "More than 40% of Major U.S. Corporations Now Have at Least One White Female or Minority Director." *Wall Street Journal* (February 23, 1982): 1.
The statistic in the headline is the result of a survey of 485 firms by Heidrick & Struggles, an executive search firm.

314. Mitchell, Meg. "A Profile of the Canadian Woman Director." *Business Quarterly* 49 (Spring 1984): 121-27.
A Conference Board in Canada survey shows that women hold 2.5 percent of corporate director posts in Canada, up from one percent in a 1977 study. The increase is due, in part, to pressure from shareholders, employees, and consumers. The School of Business Administration, University of Western Ontario, received survey responses from fifty-seven women directors and found that 64 percent serve on more than one board, more than half are age fifty-six or over, more than 66 percent have college degrees, the majority are Canadian and speak English, they are primarily from an upper-middle-class background, 40 percent attended private school, 25 percent were professionals, 21 percent corporate executives, 21 percent self-employed, and 19 percent volunteers and homemakers. One-third of the women directors work in financial services, and most report little overt sexual discrimination. Includes tables and short bibliography.

315. Morin, Stephen P. "Trying to Get Women Directors, Boston Bank Looks Close to Home." *Wall Street Journal* (December 1, 1982): 29.
The United States Trust Co., a Boston bank, chose its first three women directors in a move toward marketing to professional women. The three women chosen are Joan Goody, architect; Brunetta Wolfman, an official with the Massachusetts State Education Department; and Barbara C. Sidell, lawyer and wife of James V. Sidell, the bank's president.

316. "My Four Sons." *Wall Street Journal* (July 3, 1984): p. 27, col. 3.
Shareholders at several annual meetings express little enthusiasm for women directors. Even well-known women like Lois Wyse, Jayne Baker-Spain, and former Commerce Secretary Juanita Kreps finished last in the number of stockholder votes at Consolidated Natural Gas, Beatrice Cos., and Zurn Industries.

317. Newsom, Douglas Ann. "Directorship: A Year in the Life." *Directors and Boards* 7 (Summer 1983): 37-42.
Professor and chair of the department of journalism at Texas Christian University, Newsom relates her experiences as the first woman elected to the board of ONEOK Inc., a Tulsa, OK, diversified energy company. She credits her consumerism dissertation for her appointment to the Audit Committee. Newsom describes the decision involved in presenting the annual report and the conduct of the annual meeting.

318. Novarra, Virginia. "Non-Executive Directorships—A Message to the Chairmen." *Women in Management Review* 2 (Summer 1986): 92-95.
Founder and director of Executive Counselling, Novarra tells how she plans to get women on more company boards as nonexecutive directors or NEDS. She describes the growing trend toward more NEDs, outlines

the appointments system—the Old Boy Network—and challenges company chairmen to answer these questions: "How many women are there among your board members, shareholders, customers, employees, managers and specialists, competitors (in Britain and overseas)?" Includes references.

319. "The Number of Women on Corporate Boards Stayed at 36% in 1980 among 576 Concerns Polled by Korn/Ferry Recruiters." *Wall Street Journal* (August 4, 1981): 1.
(The headline is the complete article.)

320. Tigner, Brooks K. "Eleanor Elliott: Woman in the Boardroom." *Management Review* 74 (June 1985): 18-20.
A director of the Legal Defense and Education Fund of the National Organization for Women (NOW), Elliott spoke on the women's revolution to business and professional women of New York's International House. She is vice chair of the American Women's Economic Development Corporation and a member of the board of directors of two corporations. When selected for the board of Celanese Corporation, Elliott warned other board members that she was a militant feminist.

321. "Women Directors' Newness Limits Their Clout on Many Boards." *Wall Street Journal* (April 28, 1981): 1.
The University of Texas School of Management studied 155 women directors of 441 large corporations. Only half of the women had a background in business and few of them sat on important compensation committees. Catalyst, the New York-based organization for women's advancement, claims women are only 2 percent of the country's 16,000 corporate board members.

Women Bosses

322. Andrews, Lori B. "The Lady Is a Boss." *Parents* 59 (April 1984): 32, 34-36.

Answer a seven-point quiz to see if you are management material or to improve your management skills, then review the management experts' answers to the same questions. The quiz asks for your response to morale problems, promotions, money and risk-taking, supervision of new employees, resentment toward women managers, delegation, discipline, and asking for a raise or promotion.

323. Baron Alma S., and Abrahamsen, Ken. "Will He—or Won't He—Work with a Female Manager?" *Management Review* 70 (November 1981): 48-53.

Over 7,000 male middle- and top-level executives responded to a questionnaire about attitudes toward female executives. Eighty percent of those surveyed believe that women executives will become "commonplace" in time, but almost 52 percent feel that women are not as career-oriented as men. The authors developed a matrix to categorize male attitudes toward women in nontraditional roles. The quadrants of the matrix are: True Acceptance, Doesn't Fit In, Use 'Em, and Chauvinist American Male Pig. Includes figures.

324. Cassidy, Robert. "How We're Viewed by the Men We Boss." *Savvy* 3 (July 1982): 15, 17-18.

Management experts and researchers' findings challenge male executives who claim that working for a woman is not a problem for them. Alma Baron, professor of management at the Management Institute, University of Wisconsin, and other researchers give seven reasons why men object to working for a female manager: she is not confident, she does not have clout, she does not know how to play the game, she comes on too strong, I do not know how to treat her, working for a woman makes me look bad, and I am paying the consequences because she is only a token. Baron sees progress, however, in working relationships between men and women.

325. Castro, Janice. "More and More, She's the Boss." *Time* 126 (December 2, 1985): 64-66.

The number of women executives in the United States rose from 1.4 million to 3.5 million from 1972 to 1983, and a Harvard economist predicts many will be promoted to high executive levels over the next twenty years. Observers believe that women are behaving more aggressively, are willing to take more risks, and are more apt to be evaluated based on performance. For all their progress, women's MBAs salaries are still 20 percent less than men's within ten years after graduation. Includes photographs.

326. Cole, Diane. "Do You Have What It Takes to Be a Boss?" *Mademoiselle* 89 (December 1983): 128-29, 200-01.
Take the ten-point test to see if you are ready to be a boss. Answer these questions: (1) do you look like a boss? (2) do you work like a boss? (3) do you know when to take the initiative? (4) can you put up with work that gets you down? (5) can you keep a secret? (6) can you learn from your mistakes? (7) are your priorities right? (8) are you getting what you need from your colleagues? (9) can you delegate details? and (10) are you too ambitious for your own good?

327. Glickman, Amy. "Women Clash: Older Worker vs. Young Boss." *Wall Street Journal* (February 19, 1985): p. 37, col. 3.
A seminar at Boston's Simmons College addresses the conflict between older women and their younger female bosses (1.3 million women under age thirty-five are administrators or managers). Older women may resent the younger woman who earned a business degree and has had less difficulty on the corporate ladder, while the younger women bosses express irritation at older women's attitudes, including telling the boss the best way to do something or questioning their judgment. The conflict most likely will ameliorate as younger women managers become more mature and experienced and as women have more opportunities for education and training.

328. Harragan, Betty Lehan. "Resenting the Woman Boss." *Savvy* 2 (March 1981): 19, 22.
Harragan describes some of the cultural conditioning and psychology that accounts for hostility often experienced by women managers from the clerical women in their organizations. She advises the clerical workers to take advantage of the woman manager's experience and possible offers of help or advancement.

329. Harragan, Betty Lehan. "When Female Subordinates Undermine Your Authority." *Savvy* 2 (April 1981): 30, 32.
In the March 1981 issue, Harragan covers the frequent difficulties women clerical workers encounter in adapting to women managers. Here she examines the opposite side of the coin—problems female managers experience when working with other women, be they clerical or professional. Private discussions with other women who may try to undermine the executive woman's authority may be the best solution.

330. Helgesen, Sally. "If You Expect a Woman Boss to Be Nurturing because She's a Woman, You May Be Setting Yourself up for a Disappointment." *Glamour* 81 (July 1983): 95.
Women managers' strengths may include sensitivity and a concern for relationships between people, but it may be a mistake to assume more support just because the boss is a woman. It may be unfair to expect all women bosses to serve as mentors for young women or to give subordi-

nates special treatment simply because boss and subordinate are the same sex.

331. Hull, Jennifer Bingham. "Female Bosses Say Biggest Barriers are Insecurity and 'Being a Woman.'" *Wall Street Journal* (November 2, 1982): 31.

Korn/Ferry International executive search firm and UCLA Graduate School of Management conducted a study of Fortune 1,000 women executives. Sixty-three percent of the women, most of them vice presidents, say there are still barriers at the senior management level, and 70 percent state that women do not receive equal pay for comparable jobs. Being a woman, lack of confidence, the old-boy network, lack of geographic mobility, and limited educational backgrounds are factors cited by the executive women as hindering career progress.

332. Hymowitz, Carol. "Male Workers and Female Bosses Are Confronting Hard Challenges." *Wall Street Journal* (July 16, 1984): sec. 2, p. 21.

Many men, and women, complain about the difficulties of working for a female boss. A study of 200 retail managers, conducted by the Center for Research on Women at Wellesley College, indicated that as the number of female executives increases, so does male animosity. Research also suggests that women blue-collar managers may experience less resentment than their white-collar counterparts, once they have established their technical competence. Robert Davis, chief of staff for Transportation Secretary Elizabeth Dole, describes what it is like working for a demanding female boss.

333. Jacobson, Aileen. "Age before Duty." *Savvy* 6 (April 1985): 36, 38-39.

The author of *Women in Charge* writes about the difficulties encountered by older women working for young female executives. The social difference means that young female managers may not understand the behavior of their older subordinates, and the older women have different expectations of power. Jacobson concludes with five guidelines for making the young/old power problem into a productive relationship.

334. Johnson, Sharon. "Female Executives with Male Assistants (Don't Call Them Secretaries)." *Working Woman* 10 (March 1985): 131-32.

Wendy Rue, founder of the National Association for Female Executives, says a growing number of female executives are selecting male assistants. Author of *You're the Boss*, Natasha Josefowitz believes women may choose male assistants because of the myth that women do not want to work for a female boss. Two male assistants to executive women tell why they like their job.

335. Lerner, Harriet E. "That Was No Lady, That Was My Boss." *Nation's Business* 69 (October 1981): 80.

Psychologists believe that because everyone's first boss was a woman—their mother—many people harbor "irrational fears of female authority and power." Female socialization teaches women to suppress anger, and thus adult women often find it difficult to assume independence, competitiveness, or assertiveness as bosses. If a woman wants a position of authority, she must adopt these psychological qualities: (1) she needs to have standards of self-worth from within, (2) she must not fear her own anger and aggression, and (3) she should be self-critical without being self-depreciating.

336. O'Toole, Patricia. "Women Bosses." *Glamour* 81 (March 1983): 132, 134, 136, 138.
O'Toole recites the gains women have made in management—the number of women in management more than doubled from 1970 to 1982—then cites examples of the difficulties women managers still face. The difficulties range from age and gender to powerlessness, the "bitchy" female boss attitude, the high-pitched female voice, stereotyping of women by women, sexism, inability to say "No," and overcommitment. O'Toole concludes with encouraging news. In a poll of 602 senior executives of the largest United States' companies, it appears that "Traditional prejudices against women are disappearing."

337. Parson, Mary Jean. "He's Older, but You're the Boss." *Working Woman* 11 (August 1986): 72-74.
In this excerpt from *An Executive's Coaching Handbook* (1986), Parson writes the "wrong script" and the "right script" to show how a young female manager might deal with an older male colleague. Martha, a thirty-year-old whiz kid, was promoted over fifty-year-old George and must handle his resentment with tact and sensitivity.

338. Ramy, Norma. "Who's in Charge Here, Anyway?" *Ladies Home Journal* 100 (April 1983): 32, 34.
A secretary who earned an associate degree in business administration tells about her first few months after promotion to legal coordinator in a Chicago advertising agency. She tells how she handled former co-workers' attitudes, her first experience at interviewing and hiring, and other challenges in her new role.

339. Schnack, Mary. "Are Women Bosses Better?" *McCalls* 108 (August 1981): 39.
Natasha Josefowitz, author of *Paths to Power: A Woman's Guide from First Job to Top Executive*, believes women are better managers than men, and a new survey indicates two-thirds of all Americans would not object to having a woman boss. While some people think women managers' open-door policy is wrong, others claim that because women managers spend more time with their employees, they earn the employees' respect and cooperation. Women still hold just one percent of upper-level management positions and 6 percent of middle-level management positions.

340. Sheler, Jeffrey L., et al. "When Women Take over as Bosses." *U.S. News and World Report* 92 (March 22, 1982): 77, 79-80.
Stereotypes about female managers disappear as the number of women in management tripled since 1960 to over 3 million. The authors interviewed the following four women managers, their bosses, peers, and subordinates: Nancy Widmann, vice president of CBS Radio in New York; Beverly Daniel, founder, president, and chair of Commodity Trading Corporation in Detroit; M. Leane Lachman, president of Real Estate

Research Corporation in Chicago; and Linda Jones, district staff manager for Pacific Telephone Company in San Francisco.

341. Simpson, Janice C. "The Woman Boss." *Black Enterprise* 11 (January 1981): 20-22, 25.
Cecelia Johnson, director of the Human Rights Commission in Des Moines, IA, is one of only 107,000 black women who are managers, 2 percent of all black women who work. Adrienne Williams, operations manager for Pacific Management Systems, warns black women to learn to deal with the racism and sexism they will meet and to learn to play the corporate game. She adds that women must understand how to market themselves—by speaking up at meetings, volunteering for assignments, and cultivating senior executives.

342. Slade, Margot. "Women and Their Secretaries." *New York Times* (October 15, 1984): sec. 1, p. 16, col. 1.
Virginia Schein, business and management consultant, and psychologist Dr. Kathleen V. Shea claim that female executives' relationships with secretaries are usually one of two types, . . ."disasters or roaring successes." Differences in age, advancement, and values frequently create problems between women managers and secretaries, but John H. Woodward, management consultant, says that while a secretary may not share the woman executive's goals, the secretary must take an interest in the boss's success and support her boss's needs.

343. Staihar, Janet. "To Get to the Top, Use Intuition or Become Own Boss." *Cedar Rapids (IA) Gazette* (March 23, 1986): 3B.
The authors of two new books on women managers suggest different strategies for getting ahead. Sandi Wilson, author of *Be the Boss,* tells women to leave the corporation and start their own businesses, while Marilyn Loden advises using a feminine management style in *Feminine Leadership—How to Succeed in Business without Being One of the Boys.*

344. "Women as Bosses: The Problems They Face." *U.S. News and World Report* 95 (July 11, 1983): 56-57.
U.S. News and World Report interviewed Dr. Marilyn Machlowitz, psychologist and author of *Workaholics,* about women in management. She notes that, although women now constitute 28 percent of all managers, they hold few middle- or upper-level management positions. Her research shows that male executives still resist women in positions of power and authority, and she suggests that women be firm when supervising male workers. Support from peers and higher-level executives is crucial. Machlowitz advises new college graduates to get experience in manufacturing or sales.

345. "Working for Women." *Financial World* 154 (August 21, 1985): 15.
Wendy Rue founded the National Association for Female Executives in 1972. The organization now boasts over 77,000 members. Members pay $29 a year for six issues of *The Female Executive,* discounts on several services, and access to information-sharing networks. Rue cites as her purpose: "To encourage economic job parity with men and to establish a positive support system among women."

Obstacles

346. Andrews, Lori B. "Why It's Hard to Be One of the Gang." *Parents* 57 (October 1982): 30, 32, 34.

Andrews recounts several isolating or exclusionary tactics employed by men to keep businesswomen from top-level jobs. The tactics include (1) "in the fishbowl" or hyperscrutiny of a woman's actions, (2) personalization rather than concentrating on a woman's professionalism, and (3) male bonding or exclusion from the male group. Because isolating tactics can affect your career, the author suggests combating these tactics by tying your success to that of your male co-workers, fighting personal comments with humor, avoiding personalization by keeping your personal life private, and establishing common denominators (shared values and experiences) with your male colleagues.

347. "Barriers to Women." *Fortune* 109 (May 14, 1984): 13, 16.

Ten readers responded to *Fortune*'s April 16th article, "Why Women Aren't Getting to the Top." The responses ranged from "Men don't want us there" to "We have met the enemy, and (s)he is us."

348. "Barriers to Women (cont'd)." *Fortune* 109 (May 28, 1984): 13-14.

Readers continue to respond to *Fortune*'s April 16th article, "Why Women Aren't Getting to the Top." (See also *Fortune*, May 14, 1984). Three of the four writers claim that friendships or old-boy networks operate among male managers and to the exclusion of women. The other writer calls upon corporations to go beyond affirmative action goals in hiring and promoting qualified women.

349. Chacko, Thomas I. "Women and Equal Employment Opportunity: Some Unintended Effects." *Journal of Applied Psychology* 67 (February 1982): 119-23.

Fifty-five women managers responded to questions about factors in their hiring to determine the effect of perceived preferential treatment on job commitment, work satisfaction, role conflict and role ambiguity. When the women felt that sex was an important selection criteria, they appeared to have less commitment and job satisfaction and more role stress. The author comments on the implications for affirmative action and equal employment opportunity. Includes tables and references.

350. Collins, Glenn. "Unforeseen Business Barriers for Women." *New York Times* (May 31, 1982): p. 14, col. 2.
Dr. Carol L. Weiss and Dr. Anne Harlan of Wellesley College's Center for Research on Women studied 100 male and female managers of two large companies for three years. Results of the $260,000 study show that male supervisors frequently do not give women executives feedback on their performance, and thereby do not give them a chance to improve their performance in areas where they are weak. Contrary to the "critical mass" theory (as more women enter management positions, sexism and job discrimination will decline), the researchers discovered that after several women managers enter a company overt resistance to the women drops, but when the percent of women reaches 15 percent, male resistance becomes overt.

351. Cunningham, Mary. "Corporate Culture Determines Productivity." *Industry Week* 209 (May 4, 1981): 82-84, 86.
Now vice president for strategic planning and product development for Joseph E. Seagram and Sons, Cunningham speaks to the members of San Francisco's Commonwealth Club. In her speech, which is reprinted in this issue of *Industry Week*, she elaborates on three themes: corporate culture impacts the bottom line, humane organizations affect profit and loss statements positively, and "prejudice is an expensive luxury." In the last theme, Cunningham tells corporations how eliminating prejudice against women can be good for business.

352. Farnsworth, Clyde H. "Sexual Bias: Alice in Cowboyland." *New York Times* (December 6, 1984): sec. 2, p. 24, col. 4.
Because international organizations are exempt from antidiscrimination laws, the status of women in several international organizations still leaves much to be desired. Although 90 percent of the secretaries and clerical employees at the World Bank are women, women hold less than 3 percent of the senior-level positions at the bank. Susana Mendaro, a development economist, filed a sex discrimination complaint against the World bank five years ago, the first major suit of its kind against an international organization. The bank so far has denied Mendaro a hearing. In the meantime, Mendaro has a position with a marketing company and inaugurated the Women's International Project, an effort to help women in developing countries achieve positions of power.

353. Gallese, Liz. "Women Trained to Gain Trust of Male Bosses." *Wall Street Journal* (January 6, 1981): sec. 2, p. 1, col. 3.
Barry Stein, president of the consulting firm Goodmeasure, cites one reason women managers have trouble advancing—their male bosses protect them from difficult assignments or give them few opportunities to exercise authority. Chicago's Continental Illinois National Bank and Trust established a program to encourage dialog between male managers and female subordinates. Women hold 51 percent and 21 percent of entry- and middle-level management positions at Continental.

354. Grant, Anett D. "Women Managers: The Issue Isn't Sexuality." *Business Week* (October 29, 1984): 8.
The president of Executive Speaking Inc. in Minneapolis writes to the editor concerning the October 1 article on corporate women. She claims industrial change, not sexuality, makes it difficult for both men and women to succeed today.

355. Hymowitz, Carol, and Schellhardt, Timothy D. "The Glass Ceiling." *Wall Street Journal* (March 24, 1986): sec. 4, p. 1D, 4D-5D.
Although women now hold about one-third of all management positions, they have difficulty breaking through the "glass ceiling" to top executive jobs, because male executives do not feel comfortable working with women at that level, and believe women lack the credentials, and will be diverted by family. The most likely fields for women executives are financial services, insurance, retailing, banking, and communications. Increasingly, ambitious women are leaving corporations to start their own businesses because of frustration with their lack of progress and subtle discrimination in the corporate hierarchy.

356. Leith, Prue. "The Ladies' Handicap." *Women in Management Review* 1 (Spring 1985): 19-29.
In this reprint of the American Express Lecture on women in management given at the University of Manchester Institute for Science and Technology in May 1984, Prue Leith tells readers that one way to raise the number of women managers (currently at 10 percent) is to change attitudes and undo prejudices. She claims that women have the advantage of being natural managers because of socialization.

357. Rexford, Stephen J., and Mainiero, Lisa A. "The 'Right Stuff' of Management: Challenges Confronting Women." *SAM Advanced Management Journal* 51 (Spring 1986): 36-40.
Rexford and Mainiero claim that although many women have moved into lower- and middle-level management jobs in the last several years, organizational cultures may keep them from the top positions. They advise readers that a consensus-seeking, participative, collaborative management style will be appropriate in the 1980s and 1990s, replacing the male-oriented management system of the present. In order to succeed, women need to enhance their political skills and adopt these guidelines: (1) learn how to diagnose management situations from an anthropological approach, (2) understand the political power games that are played between men and women, (3) take a long-term approach to solving the organization's problems, (4) manage with a consensual, collaborative, and participative leadership style, and (5) develop an action-oriented style of management.

358. Rogan, Helen. "Women Executives Feel that Men Both Aid and Hinder Their Careers." *Wall Street Journal* (October 29, 1984): sec. 2, p. 35.
Further findings of a *Wall Street Journal*/Gallup Organization survey show that while most women managers have been helped by men and prefer to work for a man, they also believe that male chauvinism and social exclusion continue to deter women's progress in management. In response to a question about how being female affects job performance/

evaluation, 70 percent believe they are paid less than men of equal ability, 60 percent feel some of their views are not respected as much as a man's in certain areas, and over 40 percent feel that a male subordinate has resisted taking orders from a female boss.

359. Steinberg, Ronnie J., and Haignere, Lois. "Barriers to Advancement: The Impact of Promotion Policies on Women and Minority Managers." Paper given at the 35th Annual Meeting of the Society for the Study of Social Problems, August 23-26, 1985, Washington, DC.
Steinberg & Haignere studied barriers to women and minorities aspiring to management positions in New York State government. Eligibility requirements were found to be the primary barriers.

360. "10.10.10.10: A Decade in the Lives of . . . ." *Ms.* 11 (July/August 1982): 138.
Cunningham, executive vice president at Joseph E. Seagram and Sons, addresses the issue of major change in corporations, due, in part, to the growing number of female professionals. She advises that prejudice against women in business and the professions "is an expensive luxury."

361. Walker, Kelly B. "Falling Off the Fast Track." *Savvy* 7 (August 1986): 32-35.
The Center for Creative Leadership released a report on women who did not meet management's expectations, "Executive Derailment: A Study of Top Corporate Women." Researchers claim there were three reasons women fell off the fast track: (1) they wanted too much power and were too ambitious, (2) they had a performance problem, and (3) they were unable to "fit in" the work environment. An insert tells women how to spot career derailment warning signals.

362. Wessel, David. "The Last Angry Men." *Wall Street Journal* (March 24, 1986): 18D.
Sexism may not be as overt now, but many older males still do not feel comfortable with women bosses, peers, or subordinates. It is difficult to judge the intensity of male resentment of successful women, now that blatantly discriminatory language is "socially unacceptable."

363. "Women Executives: What Holds So Many Back?" *U.S. News and World Report* 92 (February 8, 1982): 63-64.
U.S. News and World Report interviews Lawrence D. Schwimmer, career consultant, about women's progress up the corporate ladder. Schwimmer, who gives seminars for businesswomen ("Women on the Fast Track"), claims that although more women have moved into entry-level and middle-level management positions, chauvinism and prejudice still prevent women from reaching top management positions. He believes that women are not as skilled at playing the corporate game, citing their lack of training in team sports, their socialization, their reluctance to be assertive, and their discomfort with power. However, Schwimmer states that within ten to twenty years, women will attain CEO-type positions.

364. "Women Managers May Expect to Continue to Suffer from Discrimination and Stereotypes . . . ." *Wall Street Journal* (August 23, 1984): p. 1, col. 5.

So says Peter Dubno, a New York University professor. Recent male MBA graduates are as negative toward women executives as were male MBA graduates in 1975.

Comparisons of Men and Women Managers

365. "Attitudes toward Women Executives: 1965 and Today." *Training* 22 (December 1985): 109.

In a 1965 *Harvard Business Review* survey, both men and women had fairly negative attitudes toward women executives. Twenty years later researchers found that men's views had changed more than women's. The 1985 survey of 800 female and male executives asked questions about general feelings toward female executives, the comfort level in working for a woman boss, whether women are temperamentally unfit for management, whether women must be like men to succeed in business, whether women want or expect positions of authority, and whether the business community will wholly accept women executives. In answer to the last question, two in ten men and four in ten women still believe the business community will never completely accept women executives.

366. Baron, Alma S. "The Achieving Woman Manager: So Where Are the Rewards?" *Business Quarterly* 49 (Summer 1984): 70-73.

Baron describes Donnell and Hull's research comparing male and female managers and defining high, average, and low achievers. They found no significant differences in how male and female executives manage. High achievers are concerned for people and production, they are willing to relocate for career advancement, and their subordinates are committed to and satisfied in their work. Women who are high achievers may not succeed because of the organizational environment, i.e., an environment that does not encourage achieving behavior. Table I analyzes women managers based on personality traits. Includes references.

367. Blakely, Mary Kay. "Why Would She Want To? (Women Executives)." *Working Woman* 10 (April 1985): 105, 109, 111.

In response to the article on page 104 ("Why Can't a 'Working' Woman Be More Like a Man?"), Blakely offers a variety of responses. The director of the Fort Wayne Women's Bureau says the "Bluebird Theory" explains why men's self-confidence took them into the boardrooms while women—the Robins and Cardinals—are still assistants and "support staff."

368. Blanchard, Kenneth H., and Sargent, Alice G. "The One Minute Manager Is an Androgynous Manager." *Training and Development Journal* 38 (May 1984): 83-85.
Blanchard and Sargent claim that the male task-oriented and female people-oriented styles must join to form a new androgynous, situational management style. They present two lists: eleven ways for male and female managers to become androgynous. Number eleven on the women's list is "Take more risks with power."

369. Boulgarides, James D. "A Comparison of Ethics of Female Students, Male Students, Business Executives and Women Managers." *Equal Opportunities International (UK)* 2 (3) (1983): 12-17.
The author surveyed business school students, business executives, and women managers to determine whether women will have an impact on the ethical behavior of business as they assume management roles. Women business students were more ethical than male business students, but male executives had the strongest ethical profile. Includes tables and references. Appendix: Ethics Survey. Cases 1-10.

370. Boulgarides, James D. "A Comparison of Male and Female Business Managers." *Leadership and Organization Development Journal* 5 (5) (1984).
The author studied 108 male and 108 female managers in the Los Angeles area using the Allport System of Values and the Decision Style Inventory. He found no significant differences in male and female managers with regard to demographics, personal values, or decision styles. There was, however, a statistically significant difference in the average salary between the two groups. Includes nine tables, references, and Appendixes I and II.

371. Buckley, William F., Jr. "Welcome to a Man's World." *Vogue* 173 (August 1983): 301, 380.
Buckley claims that today's man who is indifferent to the subject of women's rights cannot be accused of indifference to injustice, because the real secret is this—access to the men's world is really not worth it. He concludes that women covet membership in a man's world because we covet that from which we are excluded. Harriet Pilpel, general counsel to Planned Parenthood and the American Civil Liberties Union, responds to Buckley's argument.

372. Burke, Ronald J. "Career Opportunities of Type A Individuals." *Psychological Reports* 53 (December 1983): 979-89.
One hundred twenty-two lower-level male and female managers answered a questionnaire designed to assess nine career anchors—technical functional, managerial, autonomy, service, security-organizational, security-geographical, identity-status, variety, and creativity. They also responded to the fifty-two item Jenkins Activity Survey, which assesses Type A behavior. Female managers scored higher than men on Technical-Functional and Service anchors and had higher Type A scores than men. Includes tables, references, and Appendix A: Career Anchors or Orientations.

373. Camden, Carl, and Witt, Jan. "Manager Communicative Style and Productivity: A Study of Female and Male Managers." *International Journal of Women's Studies* 6 (May/June 1983): 258-69.

Camden and Witt review the research on the effectiveness of feminine and masculine management styles and describe their research which replicates and extends previous research by Baird and Bradley. They examined the differences in communication styles between male and female managers and investigated the relationship between managers' communication styles and employee productivity.

374. Chusmir, Leonard H. "Motivation of Managers: Is Gender a Factor?" *Psychology of Women Quarterly* 9 (March 1985): 153-59.

Sixty-two male and sixty-two female managers answered two Thematic Apperception Tests (TAT) to determine their need for Achievement (nAch), Affiliation (nAff), and Power (nPwr). The women scored higher than their male counterparts on the need for Achievement and Power. There were no significant differences in the need for Affiliation. Chusmir claims that his findings imply that women who enter management "are likely to have greater managerial potential and may be more success prone than the men managers." Includes references.

375. Chusmir, Leonard H. "Personnel Administrator's Perception of Sex Differences in Motivation of Managers: Research-Based or Stereotyped?" *International Journal of Women's Studies* 7 (January/February 1984): 17-23.

One-hundred seventy-three personnel administrators (eighty-eight males, eighty-five females) responded to an opinion survey. Results indicate that the administrators believe female managers to be lower in "need Power," the same as males in "need Achievement," and higher than males in "need Affiliation." Chusmir recommends that potential managers be tested for all three motivational drives. Includes tables.

376. Cohen, Lynn R. "Minimizing Communication Breakdowns between Male and Female Managers." *Personnel Administrator* 27 (October 1982): 57-58, 60, 89.

Male managers have problems treating female colleagues as peers because of nonverbal courting and quasicourting messages—body movements, facial expressions, gestures, use of space, body rhythms, eye contact patterns, postural configurations, dress, and interior design. Cohen cites examples of how quasicourtship cues signal status: women allow people to come close to them, thus shrinking their personal space; women keep their limbs close to their bodies which reduces their body size and consequently their power; women smile more frequently which indicates lower status and position power; and women prolong eye contact which is considered a courting cue. Cohen concludes that even when women have a position of higher power or status, their body language and nonverbal messages undermine that power.

377. Cohen, Lynn R. "Nonverbal (Mis)Communication between Managerial Men and Women." *Business Horizons* 26 (January/February 1983): 13.

Male and female managers experience some communication problems because of nonverbal communication patterns that Cohen calls courting cues and quasicourting cues. She lists these courtship cues—grooming, prolonged eye contact, breast presentation, chest presentation, pelvic roll, and touching—and claims that such cues can indicate your power and status to others.

378. Colwill, Nina L. "Lucky Lucy and Able Adam: To What Do You Attribute Your Success?" *Business Quarterly* 49 (Spring 1984): 93-94.
Colwill reminds readers that a woman's job performance is generally viewed more negatively than a man's for three reasons: (1) women's successes are often attributed to luck and men's successes to ability, (2) women are not expected to perform as well as men, and (3) women's performance is seen as poorer than men's, even when identical. Colwill argues that women themselves may attribute their success to luck. Includes table and references.

379. Debats, Karen E. "The Weaker Sex." *Personnel Journal* 62 (June 1983): 444.
A study of male and female executives conducted by professors at UCLA and the University of Santa Clara shows that female executives are more committed to their careers. One of the researchers, Dr. Warren Schmidt, claims, "In general, the men were less willing than the women to move to a new city or to change their lifestyle for a better-paying job. . . .The female executives as a group were more willing to work long hours, give up home activities that conflicted with work, and relocate to accommodate career opportunities." Schmidt attributes women's dedication to the fact that they have had to work harder to overcome the barriers and prejudices against women in the corporate world.

380. Eisenberg, Lee, and Grunwald, Lisa. "A Census of America's New Leadership." *Esquire* 104 (December 1985): 65-66, 70, 74.
Esquire surveyed the men and women nominated for the *Esquire Register* to determine what they had in common—people under forty who had demonstrated unusual creativity, drive, originality, thought. A chart on page seventy compares the men and women regarding children, career versus family, average annual income, happiness, creativity, weight, eating habits, fear of cancer, fear of heart attack, and use of nuclear weapons.

381. Forgionne, Guisseppi A., and Peeters, Vivian E. "Differences in Job Motivation and Satisfaction among Female and Male Managers." *Human Relations* 35 (February 1982): 101-18.
Professors at California State Polytechnic University compared job satisfaction and motivation of male and female managers. The managers responded to a questionnaire of twenty-five biographical and job descriptive items. Male first-level managers and male managers with large households indicate greater job satisfaction than their female counterparts, and male managers also indicate greater overall motivation than female managers. The authors call for additional research to explain the sex-related differences in job satisfaction and motivation. Includes tables, references, and Appendix A: Job Questionnaire.

382. Gould, Robert E. "Why Can't a 'Working' Woman Be More Like a Man?" *Working Woman* (April 1985): 104, 107, 109.

Surveys of male graduate business students taken in 1975, 1978, and 1983 show that their attitudes were consistently negative toward women managers. Gould, the author of *Men in the 80s: Old Questions, New Answers*, describes the early socialization that contributes to this attitude and advises women on ways to change men's attitudes in the workplace.

383. Instone, Debra; Major, Brenda; and Bunker, Barbara B. "Gender, Self-Confidence and Social Influence Strategies: An Organizational Simulation." *Journal of Personality and Social Psychology* 44 (February 1983): 322-33.

Twenty-four male and twenty-four female university students participated in a study to determine whether men and women in positions of equal power influence subordinates in a similar manner. The researchers concluded that, given equal access to power and influence strategies, males and females supervise in a similar manner. Some gender differences were observed. Females made fewer influence attempts and used fewer reward strategies and more coercive strategies with both compliant and noncompliant subordinates. Includes tables and references.

384. Izraeli, Dafna N.; Izraeli, Dove; and Eden, Dov. "Giving Credit Where Credit Is Due: A Case of No Sex Bias in Attribution." *Journal of Applied Social Psychology* 15 (1985): 516-30.

Male and female Israeli managers answered questionnaires after reading short stories that reflected four leadership styles: initiating structure, production emphasis, consideration, and tolerance for freedom. Table I shows attribution by sex of manager and leadership style for four attributions: ability, effort, luck, pull. Includes tables and references.

385. Jago, Arthur G., and Vroom, Victor H. "Sex Differences in the Incidence and Evaluation of Participative Leader Behavior." *Journal of Applied Psychology* 67 (December 1982): 776-83.

Jago and Vroom test the hypothesis that females employ a more participative management style by studying 161 female undergraduates, graduate students and managers, and 322 male colleagues. Their findings show that women use group decision-making processes more frequently than males and one-to-one consultation less frequently. Includes tables and references.

386. Josefowitz, Natasha. "Women Executives: The Accessability Factor." *Ms.* 10 (February 1982): 89.

The author of *Paths to Power: A Woman's Guide from First Job to Top Executive* discusses differences in how male and female executives handle accessibility. Josefowitz found that women managers were twice as accessible to their employees as men managers because of socialization, lower self-esteem, and aspirations in regard to position and salary, and because they have trouble saying "no" to demands on their time. She concludes with lists of costs and benefits to being an accessible manager.

387. Knudson, Ann D. "Young Management Women: A New Look." *Journal of NAWDAC* 45 (Winter 1982): 3-9.
Knudson studied almost 800 management students at a large midwestern university to determine whether women were less assertive than men. Using the Adult Self Expression Survey, the author found no significant difference in the assertive behavior of males and females.

388. LaBier, Douglas. "Madness Stalks the Ladder Climbers." *Fortune* 114 (September 1986): 79-80, 84.
A psychoanalyst and author of the book *Modern Madness* says career-oriented men and women between the ages of twenty-five and forty-seven in his eight-year study exhibit behavior that ordinarily indicates a neurotic personality—anxiety, depression, eating and sleeping problems, and overuse of drugs and alcohol. LaBier claims that these people do not separate their careers from their identities, but these managers also want personal fulfillment. The author gives examples of two women managers who fall in this category.

389. Liden, Robert C. "Female Perceptions of Female and Male Managerial Behavior." *Sex Roles* 12 (February 1985): 421-32.
Eighty-eight percent of the female employees in nine branches of a major bank preferred to work for male managers. Situational variables rather than sex differences may account for this preference. The male managers had significantly more experience than the female managers. Includes tables and references.

390. "Living in a Man's World." *Vogue* 173 (August 1983): 300, 380-81.
An anonymous woman executive laments the fact that as she advanced in the corporate world, she began to think and act more like a man, causing her to compromise some of her human values "as a woman." She relates how difficult it was to negotiate a contract with Japanese men until the point where she felt they no longer regarded her as a woman. The author poses the question ". . .whether we must compromise our sense of values as women to maintain our positions of power."

391. Lublin, Joann S. "The Best Managers May Be Women." *Wall Street Journal* (July 6, 1982): 1.
Tests conducted by Johnson O'Connor Research Foundation show that women may prove to be the best managers. In the test of 250,000 men and women, women had higher scores than men in six areas.

392. Mai-Dalton, Renate R., and Sullivan, Jeremiah J. "The Effects of Manager's Sex on the Assignment to a Challenging or a Dull Task and Reasons for the Choice." *Academy of Management Journal* 24 (September 1981): 603-612.
Male and female college students and banking executives answered a questionnaire about assigning challenging or dull tasks to employees. Male respondents preferred a female employee for the dull task and a male employee for the challenging task, while female respondents answered the opposite preference, a female employee for a challenging task and a male employee for a dull task. Includes references.

393. "Male vs. Female: What a Difference It Makes in Business Careers." *Wall Street Journal* (December 9, 1986): p. 1, col. 5.

Two executive search firms surveyed female and male corporate officers and found significant differences in men and women's career patterns. The Korn/Ferry International study of male officers found that male officers are an average age of fifty-one, work fifty-five hour weeks, and earn $215,000 a year while the Heidrick & Struggles study of female officers claims the typical female officer is forty-four, works the same fifty-five hour week, and earns $116,810. Eighty-two percent of the women say they have had to make personal sacrifices for their careers—20 percent never married, 20 percent are separated or divorced (five times the male rate), and over 50 percent are childless while 95 percent of the men had children.

394. Metcalfe, Beverly Alban. "Current Career Concerns of Female and Male Managers and Professionals: An Analysis of Free-Response Comments to a National Survey." *Equal Opportunities International (UK)* 3 (1) (1984): 11-18.

Male and female members and fellows of the BIM (British Institute of Management) answered a questionnaire about the effects of job changes on personal and career development. There were significant differences in the managers' responses—male managers most frequently encountered job changes as a result of company reorganization. Female managers cited a spouse's job relocation as the reason they changed jobs. Women also commented on the advantages and disadvantages of fulfilling both corporate and family roles and the problems of being female in male-dominant organizations. Appendix: Brief Description of the Research Project and information about the questionnaire. Includes references.

395. Millard, Richard J., and Smith, Kay H. "Moderating Effects of Leader Sex on the Relation between Leadership Style and Perceived Behavior Patterns." *Genetic, Social, and General Psychology Monographs* 111 (August 1985): 303-16.

Male and female managers in a large governmental service agency completed the Least Preferred Co-Worker Scale (LPC) and the Leader-Member Relations Scale, and their subordinates answered the Leader-Behavior Description Questionnaire. There were no significant differences between male and female managers on the LPC scale. Includes tables and references.

396. "Open Doors: Female Bosses Are Twice as Accessible to Subordinates as Male Ones." *Wall Street Journal* (August 4, 1981): 1.

So writes San Diego State researcher Natasha Josefowitz. She advises women to learn to say "no," and encourages male managers to increase their rapport with subordinates.

397. Palmer, David D. "Personal Values and Managerial Decisions: Are There Differences between Men and Women?" *College Student Journal* 17 (Summer 1983): 124-31.

Five-hundred ninety-five female and male business students in an undergraduate management course completed questionnaires to evaluate the strengths of six values—theoretical, economic, aesthetic, social, political, and religious—and participated in a classroom simulation to measure their decision-making preferences. Results indicated that female students were more strongly oriented toward aesthetic and social values than toward theoretical values, and that men's and women's managerial decision-making patterns were similar. Includes tables and references.

398. Powell, Gary N., and Butterfield, D. Anthony. "Sex, Attributions, and Leadership: A Brief Review." *Psychological Reports* 51 (December 1982): 1171-74.

The authors reviewed research on attributions to male and female managers and found that (1) causal attributions for successful performance and evaluations of performance often differ for female and male leaders, (2) female leaders are not evaluated or perceived differently from male leaders when engaging in the same behavior, (3) when group performance is high, both female and male leaders are evaluated more highly, and (4) female raters may tend to give higher evaluations to leaders and see more behaviors of leaders than male raters. They recommend additional research into the effects of raters' sex-role identity and sex. Includes references.

399. Powell, Gary N.; Posner, Barry Z.; and Schmidt, Warren H. "Sex Effects on Managerial Value Systems." *Human Relations* 37 (November 1984): 909-21.

One-hundred thirty men and women members of the American Management Association answered a survey investigating managers' values, expectations, and approaches to ethical issues. Contrary to stereotype, researchers found that (1) women managers were more concerned about success versus family/home life than male managers; (2) women rated high productivity, efficiency, good organizational leadership, and organizational stability as more important than men; and (3) women managers considered ability, skill, ambition, cooperation, and flexibility as more important than did the male managers. Includes tables and references.

400. Powell, Gary N.; Posner, Barry Z.; and Schmidt, Warren H. "Women: The More Committed Managers?" *Management Review* 74 (June 1985): 42-45.

The authors conducted a study to determine the relative degrees of commitment of male and female managers to their careers as opposed to their home and family life. They surveyed 1,302 men and 156 women members of the American Management Association and found that women managers put more emphasis on success in their jobs at the expense of their personal lives than did the male managers. The researchers concluded that female managers were more committed to their careers than male managers of the same age, salary, education, and managerial level. Includes tables.

401. Rosen, Benson; Templeton, Mary Ellen; and Kichline, Karen. "The First Few Years on the Job: Women in Management." *Business Horizons* 24 (November/December 1981): 26-29.

Researchers report on a questionnaire answered by 121 female and male managers. The respondents answered questions about motivations for working, work-related contacts, treatment on the job, dual-career problems and career progress. They offered these ten items of advice to women considering a management career: (1) obtain information about company attitudes toward women, (2) choose your first job carefully, (3) be sensitive to dual-career conflicts, (4) do not begin your career with a chip on your shoulder, (5) listen to advice, take responsibility, (6) develop self-confidence and assertiveness, (7) observe a successful role model, (8) get a mentor, (9) become part of a women's support network, and (10) read *Games Mother Never Taught You, Managerial Woman,* and *The Gamesman.*

402. Ryan, Edward J.; Watson, John G.; and Williams, John. "The Relationship between Managerial Values and Managerial Success of Female and Male Managers." *Journal of Psychology* 108 (May 1981): 67-72.

One-hundred twenty-two female and 130 male managers who are members of the Association of Records Managers and Administrators completed the Personal Values Questionnaire (PVQ) which includes five categories of values: goals of business organizations, personal goals of individuals, groups of people, ideals associated with people, and ideas about general topics. Significant differences in values between male and female managers were noted on these scales: compromise, emotions, equality, government, liberalism, stockholders, leisure, autonomy, skill, tolerance, and organizational stability. The female mean exceeded the male mean on all eleven scales. Includes references.

403. Rynes, Sara, and Rosen, Benson. "A Comparison of Male and Female Reactions to Career Advancement Opportunities." *Journal of Vocational Behavior* 22 (February 1983): 105-16.

Managerial, professional, and technical men and women enrolled as MBA students answered questions about opportunities for career advancement. The authors found that men and women have similar attitudes toward career advancement and the importance of taking risks such as relocation, employer changes, and functional changes for career progress. Both sexes also had similar salary expectations. Includes tables and references.

404. Schmidt, Warren H., and Posner, Barry Z. "Male and Female Managers: Some Unexpected Differences." In *Managerial Values in Perspective.* American Management Association, 1983. pp. 16-20.

One-hundred thirty men and 130 women answered a survey about work/personal values. Both sexes rate effectiveness as an organization's highest goal, but female managers ranked good organization and organizational stability significantly higher than did males. Researchers found, contrary to traditional opinion, that female managers are more career oriented than male managers. Includes exhibits.

405. Scott, Dow. "Trust Differences between Men and Women in Superior-Subordinate Relationships." *Group and Organization Studies* 8 (September 1983): 319-36.

Male and female program agents of a state cooperative extension service answered questionnaires to determine the effect of gender on trust, i.e., whether subordinates trust women superiors as much as men. Results indicated that women did not express higher levels of trust than men, and respondents did not trust male superiors more than female superiors.

But trust levels were significantly higher when respondents reported to someone of the same sex. Includes tables and references.

406. Serlen, Bruce. "Mutterings from the Men's Room." *Working Woman* 8 (May 1983): 112-15.

Serlen interviewed middle-management men about their attitudes toward competing with female colleagues. The men, thirty to forty-five years old, feel resentment and express their feelings by questioning the women managers' sexual mores. The men complain about aggressive women and use tactics such as commenting on a woman's appearance or apologizing for using strong language in front of a woman to emphasize the difference between male and female managers.

407. Shockley-Zalabak, Pamela Sue. "The Effects of Sex Differences on the Preference for Utilization of Conflict Styles of Managers in a Work Setting: An Exploratory Study." *Public Personnel Management* 10 (Fall 1981): 289-95.

Thirty-one male and thirty-eight female managers answered the Hall Conflict Management Survey to compare their conflict styles. The survey measured preference for win-lose, yield-lose, lose-leave, compromise, and synergistic conflict styles in various situations. Shockley found that male and female preferences for conflict styles were identical in all situations. Includes tables, footnotes, and bibliography.

408. Smeltzer, Larry R., and Werbel, James D. "Gender Differences in Managerial Communication: Fact or Folk Linguistics?" *Journal of Business Communication* 23 (Spring 1986): 41-50.

The authors studied thirty-nine female and forty male MBA students to determine whether females use a different communication style than males in management communication. They found no difference between men and women in terms of passive versus active communication style or in other measures of communication quality. Includes tables and references.

409. Solomon, Laura J., et al. "Corporate Managers' Reactions to Assertive Social Skills Exhibited by Males and Females." *Journal of Organizational Behavior Management* 4 (Fall/Winter 1982): 49-63.

Sixty-seven male and thirty-eight female middle- to upper-level managers in a Fortune 500 company participated in a study of assertive communication styles. The respondents rated audiotaped conversations as directly assertive, empathetic plus assertive, or self-effacing plus assertive and saw assertive males and assertive females as equally "likeable, socially skilled and interpersonally effective." Includes tables and references.

410. Staley, Constance Courtney. "Managerial Women in Mixed Groups: Implications of Recent Research." *Group and Organization Studies* 9 (September 1984): 316-32.

Staley reviews recent research on the quality and quantity of female participation in mixed groups and relates the findings of this research to management training programs designed to improve such interactions. She suggests that this body of research be used in three ways: (1) to prepare women managers for both male and female reaction to their participation in mixed groups, (2) to help women understand their own behavior in mixed groups, and (3) to devise coping skills for women in mixed groups. Includes references.

411. Steinberg, Rhona, and Shapiro, Stanley. "Sex Differences in Personality Traits of Female and Male Master of Business Administration Students." *Journal of Applied Psychology* 67 (June 1982): 306-10.

Steinberg and Shapiro used three personality measures—the Sixteen Personality Factor Questionnaire, the California Personality Inventory, and the Rathus Assertive Inventory—to test the statement that females do not possess personality traits characteristic of senior managers. The seventy-one male and female MBA students who participated in the study did not differ significantly on most personality measures. Includes tables and references.

412. Stevens, George E. "Women in Business: The View of Future Male and Female Managers." *Journal of Business Education* 59 (May 1984): 314-17.

The number of women MBA graduates increased almost 13 percent from 1973/74 to 1978/79—from 6.6 percent to 19.1 percent. Stevens questioned 226 senior business students to determine their attitudes toward women managers. The students answered the WAMS (Women As Managers Scale). The findings support Stevens' thesis that future managers will have more positive attitudes toward women in management. Includes tables and references.

413. "Success or Money?" *Wall Street Journal* (September 17, 1985): p. 1, col. 5.

A *Working Woman* magazine survey found that executive women aim for success in their careers, while their male counterparts desire financial gain. A good family life was a higher priority for males than for females, and female executives said that work success was a sexual stimulant.

414. Trempe, Johanne; Rigmy, Andre-Jean; and Haccoun, Robert T. "Subordinate Satisfaction with Male and Female Managers: Role of Perceived Supervisory Influence." *Journal of Applied Psychology* 70 (February 1985): 44-47.

Researchers conducted a study of eighty-seven semiskilled men and women to determine their satisfaction with male and female supervisors and the degree of upward influence these supervisors held. The results show that subordinates were not as concerned with sex of the supervisor as they were with the degree of influence that the supervisor exerted. Male and female managers were rated equally regarding their concern for employees. Includes references.

415. Tsui, Anne S., and Gutek, Barbara A. "A Role Set Analysis of Gender Differences in Performance, Affective Relationships, and Career Success of Industrial Middle Managers." *Academy of Management Journal* (September 1984): 619-35.

Tsui and Gutek evaluated performance effectiveness of male and female managers by studying 295 male and female middle-level managers and their superiors, subordinates, and peers. The research indicated no pro-male bias in performance effectiveness. Additionally, they found that women managers seemed to be promoted faster and were more satisfied in their jobs than were male managers. Includes references.

416. Usher, Denise. "Male and Female Managers Compared." *Equal Opportunities International* 2 (3) (1983): 1-6.

The author wrote her undergraduate dissertation on the comparison between successful male and female managers. In this article she reviews sex-role stereotypes about women managers and outlines some problems they face. Usher surveys the literature that concludes men are more successful than women and research that concludes the opposite. The evidence indicates that successful managers have characteristics generally attributed to men. Includes tables and references.

417. West, Candace. "Why Can't a Woman Be More Like a Man? An Interactional Note on Organizational Game-Playing for Managerial Women." *Work and Occupations: An International Sociological Journal* 9 (February 1982): 5-29.

West reviews the research on organizational communication, then specifically discusses these speech habits: turn-taking, negotiation of simultaneous speech, and interruptions in cross-sex and same-gender communications. She concludes that the interactions between men and women in the workplace must be transformed before the structure of those organizations will change. This concept is important for "women in management" training seminars. Includes one table, references, notes, and appendix.

418. Wiley, Mary Glenn, and Eskilson, Arlene. "The Interaction of Sex and Power Base on Perceptions of Managerial Effectiveness." *Academy of Management Journal* 25 (September 1982); 671-77.

Academic researchers studied the effect of expert power and reward power when used by male and female managers. Ninety-five managers answered a questionnaire regarding an individual's power and performance, and findings indicated that the researchers' hypotheses held true, i.e., (1) male managers are viewed as more effective when using expert power, and female managers are evaluated as more powerful when using reward power; and (2) managers using expert power are seen as more effective managers than managers using reward power. Includes table and references.

419. Wiley, Mary Glenn, and Eskilson, Arlene. "Scaling the Corporate Ladder: Sex Differences in Expectations for Performance, Power, and Mobility." *Social Psychology Quarterly* 46 (December 1983): 351-59.

Middle managers in a mid-career MBA program participated in a study designed to answer the question, "Under what conditions do sex-based status rankings cease to influence expectations and evaluations of performance, power, and upward mobility within an organization?" Respondents expected men and women promoted to the same management position to have similar levels of performance, but men were expected to achieve greater success in the organization based on perceived support from superiors. Includes tables and references.

420. "Women Managers: A Profile." Management Review 75 (September 1986): 6.
Professors at the University of Michigan conducted a study on women managers. Findings of the study were reported in "A Managerial Profile: The Woman Manager." The researchers concluded that "women managers are younger than their male counterparts, less likely to be married, and more likely to work for smaller companies in personnel and industrial relations positions." They also determined that changing jobs is usually financially advantageous to both men and women managers.

421. "Women Managers Have Different Styles than Male Managers, a Study Says." *Wall Street Journal* (March 12, 1985): p. 1, col. 5.
A study shows that female managers focus on the task to be done and work closely with subordinates. The study of forty female and male managers and thirty-two of their secretaries found that women managers generally have more interaction with their workers than do male managers. Professor Anne Stratham at the University of Wisconsin, Parkside, claims that male managers focus more on themselves and tend to delegate heavily.

422. "Work, Sweet Work." *Savvy* 3 (December 1982): 19.
The American Management Association's sixty-page report "Managerial Values and Expectations" reports on questionnaires sent to almost 1,500 male and female managers. Some findings of the report show that "female managers are more career-oriented than male managers," are more willing to work longer hours than men, and get more satisfaction from their careers than their home lives.

423. Zappert, Laraine T., and Weinstein, Harvey M. "Sex Differences in the Impact of Work on Physical and Psychological Health." *American Journal of Psychiatry* 142 (October 1985): 1174-78.
The authors studied men and women of the 1977 and 1978 graduating classes of a large graduate business school. The respondents answered questions about work environments, job tension, coping styles, work and home life balance, and physical and psychological symptoms. Zappert and Weinstein found that the women exhibited significantly more psychological and physical stress symptoms. Includes tables and references.

Advice Literature

424. "Advice to Women on the Move to Management." *Training and Development Journal* 36 (January 1982): 8.
The president of a West Coast executive search firm claims that women need to show a "leadership" presence to qualify for management. The required qualities include dressing for a management role, communication skills, a business first attitude, a sense of priorities, a willingness to work harder, and seeking a job with a "track of opportunity."

425. Allison, Mary Ann, and Allison, Eric W. "Managing Men." *Working Woman* 10 (October 1985): 37-38, 40.
To help women executives sort out the conflicting advice on how to manage male subordinates, the authors offer eight strategies. They advise taking charge without being overly aggressive and addressing the special problems of managing men who are older or younger than the female manager.

426. Ash, Mary Kay. "How to Play Boss: From Mary Kay's People Management." *Cosmopolitan* 199 (August 1985): 84, 90.
Mary Kay gives readers twenty-three tips on supervisory skills excerpted from her book *Mary Kay on People Management* (Warner Books, 1984). Examples include build with people, be a follow-through person, be a risk-taker, be a problem-solver, set the pace for your staff, and apply golden-rule management techniques.

427. Bryer, Carol Ann, and Zalupski, Vilma. "Women in Management: Two Points of View: Meeting the System." *Community and Junior College Journal* 52 (October 1981): 7-9, 12-13.
The authors offer women some suggestions for "meeting" rather than beating the system. They advise securing support from males in the system, joining organizations that have goals in common with women's groups, building bonds across sex, race, and nationality, and developing a sense of teamwork.

428. Chapman, Fern Schumer. "Competing with the Boys." *Fortune* 114 (June 9, 1986): 205-06.
Chapman reviews four new advice books for women executives: Kathryn B. Stechert's *Sweet Success*; Charlene Mitchell's *The Right Moves: Succeeding in a Man's World without a Harvard MBA*; Madilyn Loden's *Feminine Leadership: or How to Succeed in Business without Being One*

of the Boys; and Toni Scalia's *Bitches and Abdicators*. She sees a common flaw in all four titles—the implication that business success is dependent on personality and politics, not education and expertise.

429. Cornwall, Deborah J. "Accept Responsibility for Your Own Future—Work with Your Manager to Obtain It." *AMA Forum* 73 (December 1984): 32-34.

To make life easier for yourself and your manager, Cornwall advises: (1) act as if you have a legitimate place in the business world, (2) avoid the stereotypes of executive women, (3) don't allow a manager to distract you from your career goals, and (4) learn the politics required to compete for power and leadership. Her final advice is accept responsibility for your own future and work with your manager to obtain it.

430. Crosthwaite, Carol. "Working in a Man's World: Are Women Making Progress?" *Vital Speeches of the Day* 52 (January 1, 1986): 78-80.

In a speech to the National Council of Jewish Women, Carol Crosthwaite, division staff manager of corporate relations for Southwestern Bell Corporation, states that although trend-watcher John Naisbitt believes many American institutions will be run by women in the near future, women still only hold a small number of officer and CEO positions in business. Crosthwaite claims that women have determined their own definition of success, different from the traditional male view of corporate success. She gives seven practical tips for working in a man's world: give up thinking you can change other people; do not make an issue of being a woman; keep yourself above any tactics which men—or other women—may use against you; help other women; be competent; know your strengths and use them; have some fun.

431. Cunningham, Mary. "What Price Good Copy?" *Newsweek* 100 (November 29, 1982): 15.

Now senior executive at Joseph E. Seagram and Sons, Mary Cunningham writes about the treatment she received from the press when she worked at Bendix for Bill Agee. She offers readers these hints for evaluating news stories: be wary of melodrama passing for news; be suspicious of the use of unnamed "reliable" sources, be cautious of stories about personalities or egos as opposed to business issues.

432. Douglass, Donna N. "For Women: How to Get Where You Want to Go." *Supervisory Management* 29 (May 1984): 30-36.

In this excerpt from *Choice and Compromise—A Woman's Guide to Balancing Family and Career*, Douglass shares five rules for successful women managers: (1) have a healthy disrespect for "big shots," (2) face the fact that competition exists, (3) learn to delegate effectively, (4) meet deadlines, and (5) accept the managerial role and aim for respect, not love, from your subordinates.

433. Dreyfuss, John. "Women Executives' Advice for Business Success: Take Risks." *Los Angeles Times* (November 7, 1984): sec. 5, p. 1, 13.

Five women owners and directors of multimillion dollar companies spoke on the subject of entrepreneurship to Women in Management students at UCLA's Graduate School of Management. The speakers were

Julia Thomas, Janice Jones, Adrienne Hall, Ellen Magnin Newman, and Nina Blanchard.

434. Edelman, Gay Norton. "Can You Call Yourself a Pro?" *Mademoiselle* 89 (October 1983): 152-53, 238, 240.

Take this short ten-point multiple choice quiz to determine your professionalism. The author asks questions about loyalty, individuality versus conformity, behavior at office parties, appropriate dress, telephone etiquette, diplomacy, and accepting tough assignments. A lengthy discussion of the appropriate response follows each question.

435. Freedman, Alix M. "How to Do Everything Better." *Wall Street Journal* (March 24, 1986): 25D.

Freedman claims that most of the recent business books for corporate women start with the premise that women are lacking in the skills, experience, or personal attributes that can mean success. The author goes on to offer advice to women on how they can improve themselves or adopt the strategies males use. Includes notes on five recent titles.

436. Gates, Mary M. "Changing Role of Women in Voluntarism; Address, February 27, 1981." *Vital Speeches of the Day* 47 (May 1, 1981): 436-39.

A member of the board of regents of the University of Washington, Gates delivered a speech on women and voluntarism to the YWCA in Seattle as part of a seminar on civic responsibility and the corporate woman. She reviews the changes in women's volunteer efforts in the past several years, indicating that most volunteers in the United States now hold full-time jobs, and that women may be asked by their companies to volunteer as a company representative. Gates reviews the advantages to being an administrative volunteer: the chance to learn about a new field or organization, variety, new contacts, visibility, experience in fund-raising, recruiting, budgeting, and public relations.

437. Gubernick, Lisa. "First Encounters of the Business Kind." *Mademoiselle* 89 (December 1983): 126-27, 196.

Gubernick advises young women in management on business behavior or etiquette. In this article she covers decorating your office, running meetings, business lunches and business travel. She suggests watching others in your organization for cues on what is appropriate.

438. Handler, Janice. "A Corporate Twist on the Feminine Mystique." *Wall Street Journal* (March 25, 1985): p. 28, col. 3.

Handler, assistant general counsel of a Fortune 500 company, questions whether women have given up one "feminine mystique" for another— this time for a "career" (years of training, long hours, entry-level low salaries) rather than a job and the title "superachiever." She urges working women to beware the superwoman, workaholic, and millionaire-at-36 myths and concentrate instead on basic social and corporate change. "After all," says Handler, "the Feminine Mystique can, and in some cases has, evolved into the Fast-Track Mistake."

439. "How to Succeed in Business." *Mother Jones* 9 (June 1984): 11.
A *Mother Jones* writer tells, tongue-in-cheek, the story in a recent issue of *Fortune* magazine about a corporate executive who had to tell a woman manager to cross her legs or keep her knees together when she sat. He says this tip may cause some debate, because men have traditionally advised businesswomen to do the exact opposite.

440. Jaffa, Elliott. "Getting Chutzpa." *Working Woman* 7 (November 1982): 34.
A behavioral psychologist who conducts seminars in aggressive marketing, creative problem solving and motivational management, advises women managers to arm themselves with a little chutzpah. He reminds them that being successful is sometimes less important than taking risks and that the worst thing that can happen to you when you ask for additional staff, equipment, or promotions is being told "no."

441. Josefowitz, Natasha. "The New Kid on the Block." *Essense* 14 (January 1984): 21.
Josefowitz, author of *Paths to Power*, counsels women who have become first-time supervisors. She suggests these steps: (1) talk to each of your subordinates individually about supervision in your area before you change anything, (2) strive for your employees' respect, not their affection, and (3) make your employees aware of your standards, and (4) reward good performance.

442. Kennedy, Marilyn Moats. "How to Deal with a Boss and Co-workers Who Respect but Don't Like You." *Glamour* 83 (March 1985): 146, 148.
The author of *Office Politics* claims there may be four reasons why bosses, peers, or subordinates may not like you: (1) jealousy, (2) the hostility may not be personal, (3) the hostility may be caused by economics, and (4) there may be no reason at all. Moats gives advice for dealing with the hostile colleagues.

443. Kennedy, Marilyn Moats. "Just Been Made the Boss? All the Best Ways to Make Sure You Get the Support You Need." *Glamour* 83 (May 1985): 108, 116.
Kennedy, the author of *Salary Strategies*, offers advice on how to handle these situations when you have just been promoted to boss: (1) you moved up from the ranks, (2) you have been promoted quickly, (3) you have changed departments, and (4) you came in as the outsider. Reprinted from *You're the Boss* by Natasha Josefowitz.

444. Kornbluth, Jesse. "The Perils of Personal Publicity." *Savvy* 6 (August 1985): 50-55.
Executive women comment on their experiences with the press, and Kornbluth gives the "Ten Commandments of Dealing with the Media," including know who you are talking to, keep your personal life personal, and follow your company's media policy.

445. Kron, Joan. "The New Double Standard." *Wall Street Journal* (March 24, 1986): 27D.
Kron describes office etiquette mentioned in some of the books by Miss Manners (Judith Martin) and Letitia Baldridge (*Letitia Baldridge's Guide to Executive Manners*). The best advice is treat everyone the same.

446. "Life at the Top." *Vogue* 174 (August 1984): 314-15, 317, 319, 417-19.
Nineteen successful women tell *Vogue* readers how they work and play, what they enjoy about their life and their success, their thoughts on exercise and fashion, and their opinion on the question "Is your work world a man's world?"

447. Machlowitz, Marilyn. "Gaining Visibility." *Working Woman* 8 (August 1983): 24, 26.
Machlowitz advises women managers that visibility—displaying and magnifying your accomplishments—increases your marketability. She proffers these tips for making yourself visible: do a good job, look the part, get out there, join, cut across levels, remember that you are always on display, tackle tough assignments, bring your work out into the open, be modest, reposition yourself at career junctures, and modify your routines.

448. McFadden, Maureen. "Sudden Success." *Working Woman* 11 (June 1986): 94-95.
McFadden offers these hints for women who have suddenly been promoted to management positions: accentuate the positive, ask for feedback, learn by your mistakes, and ask questions. Several women describe how they learned to handle the additional pressures and responsibilities of promotions to management.

449. McNair, Marcia, and Ray, Elaine C. "You're the Boss: The Essence Guide for Managers and Supervisors." *Essence* 15 (March 1985): 75-82.
This article gives advice, tips, and resources for black women, whether just entering the workforce or moving up to boss. The short segments cover moving from secretary to supervisor, networking, upgrading your image, do's and don'ts for black managers, decision making, racism and sexism at the top, firing employees, and managing your staff, your time, and home and family life. A Bureau of the Census chart shows where black women managers are in various industries. The article concludes with a suggested list of nine books on management.

450. Moe, Ann M. "Women and Work: A Time for New Strategies." *Vital Speeches of the Day* 49 (September 1, 1983): 699-701.
Senior Vice President and manager of Rainier National Banks Moe addressed the 1983 Women Plus Business Conference in Seattle on past strategies for women's success: focusing on (1) the definition and awareness of businesswomen's problems, (2) the "institutionalization" of women's issues, (3) the adaptation and adoption of outwardly obvious techniques for success, and (4) zeal for improvement. She proposes these new strategies for the 80s: (1) be as much of an individual as a member of the group, (2) put achievement of real business objectives at the center of

your attention, (3) develop experience and achieve technical skills, and (4) become a leader of some nonwomen's issues.

451. Nelton, Sharon. "Getting It All Done." *Working Women* 10 (December 1985): 92-95.
Working Woman interviewed eight male and female executives in companies with $6 million to $2 billion in sales to learn about their work habits. Some, such as Jane Evans, president of Monet Jewelers, arrive early at the office to get a head start, others describe their techniques for dealing with phone calls, paperwork, mail, agendas, and priorities.

452. "Olin Corporation Retains Management Consultant Jean Driscoll to Advise Its Top Two Female Managers Monthly on Management Effectiveness." *Wall Street Journal* (August 4, 1981): 1.

453. O'Toole, Patricia. "Working Papers: Success Mania." *Vogue* 172 (April 1982): 178, 180.
O'Toole evaluates the power tactics described in the recent rash of success books and concludes that the style suggested is negative or oppressive power. She regrets that writers of the "getting ahead" books prey on women's self-doubt by touting gamesmanship and gimmicks and suggests instead that men and women enlist cooperation or "productive" power to achieve their workplace goals.

454. Raffel, Dawn. "The Professional Attitude." *McCalls* 111 (May 1984): 56, 58.
A professional attitude is as important as technical skills. Joni Evans, a publisher and editor-in-chief of Linden Books, says "Attitude counts for about seventy-five percent and skills about twenty-five percent." Raffel gives these hints for gaining that professional edge: (1) take the initiative, (2) project confidence under pressure, (3) be openminded and flexible, (4) take responsibility for your successes and failures, (5) keep your private life (reasonably) private, and (6) treat others with courtesy and respect.

455. Smith, Anne Mollegen, and Dill, Diana. "The Real Truth about Success from 100 Women Who've Been There." *Glamour* 82 (March 1984): 242-45, 321, 323, 327, 329, 331, 333.
The editors of *Glamour* questioned 100 of America's most successful women on their secrets of success. They responded to inquiries about how to choose the right career, the importance of who you work with, what gets the biggest raise, visibility, how to move up the management ladder, what to do when you are blocked, and how to handle job changes.

456. Stamell, Marcia. "How to Survive Once You've Arrived." *Mademoiselle* 89 (October 1983): 143-45, 234.
Stamell reviews the experts' advice to women on how to handle promotions and new responsibilities. Suggestions include tips on how to manage former co-workers, gaining acceptance from new peers, and learning from your new boss. The emphasis is on moving from secretary to executive.

457. Stead, Bette Ann. "Why Does the Secretary Hate Me and Other Laments of the Professionally Educated Woman Employee." *Vital Speeches of the Day* 48 (May 1, 1982): 434-40.
Stead, professor of marketing at the University of Houston, spoke on March 21 to the Society of Women Engineers, saying there are four on-the-job problems that are unique to women: (1) why does the secretary hate me? (2) what's the importance of "image"? (3) can the dual-career family really work? and (4) the current climate for women is gloomy. She advises women to be prepared by working on an MBA, getting career counseling, writing down the next two or three jobs they want, keeping their technical expertise current, and becoming an effective public speaker.

458. Taylor, Anita. "Women as Leaders." *Vital Speeches of the Day* 50 (May 1, 1984): 445-48.
Chair of the department of communication at George Mason University, Anita Taylor spoke on the topic of women leaders to the GROW Conference of Kentucky Women Researchers on February 23, 1984. She claims that women's nurturing nature, discrimination, sex-role socialization, and capitalism have kept them from leadership positions, but that leadership in the future will require many skills "for which women are uniquely qualified." She concludes that to be effective leaders, women must demand certain rights: (1) insist on equal pay for work of equal worth, (2) insist on equalizing the load at home, and (3) insist on the rights of all men and women for safe and affordable child care.

459. Wachtel, Eric, and Tifft, Susan. "Exceptions to the Rules?" *Savvy* 4 (November 1983): 37-43.
The authors compare career advice in *How to Hold onto Your Job* by Wachtel to that from three notable women executives and find that the practical advice given by those in the field frequently differs from that in the "how to" management books. Elaine S. Reiss, senior vice president at Ogilvy & Mather; Janet Long, regional director of Home Box Office, Inc.; and Sandra D. Kresch, vice president of marketing, Time Video Information Services, relate first-hand management problems and solutions.

460. Wiley, Kim Wright. "Chairman of the Bored." *Savvy* 7 (January 1986): 46-49.
Even executive women sometimes admit to being bored on the job. Boredom ranges from "temporary restlessness" to "chronic, almost desperate boredom" and can be cyclical. Wiley concludes with a list of "Ten Ways to Combat On-the-Job Boredom."

461. "Women and Corporate Culture." *Management Review* 72 (November 1983): 6.
Sharon Crain, of Crain & Associates Career Counselors, says women are still seen as lacking in business skills. Crain gives seminars and lectures for women on such topics as self-presentation, speaking, and dress. She advises women to walk with confidence and develop a more business-like speech pattern.

Psychology of Women in Management

462. Abeel, Erica. "Dark Secrets." *Esquire* 101 (June 1984): 258-60, 262, 264, 266.

The author of *I'll Call You Tomorrow: And Other Lies between Men and Women* interviewed psychoanalysts to find what women's current anxieties are. Although women have made gains in the corporate world, their primary anxiety remains the same—fear of abandonment, rejection, and loss of love. Successful professional women now face a double bind—being viewed as sex object and success object. One psychoanalyst claims that as more women define themselves through their work, they will lose the old anxieties.

463. Betz, Ellen L. "Two Tests of Maslow's Theory of Need Fulfillment." *Journal of Vocational Behavior* 24 (April 1984): 204-20.

Betz questioned three groups of women college graduates—professional/managerial, clerical/sales, and homemaking—to determine the relationship between need importance and need deficiencies and between need deficiencies and life satisfaction. The findings, which may be used to study women's career development processes, indicate that female managerial/professionals may have lower deficiencies in esteem than homemakers, but they may have a greater need for security/safety and autonomy. Includes tables and references.

464. Beutell, Nicholas J. "Correlates of Attitudes toward Women as Managers." *Journal of Social Psychology* 124 (October 1984): 57-63.

Beutell studies undergraduate and graduate business students to determine the effect of birth order, sex, and work values on their attitudes toward women managers. He used the WAMS (Women As Managers Scale), an instrument that asks respondents to rate twenty-one statements about women as managers. His findings indicate that women had more favorable attitudes toward women managers than did men and that work values were predictors of attitudes toward women managers among MBA students.

465. Blotnick, Srully. "Unsexed by Success: Has the Bedroom become Your Bored-Room?" *Harper's Bazaar* (September 1985): 236, 243, 472.

The author of *Otherwise Engaged: The Private Lives of Successful Career Women*, Blotnick describes his findings from a twenty-five year study of 3,000 women executives. He concludes that fear of intimacy and commitment harm a woman's sex life as well as her chances for career advancement. For success at work and sex, Blotnick advises executive women to take their personal lives as seriously as their careers.

466. Buono, Anthony F., and Kamm, Judith B. "Marginality and the Organizational Socialization of Female Managers." *Human Relations* 36 (December 1983): 1125-40.

Assistant professors of management at Bentley College, the authors use the sociological theory of marginality to explain the low number of women in top executive positions. The authors describe three other theories that are used to explain women's lack of progress in management: the dual labor market explanation, the female societal role explanation, and the organization structure explanation. Three steps should be taken to effectively integrate women managers into their organizations: anticipatory socialization, organizational "encounter," and change and acquisition of group norms and values. Buono and Kamm offer business schools specific suggestions for preparing their female students for managerial careers. Includes extensive bibliography.

467. Chassler, Sey. "Executive Peter Pans and Wendys: Can They Succeed in Business?" *Working Woman* 9 (September 1984): 168-69.

Chassler explains the theories of Dr. Dan Kiley, the author of *The Peter Pan Syndrome* and *The Wendy Dilemma*. He cites examples of both personality types, describing Cathie Black of *USA Today* and Mary Cunningham, vice president of Joseph E. Seagram and Sons, Inc.

468. Chusmir, Leonard H. "Male-Oriented vs. Balanced-as-to-Sex Thematic Apperception Tests." *Journal of Personality Assessment* 47 (February 1983): 29-35.

Chusmir used two instruments, Thematic Apperception Test (male-oriented) and Thematic Apperception Test (balanced-sex) to measure need achievement, need affiliation, and need power of 124 (sixty-two male and sixty-two female) managers. In the first, male-oriented Thematic Apperception Test (TAT), males and females responded the same, but women selected stronger affiliation imagery stories than did men in the balanced-sex TAT. Includes tables and references.

469. Colwill, Nina L. "Fear of Success in Women: Organizational Reality or Psychological Mythology?" *Business Quarterly* 49 (Fall 1984): 20-21.

Since Matina Horner introduced the concept of fear of success in women in 1968, the psychological literature on women's motive to avoid success has grown. More recent studies indicate, however, that the results of Horner's study may have been a "rational response to a specific social situation," not a "deeply rooted personality trait." Colwill supports this statement, noting that (1) by slightly varying the sentence that is presented to subjects, researchers have been able to produce greater "fear of success" in men than in women, (2) "fear of success" appears to be declining in both women and men, and (3) "fear of success" does not predict poor performance in a competitive situation. She concludes that successful men and women executives alike are well aware of both the positive and negative consequences of high achievement. Includes references.

470. Crino, Michael D.; White, Michael C.; and DeSanctis, Gerry L. "A Comment on the Dimensionality and Reliability of the Women as Managers Scale (WAMS)." *Academy of Management Journal* 24 (December 1981): 866-76.

Researchers sent questionnaires containing the WAMS (Women As Managers Scale) and demographic items to business students and managers to test for "differential subgroup reliability." The data show that the WAMS may be more reliable when used with students rather than managers, and may be more reliable for males than for females. They warn other researchers against using the WAMS when other measures might be more appropriate. Includes tables and references.

471. Crino, Michael D.; White, Michael C.; and Looney, Stephen W. "In the Eye of the Beholder: A Reply to Ilgen and Moore." *Academy of Management Journal* 28 (December 1985): 950-54.

The authors respond to a paper by Ilgen and Moore (1983) that is critical of their 1981 study on the dimensionality and reliability of the Women As Managers Scale (WAMS). They claim that a careful reading of their original paper, a review of the development of the WAMS, and the use of a standard psychometric theory text reveal that Ilgen and Moore did not clearly show any flaw in the work of Crino, White, and DeSanctis (1981). Includes table and references.

472. Cullen, John B., and Perrewe, Pamela L. "'Superiors' and 'Subordinates' Gender: Does It Really Matter?" *Psychological Reports* 48 (April 1981): 435-38.

Cullen and Perrewe used data from a 1972/73 Quality of Employment survey conducted at the University of Michigan to determine whether the gender of supervisors and subordinates influences perceptions of superiors' behaviors. Their findings showed no correlation between sex of superiors and subordinates' perceptions of superiors' behavior. They indicate a need to study next whether the gender of superior and subordinate affects such subordinate behaviors as turnover and absenteeism.

473. Dubno, Peter. "Attitudes toward Women Executives: A Longitudinal Approach." *Academy of Management Journal* 28 (March 1985): 235-39.

Dubno measured positive and negative attitudes toward women executives over an eight-year period (1975 to 1983) to determine trends and changes in attitudes. MBA students at three graduate business schools responded to the Managerial Attitudes Towards Women Executives Scale (MATWES) three times in the eight-year period. Results indicated male MBA students had consistently negative attitudes toward women managers, while female students held consistently positive attitudes toward women managers. Dubno concludes that women executives might expect discrimination and stereotyping to continue, as he found no change in males' negative attitudes toward women managers. Includes tables and references.

474. Ezell, Hazel; Odewahn, Charles A.; and Sherman, J. Daniel. "Effects of Having Been Supervised by a Woman on Perceptions of Female Managerial Competence." *Personnel Psychology* 34 (Summer 1981): 291-99.

Three-hundred sixty men and women managers (56 percent male, 44 percent female) in state public welfare agencies who were enrolled in or had completed a management training program participated in a study to determine whether the perception of a woman manager's competence varied depending on whether an individual had or had not been supervised by a woman. The respondents answered questions about women managers' adaptation or alteration of their work environments, their ability, and their motivation to manage. The primary finding was that people who have worked for women managers had a more positive perception of women's motivation to manage. Includes tables and references.

475. Garland, Howard; Hale, Karen F.; and Burnson, Michael. "Attributions for the Success and Failure of Female Managers: A Replication and Extension." *Psychology of Women Quarterly* 7 (Winter 1982): 155-62.

Researchers from the University of Texas at Arlington surveyed 110 (fifty-two male and fifty-two female) employees of a state human services agency regarding their attitudes toward women in management and attributions for success or failure of women managers. The survey results indicated that a male's positive attitude toward women managers will cause him to attribute her success to ability or effort, and females with positive attitudes toward women managers attribute their failure to the job, not to a lack of ability. Includes two tables and references.

476. Ilgen, Daniel R., and Moore, Carol F. "When Reason Fails: A Comment on the Reliability and Dimensionality of the WAMS." *Academy of Management Journal* 26 (September 1983): 335-40.

Ilgen and Moore question the findings of Crino, White, and DeSanctis in their 1981 report on the reliability and dimensionality of the Women As Managers Scale (WAMS). They do agree that since the scale was developed in the mid-1970s, the situation for women managers has changed, but feel that the research of Crino, et al. does not correctly point out the weaknesses of the scale. Includes tables and references.

477. Keown, Charles F., and Keown, Ada Lewis. "Success Factors for Corporate Women Executives." *Group and Organization Studies* 7 (December 1982): 445-56.

Keown and Keown replicated Hennig and Jardim's research (1977) to see if the picture of *The Managerial Woman* is still true and to determine attitudes and leadership styles that are successful for women executives today. They provide a "Profile of Successful Corporate Women" and conclude with implications for career counselors, personnel managers, organizational development specialists, and women executives. Includes tables and references.

478. Koprowski, Eugene J. "Cultural Myths: Clues to Effective Management." *Organizational Dynamics* 12 (Fall 1983): 39-51.
Professor of management at the University of Colorado, Koprowski calls on mythology to give managers clues on dealing with three new workplace issues: the role of women, Japanese management techniques, and managers' leadership roles. Following a discussion of the stature of women in myths, women as symbols, and the duality in human nature, the author draws implications for management, concluding that conflicts between men and women in the workplace are likely to escalate. Includes bibliography.

479. London, Manuel, and Stumpf, Stephen A. "Effects of Candidate Characteristics on Management Promotion Decisions: An Experimental Study." *Personnel Psychology* 36 (Summer 1983): 241-59.
Seventy-two lower- to middle-level managers from three corporations participated in a half-day management promotion decision exercise in which researchers manipulated four candidate characteristics: potential for advancement, availability of assessment center information, current position, and sex. Females were favored for management positions when their current position was one close to the given vacancy and when they had experience in the type of work described. Includes tables and references.

480. Macleod, Jennifer S. "How about Women's 'Fear of Success'?" *EEO Today* 9 (Autumn 1982): 245-50.
A social psychologist and management consultant conducted a workshop for women managers on the fear of success. Macleod tells women that while men generally concentrate on their careers, women try to achieve in several areas—marriage, career, children—and are frequently criticized by spouse, parents, friends, or employers for neglecting one or more. She concludes that women are not afraid of success, rather they are afraid of being punished if they are successful.

481. Marshall, Judi. "The Identity Dilemmas of Being a Woman Manager." *Equal Opportunities International (UK)* 2 (2) (1983): 28-33.
A lecturer on organizational behavior in the School of Management, University of Bath, Judi Marshall classifies the literature on women as reform feminism, radical feminism, or revision and relates those categories to the literature on women in management. She describes the stress that women managers experience as a result of the male positive, female negative attitude and regrets the fact that women managers have few female role models, because many female executives identify with their male colleagues first.

482. Motowidlo, Stephan J. "Sex Role Orientation and Behavior in a Work Setting." *Journal of Personality and Social Psychology* 42 (May 1982): 935-45.
The author discusses the evolution of the concept of androgyny and behavioral correlates of androgyny, then describes his method of research. Thirty-eight female and twenty-seven male low- to middle-level managers of a large utility company completed Bem's Sex-Role Inventory. Androgynous persons scored higher on Support for Nontraditionals, Candor and Personal Assertiveness, and Active Listening.

483. Nevill, Dorothy D.; Stephenson, Beth B.; and Philbrick, Jane Hass. "Gender Effects on Performance Evaluation." *Journal of Psychology* 114 (November 1983): 165-69.

Male and female bank managers and students completed the Women As Managers Scale (WAMS) and rated the performance of male or female assistant branch bank managers using the Career Opportunities Application and the Performance Criteria for Assistant Branch Managers. The respondents' ratings of successful or unsuccessful applicants were similar, but females rated successful applicants more positively and managers who had less favorable attitudes toward women managers rated female applicants lower than male applicants. Includes references.

484. O'Donnell, Holly. "Leadership Effectiveness: Do Sex and Communication Style Make a Difference?" *English Journal* 74 (March 1985): 65-67.

Women have been entering the executive suite in increasing numbers, but there are still many negative perceptions about their managerial skills and psychological attributes. The author analyzes educational (ERIC) research on communication styles related to manager's gender and perceived effectiveness and offers ways to heighten high school students' awareness of these findings. Classroom activities might include: class discussion, interviews with community leaders for opinions on female leadership, a resource file of articles on women in management, and a list of communication characteristics of male managers/executives. Includes references from ERIC.

485. Remland, Martin; Jacobson, Carolyn; and Jones, Tricia. "Effects of Psychological Gender and Sex-Incongruent Behavior on Evaluations of Leadership." *Perceptual & Motor Skills* 57 (December 1983): 783-89.

Researchers employed Spence and Helmreich's Personal Attributes Questionnaire to investigate "the influence of psychological gender on evaluations of leadership performance by a male and female manager described as using either supportive or nonsupportive nonverbal communication with a male subordinate in a problem-solving interview." They found that, unlike previous reports, evaluations of nontraditionl sex role behavior by male and female managers were not affected by psychological gender. Includes references.

486. Ritchie, Richard J., and Moses, Joseph L. "Assessment Center Correlates of Women's Advancement into Middle Management: A 7-Year Longitudinal Analysis." *Journal of Applied Psychology* 68 (May 1983): 227-31.

One-thousand ninety-seven women managers attended a two-day management assessment in 1976 and were evaluated seven years later to determine the relationship between assessment center performance and advancement into middle management. Results of the study supported the theory that assessment center ratings predict management potential. Findings also indicated that men and women need essentially the same skills to advance in management. Includes tables and reference.

487. Snodgrass, Sara E., and Rosenthal, Robert. "Females in Charge: Effects of Sex on Subordinate and Romantic Attachment Status upon Self-Ratings of Dominance." *Journal of Personality* 52 (December 1984): 354-71.

Researchers studied thirty-six dyads (72 people) in group interactions and asked the subjects to rate themselves, the other person, and the activity in terms of leadership roles. The authors concluded that female leaders rate themselves as less dominant than male leaders, possibly due to role conflict. Snodgrass and Rosenthal suggest that women fear a perception of them as cold and unfeminine. Includes references.

488. Terborg, James R., and Shingledecker, Pamela. "Employee Reactions to Supervision and Work Evaluation as a Functon of Subordinate and Manager Sex." *Sex Roles* 9 (July 1983): 813-24.

Employees of a Fortune 500 company answered an attitude survey regarding supervision and work evaluation. Results indicate that sex stereotypes may not play a large part in a subordinate's view of supervision and work evaluation. Includes tables and references.

489. Waddell, Frederick T. "Factors Affecting Choice, Satisfaction, and Success in the Female Self-Employed." *Journal of Vocational Behavior* 23 (December 1983): 294-304.

Forty-seven self-employed women and forty-seven female managers and secretaries were compared with regard to six factors: achievement motivation, locus of control, sex-role "masculinity," and availability of models for ownership (mother, father, and other). There were no significant differences between female owners and female managers on the three variables, but owners had more parental models for ownership than either managers or secretaries. The owners exhibited a uniformly high level of job satisfaction.

490. Wexley, Kenneth N., and Pulakos, Elaine D. "Sex Effects on Performance Ratings in Manager-Subordinate Dyads: A Field Study." *Journal of Applied Psychology* 67 (August 1982): 433-39.

Researchers evaluated Schmitt and Lappin's (1980) hypothesis that people rate those like themselves with more confidence. Wexley and Pulakos studied 286 manager-subordinate dyads using the Behavioral Observation Scales (BOS) and Minnesota Satisfactoriness Scale (MSS). They found that female managers gave more variable ratings to male subordinates than to female subordinates. Includes tables and references.

491. White, Michael C.; Crino, Michael D.; and DeSanctis, Gerry L. "Critical Review of Female Performance, Performance Training and Organizational Initiatives Designed to Aid Women in the Work-Role Environment." *Personnel Psychology* 34 (Summer 1981): 227-48.

The authors list four propositions for women managers' performance appraisal and two propositions in regard to performance training for women and analyze the research relating to each proposition. Includes lengthy bibliography.

492. White, Michael C.; Crino, Michael D.; and DeSanctis, Gerry L. "Ratings of Prestige and Desirability: Effects of Additional Women Entering Selected Business Occupations." *Personality & Social Psychology Bulletin* 7 (December 1981): 588-92.

Some researchers theorize that as the number of women in high-status professions increases, the occupational prestige of those professions decreases. Replication of Touhey's study by Suchner (1979) did not support this finding. The authors studied 394 males in junior/senior management courses at a business college. Their findings are consistent with Suchner's study. They suggest reasons why their findings did not support Touhey's conclusion. Includes references.

493. White, Michael C.; DeSanctis, Geraldine; and Crino, Michael D. "Achievement, Self-Confidence, Personality Traits, and Leadership Ability: A Review of Literature on Sex Differences." *Psychological Reports* 48 (April 1981): 547-69.

The authors studied women managers' adjustment to the managerial role. Factors considered were self-confidence, achievement, fear of success, leadership ability, personality characteristics, career tactics, and career strategies. They conclude that there is a need for empirical studies of women managers, rather than commentary, and they call for measurement instruments in addition to the Women As Managers Scale (WAMS). Includes extensive references.

Women Managers in Various Fields

494. Adler, Nancy J. "Expecting International Success: Female Managers Overseas." *Columbia Journal of World Business* 19 (Fall 1984): 79-85.

Less than 3 percent of all American and Canadian expatriate managers are women. Adler surveyed international personnel managers in sixty American and Canadian corporations to find out why this figure is so low. She found that while qualified women managers are willing to work abroad, there are three obstacles to their appointment to such posts: foreigners' prejudice, dual-career marriages, and, in their own companies, selection bias for men. Includes charts and notes.

495. Adler, Nancy J. "Women Do Not Want International Careers: And Other Myths about International Management." *Organizational Dynamics* 13 (Autumn 1984): 66-79.

A survey of 700 United States' and Canadian companies shows that only 3 percent of expatriate managers are women. Adler studied male and female MBA students regarding their interest in international careers and found that men and women are equally interested in international careers—84 percent would like at least one foreign assignment. Males and females did not differ in their reasons for turning down international assignments, but respondents felt that men would have more opportunities for such assignments. Experts believe there are few women in international management because of female managers' disinterest, companies' resistance, and foreigners' prejudice, but Adler's research shows that women are as willing as men to work overseas. Includes exhibits and bibliography.

496. Adler, Nancy J. "Women in International Management: Where Are They?" *California Management Review* 26 (Summer 1984): 78-89.

Adler reviews the status of women in international management and describes a survey of United States' and Canadian firms to determine the number of male and female managers. Her findings indicate that women account for less than 3 percent of international managers. Larger companies are more likely to send women on overseas assignments, and banks have the largest number of female expatriate managers. Adler concludes with recommendations to corporations for selecting effective overseas managers, regardless of gender. Includes tables and references.

497. "Aspiring Women Learn How to Attain Organizational Power." *American Libraries* 13 (September 1982): 533-34.
Jane Covey Brown, vice president and director of marketing for Goodmeasure, Inc., warns women about the status of women in librarianship, claiming the profession must redistribute power to women at all job levels. High-level women library managers agree with Brown's statements and suggest job rotation, special administrative tasks, and an environment of experiment and risk taking as means of sharing power. Women are encourged to get first-line supervisory experience, to find mentors, and to plan their careers as men do.

498. Atkinson, Judith A. "Women in School Administration: A Review of the Research." *Review of Educational Research* 51 (Fall 1981) 311-43.
Atkinson reviews the research on women in administration, management, and leadership since 1974, then focuses on the status of minority women in educational administration. She concludes with strategies for change and directions for future research. Includes extensive bibliography.

499. Beck, Jane. "Developing Women Managers in the Hotel and Catering Industry." *Women in Management Review* 2 (Spring 1986): 31-37.
Although two-thirds of the 2.5 million people in hotel and catering are women, few hold management positions. One-hundred ten young women have participated in the Manpower Services Commission management development program designed to increase the number of women in middle- and upper-level management in these areas. The result of the program is significant—50 percent of the graduates of the first two classes were promoted within a year.

500. Bekey, Michelle. "Women in Management." *Registered Representative* (November 1982): 34-36, 38, 40-41.
A growing number of women are becoming managers in the securities industry, most in office services or operations. Many of the women began as secretaries, research assistants, or brokers, and they credit some of their success to mentors. Bekey profiles women who are branch managers, vice presidents, sales managers, and office managers.

501. Blumenthal, Karen. "Room at the Top." *Wall Street Journal* (March 24, 1986): 7D, 9D.
Although women have entered the workplace in large numbers in the last twenty years, few have reached executive positions, especially in manufacturing and heavy industry. Even in fields that traditionally employ more women—financial services, personnel, public relations—women seldom get beyond middle management. Some companies have started actively recruiting women and initiating programs to integrate them into the organization more quickly.

502. Bodec, Ben. "Why So Few Women at the Top?" *Marketing and Media Decisions* 17 (April 1982): 70-71, 118.

Bovec interviewed top women managers in advertising and discovered that sex bias still prevails in the major agencies, and women feel the only way to the top is to start their own agencies. Only five women have earned the title chair, president or managing partner in the top 100 agencies: Mary Wells of Wells Rich Greene; Charlotte Beers of Tathum-Laird and Kudner; Marcella Free of Avrett, Free and Fisher; Lois Geraci Ernst of Advertising to Women; and Lois Wyse of Wyse Advertising. The article includes numerous excerpts from interviews with women advertising executives and advertising executive recruiters.

503. "Bonanza for Women Managers?" *Computer Decisions* 16 (January 1984): 78.

Information processing may be a good field for women interested in management opportunities. The number of women MIS/DP managers increased from 6 to 10 percent in one year, according to a *Computer Decisions* salary-status survey. Examples of successful women in the field include Sharon Kaminecki, director of information systems for the Environmental Affairs and Safety Department of Standard Oil, and E. Nancy Markle, vice president of information services at the Federal National Mortgage Association.

504. Bonner, George R. "Women Executives Gaining More Status in the Advertising Industry." *Christian Science Monitor* (March 11, 1983): p. 11, col. 1.

In the past the only route to the top for a woman in advertising was forming her own agency. Today, there are more opportunities for women to advance into middle management, although men still outearn women in every category in the latest industry salary survey. Lois Wyse, founder and president of Wyse Advertising, claims there is still a client barrier, and that the climate will become more competitive for women in advertising. The president of Advertising to Women, Lois Ernst, believes there has been progress in reducing the amount of sexist advertising.

505. Brandehoff, Susan. "A New Director Tests Her Management Mettle." *American Libraries* 16 (January 1985): 47-48.

Patricia Swanson, assistant director for science libraries at the University of Chicago, was named to head the new 900,000-volume John Crerar Library in 1983. Although she finds the work rewarding, Swanson admits that she has a hard time saying "no" to people. She also believes that people with energy, skills, and creativity should be considered for management, regardless of sex.

506. Brandehoff, Susan. "Spotlight on Women Managers." *American Libraries* 16 (January 1985): 20-26, 28, 45-46.

American Libraries interviews six women library managers about their professional goals, the management style that works best for them, the most difficult decision they have made in their present jobs, whether networking and/or mentors has been important in their careers, and what education they would recommend beyond the MLS for administration. Includes photographs and descriptions of the women's careers.

507. Bussey, John. "The Industrial Revolution." *Wall Street Journal* (March 24, 1986): 14D.

Women still earned only 14 percent of all bachelor's degrees in engineering in 1984, which helps explain why so few women have become plant managers. Chrysler, Ford, DuPont, Goodyear, and Hewlett Packard have no women plant managers. Fifty-seven-year-old Patricia Carrigan was named GM's first woman plant manager in the United States in 1982.

508. "Consulting Springboard." *Business Week* (August 17, 1981): 101, 104.

Some women use management consulting as a means of gaining entry to high-level corporate positions. The advantages are versatility, problem-solving ability, familiarity with a wide variety of operating styles, risk-taking ability, and selling skills. One Michigan State University professor of management claims consulting experience is more valuable to women than industry experience.

509. Gable, Myron; Gillespie, Karen K.; and Topol, Martin. "The Current Status of Women in Department Store Retailing: An Update." *Journal of Retailing* 60 (Summer 1984): 86-104.

Gillespie and others replicate her 1977-78 research on the status of women managers in department store retailing. They compare the women in both studies by geographic area, number of executives in a firm, number of stores in a firm, and annual sales volume of the organizations. In addition, they compared the makeup (male versus female) of the boards of directors of the twenty-five largest publicly owned department stores with that of the twenty-five largest industrial firms. They conclude that while the number of women managers in retailing has increased from the time of the first study, the number of women reaching upper- or senior-level management positions is few. Includes tables and references.

510. Harragan, Betty Lehan. "Making the Right Move." *Working Woman* 8 (December 1983): 42.

Harragan advises an electrical engineer about staying in the technical arena or moving to general management. She views the engineer's assignment as administrative assistant to a senior manufacturing engineer at headquarters as evidence that the company wants her to have additional experience and credentials.

511. Haynes, Karen S. "Sexual Differences in Social Work Administrators' Job Satisfaction." *Journal of Social Service Research* 6 (Spring/Summer 1983): 57-74.

Male and female social service agency administrators answered a questionnaire about three independent dimensions (organizational structure, organizational climate, individual processes) and one dependent dimension (job satisfaction). The author concludes that male and female managers perceived internal and external barriers differently. Includes tables, references, and Appendix A: Dimensions, Variables, and Scales of Survey Instrument.

512. Hill, Raymond E., and Hansen, Jo-Ida C. "An Analysis of Vocational Interests for Female Research and Development Managers." *Journal of Vocational Behavior* 28 (February 1986): 70-83.

Using the Strong-Campbell Interest Inventory, Hill and Hansen studied female and male research and develoment (R & D) managers, technical specialists, and nontechnical managers. The interest pattern for female R & D managers resembled that of female engineers, and both male and female R & D managers were equivalent on the Enterprising theme and Basic Interest Scales. Includes tables and references.

513. Hilliard, S. Lee. "Pressing for Power." *Black Enterprise* 15 (April 1985): 42.

Pam McAllister Johnson, president and publisher of the *Ithaca Journal*, is the nation's first black woman in charge of a general-market daily (95 percent of newspaper managers in the United States are white). Previously a television, radio, and newspaper reporter, Johnson describes herself as self-competitive.

514. Hoffman, Marilyn. "Women Executives Give Tips on Progressing in the Professional World." *Christian Science Monitor* (March 8, 1983): p. 18, col. 1.

Hoffman interviewed executive women in the home-furnishings field to find out what women need to know to keep ahead in today's competitive world. The women included the director of communications for the Southern Furniture Manufacturers Association, executive editor of *House and Garden*, home fashions coordinator for Celanese Corporation, a professor at New York University, editor of *Designer* magazine, and home-fashions coordinator for J.C. Penney. Their advice: find a mentor, always be a lady, keep a smile on your face, learn to work with the people in your organization, assert yourself, capitalize on your positive or strong points, and dress for the next higher position.

515. Hymowitz, Carol. "Women Executives Have a Rough Time in Pittsburgh's Old Line Industrial Firms." *Wall Street Journal* (May 6, 1982): 31.

Although Pittsburgh is corporate headquarters for many of the largest industrial corporations, there are few women at high levels of management. The 200 members of the local Executive Women's Council work mainly in nonprofit organizations, health care, banking, and small businesses. Only three executive women qualify for membership in the elite Duquesne Club. One woman vice president claims, "The old boys' club reigns supreme in Pittsburgh."

516. Landro, Laura. "Reel-Life Struggles." *Wall Street Journal* (March 24, 1986): 12D-13D.

There are women writers, producers, and directors, but no woman has yet been named president or CEO of a major studio. Landro profiles Dawn Steel, president of motion picture production at Paramount, and Barbara Corday, president of Columbia Pictures Television.

517. Lubin, Aasta S. "Superwomen of the Financial World." *Working Woman* 9 (September 1984): 161-67.

Therapist Lubin conducted an in-depth study of five members of the Financial Women's Association of New York for her doctoral dissertation at Columbia University Teacher's College. She presents individual profiles of the five women executives. Three have MBAs and one is completing a Ph.D. All five are married, range in age from thirty-two to thirty-seven, are white women from middle-class families, have one or two children, and earn at least $50,000 a year.

518. Martin, Josh. "Brave New Managers." *Working Woman* 8 (May 1983): 100-04.

Martin reviews the status of women in data processing, noting that women represent 20 percent of project managers who earn between $24,000 to $50,000. Industry experts claim that within five years women will have made considerable gains at all levels of data processing management. Martin relates how Betty Nimi went fom a technical manager supervising fifteen people to a general manager with 180 people reporting to her.

519. "Maybe Next Year." *Wall Street Journal* (September 12, 1985): p. 35, col. 3.

Although many Wall Street investment banking firms are promoting women into management positions, progress is still slow. Morgan Stanley & Co. celebrated its 50th anniversary with a black-tie dinner for its ninety-five managing directors—all of whom are male. A separate celebration will be held for the firm's 115 principals—ten of whom are women.

520. Moran, Robert T. "Forget about Gender, Just Get the Job Done." *International Management* 41 (March 1986): 72.

The author of *Getting Your Yen's Worth: How to Negotiate with Japan, Inc.* feels that women excel in international management positions for three reasons: "women tend to approach relations and negotiations from a win-win strategy; they tend to be more respectful and culturally sensitive; and they tend to be better listeners and more sympathetic than men." Only 3 percent of international managers were women in 1984. Most of those women felt that being female was neither an advantage nor a disadvantage in their career advancement, but they sometimes had more freedom than women nationals in the countries where they were working.

521. Myers, Gwyn. "Terminal Fear." *Working Woman* 7 (July 1982): 72.

A principal in a data processing consulting firm reviews some fear of computing experienced by executives and tells women managers that a positive attitude is the key to overcoming the fear. She answers five questions most commonly asked by executives who fear computerization.

522. Reier, Sharon. "The Feminine Mystique." *Institutional Investor* 18 (July 1984): 223-24, 226.
Christine Patton started as a foreign exchange trader with Morgan Guaranty Trust fifteen years ago. Now as senior vice president in charge of global foreign exchange and global liabilities at Manufacturers Hanover Trust, she will oversee 100 interbank and corporate traders. Women now account for one-third of foreign exchange treasurers and are moving into currency planning. Reier profiles several successful female "forex" managers.

523. "Six Female Executives Operating in Minors." *Sporting News* 194 (July 12, 1982): 46.
Six women are executives of minor league baseball teams: Patty Cox Hampton, president and co-owner, Oklahoma City 89ers, and vice president of Chicago Cubs; Frances Crockett, president and general manager of Charlotte Orioles; Hilary Buzas, president of Bristol (CT) Red Sox; Michelle Myers Sprague, owner and general manager of Lodi Dodgers, L.A. farm club; Kathy Leonard, general manager of Redwood (Co.) Pioneers; and Patricia Nelly, president and general manager of Walla Walla (Washington) Padres.

524. Slipman, Sue. "Women in Management: The Trade Union's Role." *Women in Management Review* 1 (Winter 1986): 202-06.
Director of the National Council for One Parent Families, Slipman spoke at a *Working Woman* conference on the barriers and opportunities for women in the trade unions. In her words, "The unions' record is appalling. Their history, like so many other institutions, is one of exclusion of women. . . . Unions are antagonistic to equal opportunities policies." She calls on unions for positive action, i.e., quotas and/or contract compliance; flexible work arrangements; appointment of women to decision-making positions; and revision of union organization to a democratic, not an activist, structure. Slipman concludes that men have to be willing to share power. Includes chart on representation of women in trade unions.

525. Tannenbaum, Jeffrey A. "Only about 7.6% of the Principals in Management-Consulting Firms Are Women, Says *Consultants News*, a Fitzwilliams, NH, Newsletter." *Wall Street Journal* (October 10, 1985): p. 1, col. 5.

526. Trost, Cathy. "Women Managers Rise in High-Tech Firms, but They're Still a Rare Breed." *Wall Street Journal* (August 28, 1984): p. 1. col. 5.
Although women have experienced great gains in management positions at such firms as Computervision Corporation, IBM, Xerox, and Prime Computer, women still hold only 10 percent of high-tech management positions. Executive searchers claim difficulties in finding women with both management and technical skills.

527. "The Unlikely Banker Leading Samuel Montagu's Asian Assault." *International Management* 39 (July 1984): 45-46.

Barbara Thomas, once the youngest person to be appointed an SEC commissioner, is now Samuel Montagu and Co.'s regional director for international security markets and corporate finances. She is the first women to hold the position of director at Montagu, a merchant bank. Hong Kong is now home for Thomas, her lawyer husband, and one-year old son. Thomas' management style gives a great deal of freedom to her staff. She states, "I want to get the very brightest people, treat them very well, and give them a lot of independence."

528. Williams, Kaylene C.; Faltot, James C.; and Madaire, Claire. "Research Note: A Comparison of Women in Department and Specialty Store Management." *Journal of Retailing* 59 (Winter 1983): 107-15.

Researchers at the University of Delaware replicated a study of women managers in retailing done by Karen Gillespie in 1977. While the percentage of women executives rose in retailing from 33.8 to 39.3 percent from 1976 to 1980, with significant increases in the numbers of women in positions as buyer and merchandise manager, there remains a large gap between the levels of men and women managers in retailing. The authors suggest three ways to improve the situation for women: (1) communicate opportunities to women, (2) provide specialized training for women, and (3) increase networking among women. Includes tables and references.

529. "Women: Better Overseas Execs?" *Industry Week* (October 28, 1985): 13.

Robert T. Moran, professor at the American Graduate School of International Management, Glendale, AZ, states that women make better international executives, because they have less difficulty with cultural barriers. He adds that women are more formal, show more respect, and spend more time establishing relationships. Still, only 3 percent of all expatriate managers are women.

530. "Women: The New Venture Capitalists." *Business Week* (November 2, 1981): 100.

As many as 100 women now work in the field of venture capital, 10 percent of the estimated 1,000 venture capital professionals. Most of the women entered the field by circuitous routes, however, not by the MBA route. The article profiles Eng-Wong, vice president at Industrial Capital Corp. and a graduate from Wellesley with a degree in Greek; Patricia Cloherty, co-owner of her own firm and a former Peace Corps volunteer; Joy London, vice president of Patricof, who earned a master's degree in community health; and others.

Women Managers in Other Countries

531. Abelson, Michael B. "American Woman Faces Continual Culture Shock as Japanese Executive." *Los Angeles Times* (May 14, 1984): sec. 4, p. 3-4.

Thirty-six-year-old Susan Eaton is assistant manager of marketing and new business development for the United States' division of C. Itoh and Co. Ltd., a Japanese trading company. She has adapted to working in a culture that feels woman's place is in the home because she is sensitive to the cultural differences. Eaton spent five years in Japan, teaching English to schoolchildren and business executives and gaining exposure to Japanese people and customs. She feels she is more effective at Itoh, because she is not male or Asian and because she can help her Japanese bosses understand and work with their American clients.

532. Anderson, Lynn R. "Management of the Mixed-Cultural Work Group." *Organizational Behavior and Human Performance* 31 (June 1983): 303-30.

Anderson presents data on female middle-level managers in New Zealand (p. 320-22). Table 8 shows comparisons between female and male white (Pakeha) middle-level managers based on effectiveness, satisfaction, group factors, and leadership factors.

533. Ball, Robert. "Italy's Most Talked-About Executive." *Fortune* 109 (April 2, 1984): 99-100, 102.

The first woman to head a major Italian industrial firm, forty-eight-year-old Marisa Bellisario lead Italtel, the state-owned telecommunications manufacturer, from huge losses to a profit in three years. Although she won union concessions (a cut of 7,000 jobs over three years), there have been no labor problems, and sales per employee have tripled. Italtel's 300 executives and supervisory staff includes only three women besides Bellisario.

534. Barber, David. "New Zealand Tries to Give Women a Boost." *Christian Science Monitor* (August 29, 1984): 8-9.

Although New Zealand was the first country in the world to give women the right to vote (1893), there are few women in high business or government positions. A Public Service Association report states that women are underrepresented at high levels in all major institutions and hold only 7 percent of all executive or managerial positions. Anne Hercus, a lawyer and the minister of social welfare, vows that the government will ratify the United Nations Convention on the elimination of discrimination against women.

535. Borrus, Amy. "Look Whose Sun Is Rising Now: Career Women." *Business Week* (August 25, 1986): 50.
Borrus reports that sexual discrimination is still prevalent in Japan where most women are limited to clerical jobs and leave the workforce by age twenty-five. Because of an April 1986 equal-employment law, some Japanese companies are recruiting more women graduates for management positions, but the biggest gains for Japanese women have come in foreign companies. Forty percent of women college graduates hope to become managers, according to one recent survey.

536. Bowers, Brent, and Demirsar, Metin. "Women Managers and Turkey's Sexist Society." *Wall Street Journal* (May 15, 1985): 34.
Turkish women fill 5 percent of the country's management and administrative positions, and many claim that while Turkey is still a male-dominated, sexist society outside the workplace, women do not experience sexism inside corporations and the professions. However, a leader of Turkey's feminist movement claims that Turkey's women managers come from the country's intellectual and economic elite and thus have never experienced the sexism or oppression most women encounter. Includes quotes and comments from Turkish women managers.

537. Chira, Susan. "A Tough Accent for Japanese Women." *New York Times* (February 24, 1985): sec. 3, p. 1.
The rise of Japanese women into management ranks has been slow because of Japanese cultural attitudes toward women's proper role. Japanese companies strongly oppose an equal employment opportunity law proposed by the Ministry of Labor's Women's Bureau. Statistics from 1983 show that Japanese women make up 35 percent of the salaried workforce, but hold only 6 percent of management jobs. Female managers account for only one-tenth of one percent of all working women in Japan.

538. Condon, Jane. "Foreign Female Execs: Japan's 'Third Gender.'" *Wall Street Journal* (April 2, 1984): 31.
Members of Foreign Executive Women (FEW) relate their experiences in the boardrooms and conference rooms of Japan. Some women, excluded from client meetings, have difficulty battling the Japanese attitude regarding women professionals. The most effective foreign women executives have a particular skill or area of expertise and work in staff, not line, positions. FEW president Elyse Rogers advises foreign women executives in Japan to (1) be flexible, (2) respect local business practices, and (3) learn some Japanese.

539. Crew, Bob. "Women in Management." *Industrial Management & Data Systems* (July/August 1983): 9-10.
A Manchester University Institute of Science and Technology study of women managers in Britain revealed that the typical woman manager was thirty-eight years old and earned an average 9,175 pounds a year.

Women now account for 40 percent of those entering management training courses, compared to 11 percent in 1973. However, women in middle- and senior-management still earn less than their male counterparts.

540. Cromie, Stanley. "Women as Managers in Northern Ireland." *Journal of Occupational Psychology* 54 (June 1981): 87-91.

According to the *Digest of the Statistics of Northern Ireland (1979)* only 4.6 percent of working women are managers. Cromie studied ninety-nine women and seventy-nine men to determine what accounts for the small number of women managers in Ulster. He used two instruments, the twenty-item Job Involvement Questionnaire and the Women As Managers Scale (WAMS). Results indicated that women's job involvement was not significantly less than that of men's, and all women in the survey are significantly more favorable toward women as managers than were the males in the survey. Includes tables and references.

541. DeVries, Hilary. "British Working Women—Cracking Centuries of Tradition." *Christian Science Monitor* (March 8, 1984): 25-26.

As yet Britain has no affirmative action legislation, and its Sex Discrimination Act was only passed a scant ten years ago. Observers claim that Britain is a decade behind the United States in progress for working women, and say that tokenism, lack of role models, and indirect discrimination still act as barriers to women. Eleanor MacDonald, founder of the Women in Management organization in London, asserts there is a negative syndrome in Britain where women lack confidence in their skills and the general attitude is "don't make waves."

542. Ho, Suk-ching. "Women Managers in Hong Kong: Traditional Barriers and Emerging Trends." *Equal Opportunities International (UK)* 3 (1984): 7-10.

A lecturer in the department of marketing and international business of the Chinese University of Hong Kong, Suk-ching Ho divides the entry of women in management into three themes, then analyzes the content of management recruitment ads. She classifies the ads by sex, level of management, and industry, and by academic qualifications. Includes tables and references.

543. Hulihan, Maile. "Europe's Female Managers Still Fight Bias." *Wall Street Journal* (April 17, 1984): 38.

Management Centre Europe surveyed nine European countries in 1981 and found that women occupied only 6 to 13 percent of management positions. Even more important, 74 percent of the companies that had no women managers had no plans for recruiting or hiring women into management positions. Educational systems and social customs are two causes of "hidden discriminatory policies." Although the British are seen as more open to women in management, women fill only 7 percent of management positions in the United Kingdom.

544. Kaminski, Margueritt, and Paiz, Judith. "Japanese Women in Management: Where Are They?" *Equal Opportunities International (UK)* 3 (2) (1984): 10-15.
The authors review the employment situation for Japanese women with emphasis on their participation in business. Table I compares 1982 statistics on United States and Japanese business women; Table II weighs the costs and benefits for United States women, who are inside the corporate culture, and Table III lists the costs and benefits for Japanese women, who are outside the corporate culture. The authors make nine predictions about the future for Japanese women in business. Includes references.

545. Kanabayashi, Masayoshi. "Women in Japan Get Jobs These Days, Including More Management Level Jobs." *Wall Street Journal* (May 14, 1985): p. 1, col. 1.
A working women revolution is occurring in Japan—married women comprise 21 percent of Japan's labor force, two times the rate just twenty years ago. More women are moving into supervisory positions, although pay for women still lags 10 to 30 percent behind men in similar jobs. The divorce rate has also doubled in the past twenty years, as one in eight women asking for a divorce cite their husband's inability to cope with her work role. Other Japanese women eschew marriage, not wishing to combine the traditional Japanese wife's role with the demands of a management job. Although some Japanese companies are promoting women to management positions, they generally do not have the women supervising men.

546. "More than 2% of 480,000 Japanese Companies Covered in a Recent Survey Had Women Presidents." *Wall Street Journal* (February 19, 1981): 1.
The women's average age is 52.1 years and average salary was $110,000 a year.

547. Phillips, Barbara. "Uneven Paths to Progress." *Savvy* 3 (January 1982): 54-57.
Portraits of five women executives from the People's Republic of China provide stark contrasts to the descriptions of Western women. Ma Xinyun, forty-eight, is deputy director of State Cotton Mill No. 2. She has held the same position for nineteen years—the mill's director is a man. Comrade Ma earns 104 yuan a month ($62.40), but pays only three yuan a month for a two-room flat. Executive women in China have little time for beauty or clothes—most wear the traditional pantsuit.

548. Rybkina, Lyudmila. "A Man's Job for a Woman." *Soviet Life* 9 (September 1985): 36-37.
Civil engineer Valeria Filippenko, forty-three, is director of a construction firm in Kishinev. Her boss says that while Filippenko has her own style of dealing with people, he does not believe there is a female management style. Filippenko enjoys equal pay and equal status with her husband, also a civil engineer.

549. Secter, Bob. "Singapore Wants Women out of Board Room and into Bedroom." *Cedar Rapids (Iowa) Gazette* (April 2, 1984): 3A.

The genetic theories of Prime Minister Lee Kuan Yew influenced a new population policy in Singapore. A program was instituted that gave special tax breaks to educated women. The tax break increased with each addition to their families—at the same time, women without college degrees, who are reproducing at twice the rate of women college graduates, are told to use birth control. At this time, there are no women cabinet ministers, members of Parliament, judges, ambassadors or heads of top government regulatory agencies or ministries in Singapore.

550. Symons, Gladys L. "Career Lives of Women in France and Canada: The Case of Managerial Women." *Work and Occupations* 11 (August 1984): 331-52.

Symons questioned forty-three French and twenty Canadian women executives and entrepreneurs. She reports here on their career types, socialization experiences, coordination of work and family life, sponsorship or mentors, and equal opportunity in the workplace, and concludes that there are similar patterns for French and Canadian women managers. Includes one table of demographic data, notes, and references.

551. Taylor, Frank. "Women Grab Management Power in Home of Machismo." *International Management* 39 (February 1984): 24-25, 27.

Latin American women executives spend time developing themselves professionally and getting additional training, rather than demonstrating for women's rights. It is rare to find women in top management posts, however, in part because many private firms follow the traditional route and give males the management positions and females the social functions. Some of the women interviewed felt they had advantages: better money management skills, reverse "machismo" (men find it hard to say "no" to a saleswoman), and more patience.

552. "An Upward Climb for Career Women in Europe." *Management Review* 71 (September 1982): 56-57.

Management Centre Europe, the European branch of the American Management Association, conducted a survey of 420 companies in nine countries. The findings show that it is difficult for women to enter or advance in management in Europe. Only 49 percent of the 420 companies had any women in management positions. The three countries reporting the largest number of women managers were France, Portugal, and the United Kingdom.

553. "When Women Experience the Most Problems." *Personnel Management* 17 (May 1985): 11.

In an address to the first conference of the European Women's Management Development (EWMD) Network, the founder of the French women's return-to-work program (Retravailler) said to the audience that is is most difficult for women managers in an organization when they constitute 5 to 30 percent of the workforce. When women managers account for 30 to 50 percent, they have the fewest work problems. A ten-year-old IBM program to increase the number of women in professional and management jobs is described.

554. Yanelis, Vladislav. "At the Top at 37." *Soviet Life* 4 (April 1983): 50-53.

Thirty-seven-year-old Rasima Vafina manages a medical products plant in Kazan. A graduate of the Kazan Institute of Chemical Engineering, she advanced from operations engineer to shop superintendent and eventually plant manager. Includes photographs.

Dress, Travel, and Relocation

555. Angier, Natalie, and Sutton, Tina. "Dressing up the Organization." *Savvy* 5 (May 1984): 32-35.

Fashion editor Tina Sutton advises three female Harvard MBA candidates on "dressing for success" in something other than John Molloy's conservative suits. As one of the women said, "Once a woman has proven herself, she should be able to dress with confidence, in a way that makes her feel good."

556. Craighead, Susan. "Some Women Graduate from Business Suits." *Wall Street Journal* (August 14, 1985): p. 25, col. 3.

At a recent breakfast meeting, all forty-five women executives attending wore dresses, shunning the traditional corporate uniform of suit, white blouse, and bow tie. Women's clothing retailers say the suit is still de rigeur for job interviews, bankers, lawyers, and women in their first management jobs. Now that women are 33 percent of executives according to the U.S. Department of Labor statistics, "dressing for success" is more a matter of personal style and taste.

557. "Dressing for Success." *New York Times* (September 13, 1981): sec. 6, p. 158.

Writers respond to Jani Wooldridge's July 26 article "Dressing for the Top." Judge Phyllis W. Beck of the Superior Court of Pennsylvania asserts that a "very broad range of attire is acceptable to almost any employer" and that hard work, intelligence, organization, and emotional balance are paramount to success. Irene Cummin Kleeberg of New York City believes articles like Wooldridge's perpetuate the myth that women will only get ahead in business by dressing in a certain manner.

558. Firestone, R. Darlene. "Relocating Women Managers: Can Your Company Meet Their Needs?" *SAM Advanced Management Journal* 46 (Spring 1981): 40-46.

Only 5 percent of all United States' employees transferred in 1979 were women, but relocation firms expect that number to increase in the future. Women in middle-management positions are aware that "promotion by relocation" may enhance their career opportunities. Single women generally prefer urban areas, and dual-career couples are the most difficult to relocate. Corporations should examine their relocation policies to see if they are adequate for the needs of today's managers: Do they offer to manage the sale of employees' homes and offer homebuying or mortgage assistance, are there benefits for nonhomeowners, and does the company make available information on family services in the new community?

559. Foderaro, Lisa W. "First Impressions Can Have a Lasting Effect." *New York Times* (October 13, 1985): sec. 12, p. 42.

Corporate women have gone beyond man-tailored suits and bow ties to more feminine suits. The owner of Streets & Co., a clothing store for professional women, says women are wearing "softer suits" and dresses, but one observer notes that suits indicate "a certain power that dresses do not."

560. Forsythe, Sandra Monk; Drake, Mary Frances; and Cox, Charles A. "Dress as an Influence on the Perceptions of Management Characteristics in Women." *Home Economics Research Journal* 13 (December 1984): 112-21.

Seventy-seven personnel administrators evaluated videotapes of potential women managers. The administrators' perceptions of the individuals' personal characteristics necessary for management reflected the level of masculinity in the applicants' dress. The authors conclude that women can convey the message they desire by their type of dress. Includes tables, figures, and references.

561. Genova, Mary Jane. "Professional Garb and the Gender Trap." *Wall Street Journal* (August 2, 1984): p. 24, col. 3.

Genova chides female executives for their "dress for success" attire, claiming that women earning six figures have less concern for dress, wearing what makes them feel attractive and comfortable. She exhorts women managers to focus less attention on the "team uniform" and more energy on actually performing the job.

562. Gite, Lloyd L. "Making that Move: Relocating for a Better Job." *Essence* 13 (January 1983): 32, 34, 121.

Promotion often means relocation. Gite advises women to begin by planning their moves, including checking out the job market in a new location by doing research at the public library, convention bureaus, chambers of commerce, professional and social organizations, friends, and relatives. The next step is reviewing your financial situation and budgeting moving expenses. Finally, take time to adjust to your new location, make friends, and get involved in religious, social, and professional organizations.

563. Gottschalk, Earl C., Jr. "Hotel Industry Seems to Be Baffled on How to Please Businesswomen." *Wall Street Journal* (June 15, 1983): p. 37, col. 4.

Women now account for 30 percent of all business travelers, but hotels and motels disagree on treatment for female executives. Some hotels have designated floors as "women-only" or "Women's Executive Floor" and provide special amenities such as hair dryers and makeup mirrors. Other hotel chains claim women business travelers do not want special treatment, or to be isolated or segregated, they just want to be treated "like everyone else."

564. Harragan, Betty Lehan. "The Right Moves to Get Ahead." *Savvy* 3 (May 1982): 25-26.
Women in midmanagement positions realize that moving up the corporate ladder frequently means a geographic move as well. A Boyden/Management Woman survey shows that 66 percent of single female executives and 27 percent of married ones are willing to relocate. Although turning down a transfer can mean dead-ending a career, women are advised to determine first if a transfer opportunity really means a promotion and/or increased job responsibilities.

565. Hunter, Bill. "Relocation." *Working Woman* 7 (February 1982): 16, 18.
Whether it is a man or a woman asked to relocate, the spouse's career will be affected. Hunter relates the stories of three women managers who were relocated by their companies and the resulting effect on their husband's careers. Companies are beginning to consider the needs of dual-career couples in promotion and relocation plans, says Hunter, who discusses four questions relocation experts advise answering before you relocate.

566. Lublin, Joann S. "Moving Up and Out: More Women Executives Relocate to Get Ahead." *Wall Street Journal* (August 4, 1981): 1.
Women managers are now more willing to relocate for promotions according to Merrill Lynch relocation service. There is also a trend toward more men moving because of their spouse's career relocation.

567. Lublin, Joann S. "Scenes from Two Marriages." *Wall Street Journal* (March 24, 1986): 24D.
The authors of *The Two-Career Couple* (1979) divorced after twenty years of marriage because of frequent relocations due to Douglas Hall's career. Francine Hall contends that with every move she took demotions and salary cuts. Another two-career couple opted for a commuter marriage.

568. Morris, Bernadine. "Dressing for Work: Now a Softer Look." *New York Times* (September 8, 1984): 44.
The man-tailored suit was de rigeur for young business and professional women in the 1970s, but established corporate women of the 1980s prefer dresses and comfortable, unstructured suits. Frank Smith, long-time designer for Evan-Picone sportswear, describes the latest business fashions, including prices.

569. Moskal, Brian S. "Corporate Uniforms Yield to New Images." *Industry Week* (July 9, 1984): 33, 35.
An image consultant to major corporations and author of *The Professional Image*, Susan Bixler teaches wardrobe development and "visual self-marketing." She says executive women are wearing more color, dresses, and jewelry and advises wearing hemlines just below the knee.

570. "Moving Women Managers: A New Corporate Dilemma." *Training and Development Journal* 35 (September 1981): 7.

As women reach middle- and upper-level management positions, they may be forced to relocate in order to advance. So far, according to a Merrill Lynch Relocation Management survey, only 5 percent of those relocated are women. Single women prefer the cultural and recreational opportunities in urban areas. Moves are most difficult for female managers in dual-career families, especially those families with children and with husbands who earn more money. Companies should offer assistance to relocating women managers in these areas: schools, taxes, cultural and recreational facilities, sale of houses, mortgage assistance, and help in the spouse's job search.

571. Myers, Ellen A. "In Defense of the Too-Easily Maligned Secretary." *New York Times* (November 15, 1985): sec. 1, p. 34, col. 4.

The administrative aide to the academic dean of Princeton Theological Seminary takes issue with the comment that only secretaries wear bow ties. She chides corporate women for being more concerned about dress than business issues.

572. O'Toole, Patricia. "Moving Ahead by Moving Around." *Savvy* 3 (April 1982): 37-41.

Although corporate transfers dropped 25 percent in the last two years, women make up 8 percent of those now transferred, up from 5 percent only three years ago. Women executives experience many difficulties in relocation: there are few female peers and almost all male peers are married; a woman executive may be the "trailing" spouse when her husband is transferred and have difficulties finding a position in a new location; at present, only 23 percent of 600 large corporations surveyed by Merrill Lynch Relocation Management provides any kind of assistance to the relocating spouse. One answer: many two-career couples have become commuting couples.

573. Pave, Irene. "Dressing for Success Isn't What It Used to Be." *Business Week* (October 27, 1986): 142-43.

Pave claims that women in middle management may feel free to deviate from the traditional navy-blue tailored suit. Women at top management levels can probably opt for the most variety. Pave suggests that women stick to suits if they are making a presentation, and that they should always consider the corporate culture of their organization, their natural style, and common sense when making decisions about appropriate dress.

574. "The Power of Pinstripes: A Survey of Executive Dress." *Savvy* 3 (October 1982): 88-89, 91-94.

Savvy readers are asked to answer thirty-five questions about their current position and appropriate clothing for female executives. They are also asked to determine which of twelve sketches represents appropriate clothing for themselves on a "typical day on the job." The survey results appeared in the March 1983 issue. See entry 576.

575. Salmans, Sandra. "Women Dressing to Succeed Think Twice about the Suit." *New York Times* (November 4, 1985): p. 1, col. 1.
A consumer research group noted that women bought 24 million suits in 1984, 8 million more than in 1980. One fashion consultant advises that shoulder pads in dresses can be just as powerful as suits. Women in banks and law firms still opt for the dark suit, and John Molloy, author of the best-selling dress-for-success books, says it is not necessary for women to wear suits as long as their attire is dark, conservative, and asexual.

576. Solomon, Michael R., and Douglas, Susan P. "The Power of Pinstripes." *Savvy* 4 (March 1983): 59-62.
The results of an October 1982 survey of executive dress show that, for the 6,000 readers who responded, dress varies according to the type of company a woman works for, according to her position in the hierarchy, and the region of the country. Most respondents wish to be "conservatively fashionable," not trendy. Of the twelve outfits shown in the survey, the suit and blouse with a shoestring tie was the number one choice for all respondents, regardless of profession or region of the country.

577. Twidall, Heather. "The Triumph of Executive Chic." *Working Woman* 10 (November 1985): 138-40.
The author, a thirty-seven-year-old senior vice president in banking, applauds the end of the "dress-for-success" blue suit. However, the author of *Dress for Success*, John Molloy, claims women are giving corporations the wrong message by abandoning the traditional suit. Some women believe it is necessary to wear the "junior uniform" until they have reached a certain level of management, when they can begin dressing in a more feminine fashion.

578. Witty, S. "What Does the Travelling Businesswoman Want?" *Across the Board* 20 (October 1983): 53-54, 56-57.
According to a recent issue of *Working Woman* magazine, one-third of all business travelers are now women, and the number of women business travelers is increasing three times as fast as the number of male business travelers. Ramada Inn instituted a "Traveling Woman" staff-training program, some hotels have designated some floors as women-only, and others have taken measures to ensure greater security for businesswomen. The average woman business traveler is thirty-eight years old, cares more than her male counterpart about security and room temperature, and prefers downtown hotels close to her business destination.

579. "Women Execs Want Special Treatment at Hotels: Survey." *Hotel and Motel Management* 197 (November 1982): 9.
A recent survey of 150 executive women conducted by the Ritz-Carlton Hotel in Chicago shows that women business travelers want preferential treatment. Women expect the same treatment as men regarding check-in, room service, valet service, local information or telephone service, but, in addition, they want skirt hangers, shower caps, and shampoo. Eighty percent of the women surveyed are concerned about hotel security. One

survey respondent wrote that women clerks, cocktail waitresses, and women maitre d's are the rudest to women.

580. Wooldridge, Jani. "Dressing for the Top." *New York Times* (July 26, 1981): sec. 6, p. 49.
Top women executives agree that for young women or women who are job hunting, it is wise to dress in a conservative fashion, but that time and maturity allow them to exhibit more individual style and taste in their choice of business attire. The article includes photographs of top executive women and their comments on appropriate business dress.

Power

581. Antilla, Susan. "Wall Street Woos the Nation's Most Powerful Women." *Working Woman* 10 (January 1985): 38, 40.

The American Stock Exchange hosts some of the nation's most powerful women for an evening of lectures on mid-size growth companies, training in stock trading, and dinner on the floor of the Exchange. The attendees were members of the Committee of 200, a group of 240 women who own businesses with annual sales of $5 million or more or are corporate executives with "substantial profit and loss responsibility", and members of the Women's Forum, women nationally recognized in their fields.

582. Burns, Cherie. "The Extra Edge." *Savvy* 3 (December 1982): 38-43.

Because the baby boom generation finds a shortage of middle-management jobs, those who succeed will need "personal power skills" in addition to excellent job performance. Five top management women list the personal skills they find most effective.

583. Chusmir, Leonard H., and Parker, Barbara. "Dimensions of Need for Power: Personalized vs. Socialized Power in Female and Male Managers." *Sex Roles* 11 (November 1984): 759-69.

Sixty-two female and sixty-two male low- or middle-level managers took the Thematic Apperception Test (TAT) to measure Socialized Power (sPwr) and Personalized Power (pPwr) and correlate the findings with job satisfaction. The researchers, associated with the University of Colorado in Denver, determined that female managers expressed high power motives. They conclude that since motivaton is a predictor of managerial success, women managers might be more success prone than their male counterparts and organizations would do well to consider more women for managerial positions. Includes tables and references.

584. Coppersmith, James. "Women and Power in Corporate America." *Cosmopolitan* 200 (January 1986): 54.

As vice president and general manager of WCVB-TV in Boston, Coppersmith works closely with women executives and says their perception of power must change if they truly want to make it to the top. He offers ten tips on achieving power: (1) make sure you want it, (2) steal from the stars, (3) proclaim your desire to grow every chance you get, (4) be willing to travel and relocate, (5) make your boss look good, (6) be committed to the growth of your subordinates, (7) learn about psychology and human behavior, (8) compete with your company's competitors, not your colleagues, (9) develop a sense of group identity, and (10) do not fall into the male/female trap.

585. Cunningham, Mary E. "Power Steering." *Harper's Bazaar* (September 1985): 225, 234, 236, 472.

The author of *Powerplay* and president and chief operating officer of the venture-capital firm, Semper Enterprises, Mary Cunningham tells why women have a problem with power. She believes that women abdicate power, first by denying that they have any and second by ensuring that they never will—in other words, denial and avoidance. She outlines seven steps to power: know your accuser, do not overreact, read the signals accurately, build a power base, cultivate more than one mentor, sharpen your skills of detection, and understand the game.

586. Geller, Lynn. "Men on Women in Power." *Harper's Bazaar* (September 1985): 254.

Geller quotes ten men who replied to the question, "How do you feel about women in power?" Some of the answers follow: Art Buchwald, columnist and author: "Most women are lovable, but powerful women are scary"; Stephen Demorest, TV scriptwriter: "A good test is seeing how a woman with power treats a woman without power"; Walter Channing, president of an investment firm: "I like the independence of powerful women"; Walter Thomas, magazine editor: "I have a weakness for powerful women"; Ben Stein, author and columnist: "What I don't like is when powerful women feel they have to keep proving their authority. . ."; and Jerry Harrison, musician: "I hate women who abuse power because I'm less prepared to deal with it."

587. Gold, Rosalind. "Exclusively for Women Managers." *Supervisory Management* 28 (April 1983): 18-22.

In addition to a competent performance, women managers need additional skills. They must build alliances, develop an influence style that convinces others to support them, and acquire power that enables them to make things happen. Gold suggests that establishing one hour a day of private time for working gives you three power points: others realize your time is valuable, you choose to be accessible or inaccessible, and you gain an hour of uninterrupted work time.

588. Huerta, Faye C., and Lane, Thomas A. "Participation of Women in Centers of Power." *Social Science Journal* 18 (April 1983): 71-86.

In a study of women's participation in the power structure in the United States, researchers determined that there have been few changes in the amount of power women possess. Huerta and Lane analyzed those in top positions of power for the years 1958, (1965, 1972, and 1978 in (1) the top ten companies, and (2) the top civilian positions in the Department of Defense and the Army, Navy, and Airforce, the White House Staff, the President's Executive agencies, judges in the United States Courts of Appeal, and those occupying positions in the order of success to the presidency. Women occupied twenty-two of the total number of 2,292 positions.

589. Kanter, Rosabeth Moss. "Influence Skills." *Working Woman* 8 (September 1983): 50, 52.

Kanter, co-founder and chair of Goodmeasure and author of *The Change Masters*, presents the first of a three-part case study to train middle managers in influence skills. She discusses these five lessons in organizational change: (1) standing still means losing ground, (2) investment in future flexibility is essential, (3) selling is characteristic of more and more work, (4) teamwork is characteristic of more and more work, and (5) others below you and around you in the organization need and want more power and autonomy.

590. Ketcham, Diane. "Office Power Rare for Women." *New York Times* (June 9, 1985): sec. 21, p. 1, col. 1.

Although Long Island businesswomen have made progress in the last ten years, there are still very few women on the boards of major Long Island corporations. There are thirty-three executives who serve as directors of the Long Island Association—only two are women. Includes photographs of five successful women executives and their comments on the advantage of visibility as a woman, sexual discrimination, and personal relationships.

591. Kuzela, Lad. "Women on the March." *Industry Week* (November 10, 1986): 119-22.

The number of groups for female executives and businesswomen is increasing, and their goal is political and financial power. Eighty percent of the members of the Committee of 200, founded in 1981, own and operate their own businesses, and members of the Association of Black Women Entrepreneurs, founded in Los Angeles in 1984, claim a 20 percent increase in their businesses as a result of their cooperation. Child care has become an issue for many of the women's groups, including the National Association for Female Executives (NAFE) which is funding a study on child care services.

592. O'Brien, Patricia. "Women and Power." *The Collegiate Career Woman* (Winter 1982/83): 17-20.

Five outstanding women discuss leadership and power: Jeane J. Kirkpatrick, United States Ambassador to the United Nations; Hannah Gray, president, University of Chicago; Paige Rense, editor, *Architectural Digest*; Carol Bellamy, president, New York City Council; and Mary Anne Dolan, editor, *Los Angeles Herald Examiner*. The women agree they are independent, did not plan their careers, and had an early role model.

593. O'Brien, Patricia. "Women and Power." *Notre Dame Magazine* 11 (May 1982): 11-15.

O'Brien, a newspaper correspondent and the author of *Staying Together* and *The Woman Alone*, interviewed five successful women about leadership and power. Includes photographs and direct quotes.

594. Smith, Howard L., and Grenier, Mary. "Sources of Organizational Power for Women: Overcoming Structural Obstacles." *Sex Roles* 8 (July 1982): 733-46.

Smith and Grenier analyze structural sources of power—centrality, coping with uncertainty, and control over resources—and discuss ways that women can recognize and use these organizational sources of power. Hickson (1971) defined the term centrality as "participation in activities critical to the organization's survival or relevant to the organization's current pressing problems." Resources include persons, information, and capital assets. Includes references.

Women Business Owners

595. Alexander, Ron. "4,000 Women Talk Business." *New York Times* (October 30, 1981): sec. 2, p. 6, col. 2.

Women Business Owners of New York sponsored a five-day conference with more than seventy workshops and seminars. The third biennial conference was held "to promote the significant participation of women in the economy." Mayor Koch proclaimed this Women in Business Week and sixteen women received Entrepreneurial Woman Awards. Four thousand women attended workshops and seminars on business credit, stress, computers, career changes, sales, finance, and senior management.

596. Archer, Madeline Cirillo. "You Can't Take It with You." *Savvy* 4 (March 1983): 25, 29.

Women who leave corporations to start their own companies should be aware of the possibility of a lawsuit regarding the use of "proprietary information" they picked up in their former positions. Some types of proprietary information: patents, copyrights, trade secrets, customer or client lists, strategies, and methods. Some employees are required to sign noncompetition agreements upon leaving a company to establish a business.

597. Bettner, Jill, and Donahue, Christine. "Now They're Not Laughing." *Forbes* 132 (November 21, 1983): 116-19, 122-24, 128, 130.

Women now own one-fourth of the country's 13 million small businesses and the number of female-owned businesses is growing three times that of men, but 45 percent of those women-owned businesses are in the service sector. More women are leaving the corporate world to become "the new immigrants," because they feel blocked. A chart shows that while female entrepreneurs are most often found in retailing and services, they have made significant gains in nontraditional areas like construction and manufacturing. See pp. 122-24 for word portraits of nine female entrepeneurs. Includes photographs.

598. Black, Joanne. "Five Key Questions for Women in Business." *Business Quarterly* 47 (Spring 1982): 41-46.

The author, senior vice president of marketing at the Travelers Check Division, American Express Company, warns women in business to ask themselves five key questions in this order: Why do I want to go into business anyway? How do I want to work and what style and pace of work do I like? What am I supposed to do now (after a promotion)? Do

I have the confidence to bend, not break the rules (i.e., am I willing to lose)? and Am I willing not to be a businessperson, but business woman? She concludes by calling on all successful businessmen and businesswomen to be tough, logical, and sensitive and encouraging women to acquire a broad range of business experience.

599. Brown, Kimberly A., and Perkin, Carol. "The Savvy 60." *Savvy* 6 (April 1985): 50-59.
Savvy publishes the second annual report on the top sixty United States' businesses run by women, i.e., companies with annual sales of $15 million or above. Forty-nine of the companies are privately held. The authors list the selection criteria and include photographs and brief biographies of several of the women. See pages 54 to 57 for charts of the companies by rank, executives, 1983 and 1984 revenues, growth, number of employees, and industry. Insert on page 58 lists the ten fastest growing companies.

600. Carson, Teresa; Michael, Debra; and Baum, Laurie. "Honey, What Do You Say We Start Our Own Company?" *Business Week* (September 15, 1986): 115.
The Center for Family Business reports a rise in the number of husband-and-wife management teams. Although some husband-wife businesses are very successful, others fail because the couple cannot communicate, cannot separate work from play, do not share the same goals, or have not established a clear division of labor.

601. Conway, John A., ed. "Who Needs Bosses?" *Forbes* 137 (January 13, 1986): 10, 12.
Conway reports on the status of nine women small business owners who were profiled in a November 21, 1983 article. The nine include thirty-eight-year-old Lane Nemeth, owner of Discovery Toys; Diana Guetskow, who started Netword; and Linda Richardson, owner of the Richardson Group, with annual billings of $2.5 million.

602. Edwards, Audrey, and Hauser, Marilyn Landis. "Do You Have What It Takes to Start Your Own Business?" *Essence* 14 (March 1984): 64, 66.
Many black women are choosing to start their own businesses, looking for power, freedom, control and wealth. Edwards and Hauser offer readers a ten-point quiz designed to test a woman's business sense.

603. Fooner, Andrea. "Dad & Daughter, Inc." *Working Woman* 8 (January 1983): 78-82.
In the past two years, reports Center for Family Business Vice President Don Jonovic, 30 percent more women have attended the management and succession seminars conducted by the Center for Family Business. Fooner relates the stories of several women who are taking over the family business, following in their fathers' footsteps.

604. Galante, Steven P. "Small Business Conference Opens Today . . . ." *Wall Street Journal* (August 18, 1986): 23.
One thousand one hundred twenty-eight delegates will attend the White House Conference on Small Business. Thirty percent of the delegates are women, twice the number in 1980, and 60 percent of the businesses have fewer than twenty-five employees. Article includes the top ten proposals for action at the conference.

605. Galante, Steven P. "Venturing out on Their Own." *Wall Street Journal* (March 24, 1986): 4D.
Bureau of Labor Statistics figures show that the number of self-employed women rose 43 percent from 1975 to 1985. More and more women are leaving corporations to achieve greater wealth, autonomy, and personal satisfaction.

606. Gottschalk, Earl C., Jr. "Distaff Owners: More Women Start up Their Own Businesses, with Major Successes." *Wall Street Journal* (May 17, 1983): 1.
A spokeswoman for the U.S. Small Business Administration claims, "The 1970s was the decade of women entering management, and the 1980s is turning out to be the decade of the woman entrepreneur." The number of self-employed women rose 35 percent from 1977 to 1982, from 1.7 to 2.3 million. Factors that contributed to this dramatic increase are (1) women leaving corporations to start their own businesses because they see little chance for advancement to management positions, (2) recession and layoffs, and (3) it is socially acceptable for women to own their own businesses.

607. Graham, Diane. "Women Gain Clout through Roundtable." *Des Moines (Iowa) Register* (April 27, 1986): sec. F, p. 1.
According to the U.S. Small Business Administration women are starting small businesses at three times the rate of men. One hundred Iowa women business owners have initiated the Roundtable, a state chapter of the National Association of Women Business Owners (NAWBO). Eleven of the members served as delegates to the 1986 White House Conference on Small Business.

608. Gumpert, David E. "Doing a Little Business on the Side." *Working Woman* 11 (October 1986): 41-42, 45.
The Small Business Administration's Office of Women's Business Ownership is studying home-based businesses. There are at least two prerequisites for part-time entrepreneurship, says Gumpert: the type of business should lend itself to part-time work, and your full-time job should allow for a part-time business. An insert tells how a part-time business can be "100 percent professional."

609. Harragan, Betty Lehan. "Father Doesn't Always Know Best." *Savvy* 3 (November 1982): 21-22.
Harragan recommends that daughters of the owners of small, privately held industrial firms consider the conflicts and choices carefully before seeking to follow their fathers into the business. Frequently long-time employees who wield a lot of power can be obstacles to a daughter's succession to the CEO spot. Independent careers in related fields may

give these young women an edge if they later decide to return to the family business.

610. Hewson, M. "Sanford & Daughter." *McCalls* 109 (September 1982): 52-53.
Daughters constitute 30 percent of the enrollment in the Center for Family Business seminars after only two years. There is a growing trend toward the participation of daughters in family businesses, in part because of the need for staff cutbacks in today's economic climate. Women frequently have worked in other firms and gained experience before assuming responsibility in the family business, in contrast to sons who may only have worked for their fathers.

611. Lawson, Carol. "Big Increase in Women Starting Own Businesses." *Des Moines (Iowa) Register* (August 8, 1985): 4E.
The American Woman's Economic Development (AWED) Corporation, a nonprofit group, has helped almost 800 aspiring women business owners in the past eight years. The number of women business owners in the United States rose almost 2.5 million since 1976. AWED's nine-session course costs $175 and provides women information in banking, marketing, selling, advertising, public relations, insurance, and developing business plans.

612. Lovenheim, Barbara. "Stay at Home and Work." *Redbook* 162 (March 1984): 75-77, 150.
U.S. Department of Labor statistics show there are 2.8 million self-employed women in the United States today. Many opt for their own businesses because of the conflicts of family and full-time career. The National Alliance of Home-Based Businesswomen published the directory *Women Working Home*, available for $12.95 from WWH Press, P.O. Box 237 RB, Norwood, NJ 07648. Lovenheim lists thirteen steps to take when considering starting your own business.

613. Lublin, Joann S. "Female Owners Try to Make Life Easier for Employees—Sometimes Too Easy."
Women small-business owners are more likely than men to offer child care, flexible hours, sick leave, part-time work, and sabbaticals to recruit and retain working parents and reduce the stress of combining career and family. Sometimes, however, a woman owner's desire to help her employees conflicts with good business and the bottom line of profits, and occasionally employees abuse the special privileges. The article includes stories and quotes from women entrepreneurs and their employees, one of whom claims, "I would only work for women-owned companies."

614. Macweeney, Alen. "Like Father, Like Daughter." *Fortune* 108 (October 3, 1983): 180-89.
Macweeney gives readers a pictorial essay on daughters who are running or being groomed to run their fathers' companies. Ten of the eleven companies described are private. One daughter states, "I am my father's son; we have always been very close."

615. "Model Portfolio: An Executive Quits to Start Her Own Firm."
Money 13 (February 1984): 49, 52.
Financial planners offer suggestions to Janet Conley, a forty-three-year-old mother of three who left a $50,000-a-year position at Polaroid to start her own promotional exhibits business. Their advice ranges from mutual funds and real estate, to tax-free municipal bonds, and top-grade $20 gold coins.

616. Moskowitz, Daniel B., and Pave, Irene. "Battling Another Bias in Business Lending." *Business Week* (May 27, 1985): 68, 70.
Even women who own successful businesses frequently have difficulty getting a line of credit without a spouse's signature. Women's organizations are campaigning for laws that forbid questions about a woman's marital status when she applies for a business loan, similar to the Equal Credit Opportunity Act which regards marital status as irrelevant when women apply for personal loans.

617. Nelton, Sharon. "A Business of Her Own." *Nation's Business* 72 (November 1984): 70-72.
U.S. Small Business Administration statistics point out that women are starting businesses four times as fast as men; women own 3 of the 13 million sole proprietorships in the United States; and women-owned businesses contribute $40 billion to the country's economy each year. However, women-owned businesses receive only one-half of one percent of government contracts. The National Association of Women Business Owners, with almost thirty chapters nationwide, developed a plan to team NAWBO companies with larger companies in order to obtain government contracts, get women more capital, and increase the number of women on corporate boards.

618. "Paying to Keep the Home Fires Burning." *Business Week* (March 12, 1984): 84, 87.
The growth in the number of professional and managerial women and dual-career couples makes housecleaning businesses lucrative. When Leone Ackerly started Mini Maids of America Inc. in 1973, she was the sole employee. Today she and her husband William own a $3.8 million company with thirty-six franchises. Other popular services include after-school sports services for children, take-out dinner services, clothes consultants, nanny services, and personal shopping services.

619. Ray, Elaine C., and McNair, Marcia, eds. "The Essence Guide to Starting Your Own Business." *Essence* 14 (March 1984): 69-76.
This article includes tips and hints for starting your own business and brief information on six women.

620. Reagan, Ronald. "Women Business Owners of New York: Remarks at the Conference Luncheon, April 5, 1984." *Weekly Compilation of Presidential Documents* 20 (April 9, 1984): 481-87.
President Reagan addresses the members and friends of Women Business Owners of New York, pointing out that his administration has appointed more than 1,400 women to top government posts. He describes the aim of the three-point National Initiative Program to help women business owners: (1) the Advisory Committee on Women's Business Ownership,

(2) the Interagency Committee on Women's Business Enterprise, and (3) national conferences for women in business.

621. Rich, Stanley R., and Gumpert, David E. "Business Plans: What Turns Investors On, What Turns Them Off." *Working Woman* 11 (January 1986): 38-40, 42.

Rich and Gumpert list four do's and four don'ts for business owners who are preparing business plan for investors. The advice is adapted from *Business Plans That Win $$: Lessons from the MIT Enterprise Forum.*

622. Saddler, Jeanne. "Businesswomen Don't Face Loan Bias, Study Finds." *Wall Street Journal* (July 24, 1986): sec. 1, p. 10, col. 2.

The Small Business Administration funded a study which showed that women business owners have no more trouble than their male counterparts obtaining bank loans. The National Association of Women Business Owners disputes the findings of the study, claiming that women received much smaller loans than men in the study. The Association further criticized the SBA for limiting the study to mature businesses, noting that women are four times more likely than men to start new businesses.

623. Scholl, Jaye. "The Savvy 60." *Savvy* 5 (February 1984): 32-36, 38-40, 42-43.

Savvy surveyed the top public and private companies run by women. Charts list the top sixty companies, the executives, 1982 revenues, number of employees, and a description of the business. Only fifteen of the corporations are public. Although women own 25 percent of all small businesses in America, 42 percent of those businesses have a gross income of less than $5,000 per year, and three-quarters of the enterprises are in the fields of retailing and service. Includes photographs of eight well-known women.

624. Therrien, Lois, et al. "What Do Women Want? A Company They Can Call Their Own." *Business Week* (December 22, 1986): 60-62.

According to the Small Business Administration, from 1977 to 1983 women started twice as many businesses as men. By 1983, 25 percent (3.25 million) of all small businesses were owned by women. The women-owned companies earned $98.3 million in 1983, but that is only 10 percent of all business receipts. Women are most likely to start service businesses, and their greatest difficulty is raising capital. Felice Schwartz, president of Catalyst, claims that women entrepreneurs generally employ a more egalitarian management style than men.

625. Walker, Kelly B. "The Savvy 60." *Savvy* 7 (April 1986): 39-44, 46, 49, 91-92.

Savvy's third annual report on the top sixty United States' businesses run by women finds that service companies experienced the greatest growth in the last year. The criteria for 1986 are more stringent: the company must be run by a woman and earn $20 million or more in annual sales. See pages 40 to 43 for a rank order listing of the sixty companies, the names of their executives, fiscal year revenues and revenue growth (1984 to 1985), number of employees, and industry.

626. Wechsler, Jill. "Here's How to Make Small Businesses Grow." *Working Woman* 11 (July 1986): 40.

One-third of the 1,000 elected delegates to the White House Conference on Small Business are women, 200 of whom are members of the National Association of Women Business Owners (NAWBO). Mary Kelly McCurry, NAWBO president, wants the conference to establish a commission to study and prescribe economic policy for service businesses.

627. Welsch, Harold P., and Young, Earl C. "Women at the Top: How Women Are Meeting the Many Challenges of Owning a Small Business." *Management World* 12 (September 1983): 32-33.

The Internal Revenue Service reports that female-owned businesses increased 43 percent between 1972 and 1979. Welsch and Young describe the findings of a study of male and female entrepreneurs by the Small Business Institute at the University of Chicago. Women start their own businesses primarily for challenge and financial independence.

628. "When the Boss's Daughter Is a Boss." *New York Times* (May 6, 1984): sec. 1, p. 74, col. 3.

Dr. Matilde Salganicoff, director of the Women in Family Business Program at the Wharton Applied Research Center, and Dr. Barbara Hollander, an organizational and family consultant, conducted a three-day development workshop for twenty women in family businesses. The women talked about commitment, emotional issues, isolation, and the perception others have of the boss's daughter. Hollander told the particpants "only one percent of women had reached upper management in publicly-owned corporations across the country, (but) a woman in a family-owned business could rise quickly to the level of chief executive officer."

629. "When a Daughter Takes over the Family Business." *Business Week* (March 29, 1982): 172.

An officer in the Center for Family Business knows of 500 daughters who are running family businesses, succeeding their fathers. They are typically only or eldest children and experience no conflict between motherhood and business, because their positions give them more flexibility in family lives. The owner of a textbook publishing house in Phoenix expects his three daughters to succeed him.

630. "When Wives Run the Family Business." *Business Week* (January 17, 1983): 118, 121.

A number of family-owned businesses are reversing roles, with the wife as boss when she is the owner or best qualified. Most female-headed family businesses are small ($1 to $3 million annual sales), but Redken Laboratories ($85 million sales) operates with founder Paula Kent Meehan as chair and husband John as president. Spouse's skills are generally complementary—one handles financial matters and one the creative side of the business.

631. Wojahn, Ellen. "Why There Aren't More Women in This Magazine." *Inc* 8 (July 1986): 45-48.

Given the increasing numbers of women in middle management and as sole proprietors of small businesses, one reader asks why *Inc* does not profile more women in business. The editors reply that the women are difficult to find: only 236 women qualify for the Committee of 200, an organization for women whose businesses earn more than $5 million in annual sales. Wojahn compares male and female entrepreneurial styles.

632. Woodward, Patricia. "Conference Helps Women Business Owners Top Multi-Billion Dollar Procurement Markets." *Business America* 9 (April 28, 1986): 18-20.

Mega Marketplace I, held in April in Washington, DC, brought together almost 800 women business owners to present information on marketing products and services to the United States government. Although women own 25 percent of all small businesses in the United States, they get only one percent of all federal contracts. Procurement administrators from almost forty federal and regional government agencies met with the women, a computer database matched women business owners with clients, and the women attended workshops and training sessions. District of Columbia Councilmember Charlene Drew Jarvis and her Women in Business Advisory Committee initiated Mega Marketplace I.

Women Entrepreneurs

633. Barrett, Karen. "A New Breed of Entrepreneur—Five Profiles in Commerce." *Ms.* 12 (January 1984): 23-27.
Barrett tells the start-up stories of five entrepreneurial ventures: an executive women's clothing store, a software company, a retailer of feminist erotica, a biotechnology company, and a liquor story proprietorship. An insert provides information on the American Woman's Economic Development Corporation (AWED), toll-free number 1-800-222-AWED in all other states, 1-800-442-AWED in New York.

634. Cook, Janet T. "Women: The Best Entrepreneurs." *Canadian Business* 55 (June 1982): 68-73.
A 1980 University of Washington Entrepreneurial Research Conference study found that job satisfaction and the need to achieve were the prime motivators for women entrepreneurs. Of 1,989 new business starts studied since 1978, 1,364 were headed by women. Three years later 47 percent of the female-owned firms were still in business, compared to 25 percent of those owned by males. Of the women-owned businesses, 614 were retail operations, 382 services, and 172 craft or cottage industries, 94 were in manufacturing, and 102 bought franchises. The article includes profiles of women entrepreneurs.

635. Devine, Marion, and Clutterbuck, David. "The Rise of the Entrepreneuse." *Management Today* (January 1985): 63-65, 105-06.
Because women still face barriers to top management in corporations, more of them are turning to self-employment. The author of *The Business Amazon*, Dr. Leah Hertz, interviewed fifty United States and fifty British women entrepreneurs and found that the American women enjoyed higher status. Seventy-three percent of the British women entrepreneurs were mothers, compared to 36 percent of United States' women executives who have children. Steve Shirley, owner of F International, and an entrepreneur herself, believes that entrepreneurs are unemployable, because they want to control their environment.

636. Diffley, Judy High. "Important Business Competencies for the Woman Entrepreneur." *Business Education Forum* 37 (April 1983): 31-33.
Using the definition that an entrepreneur is someone who owns, controls, and operates at least 51 percent of a business, Diffley studied 106 service and retail women entrepreneurs. The women answered fifty-six questions

in four categories: general competencies, managerial competencies, marketing and sales competencies, and accounting and financial competencies. Includes tables.

637. Eliason, Carol. "Entrepreneurship Training for Females Offers New Challenges to Career Educators." *Journal of Career Education* 8 (December 1981) 145-52.

Eliason is director of the Center for Women's Opportunities at the American Association of Community and Junior Colleges and director of the National Community College Small Business Training Network. She describes several efforts to provide entrepreneurship education for women including the New York-based American Women's Economic Development Corporation and the Women Business Owners Orientation Program. Eliason outlines grade school and high school activities designed to acquaint females with the small business option and concludes with guidelines for career counseling for "potential female entrepreneurs."

638. Foers, Maureen. "Women Entrepreneurs—What is the Extra Quality They Need to Succeed: A Personal Reflection." *Equal Opportunities International (UK)* 4 (3) (1985): 19-22.

Forty-five-year-old businesswoman Maureen Foers has owned her own recruitment agency, established the Northern Business School, Humberside Office Services, Northern Mailing Services, and White Rose Marketing Services. She defines woman executive versus woman entrepreneur and tells how mentors help women managers. Foers now owns the "largest independent practical commercial training center" in the United Kingdom.

639. Frankel, Greta. "Nordic Female Entrepreneurs." *Equal Opportunities International (UK)* 3 (4) (1984): 24-29.

Greta Frankel is a project leader at the Swedish Institute for Opinion Research and coauthor of *The Invisible Contract: A Study of Working Life in the 1980s*. She claims that Scandinavian women entrepreneurs lack role models, are not familiar with the techniques of starting a business, and do not have networks of contacts. Frankel discusses three case studies of women entrepreneurs.

640. Fury, Kathleen. "A Boss of One's Own." *Working Woman* 10 (February 1985): 134.

Fury takes a humorous jibe at the recent spate of stories about women entrepreneurs, claiming there are advantages to not being your own boss. The worst thing about being an entrepreneur, she says, is not having a boss to complain about.

641. Garland, Anne Witte. "The Surprising Boom of Women Entrepreneurs." *Ms.* 14 (July 1985): 94-95, 105-06.

The latest figures show that women started small businesses at six times the rate of men from 1974 to 1984. Most of the new female-owned businesses—as high as 45 percent—are in the service sector. The American Woman's Economic Development Corporation (AWED) provides training and counseling for prospective women business owners. Since 1977, almost 1,000 women have completed the training, and only five of the businesses have failed.

642. Gregg, Gail. "Women Entrepreneurs: The Second Generation." *Across the Board* (January 1985): 10-18.

The number of women-owned businesses increased over 33 percent from 1972 to 1985 and annual revenues for their 3 million businesses reach $40 billion. Many women leave the corporate world to become entrepreneurs, unhappy with organizational barriers to middle- and upper-level management. Gregg interviewed six women entrepreneurs and compared their experiences with women entrepreneurs in a study done by Professor Robert D. Hisrich, Boston College, and Candida Brush, a management consultant. Includes photographs and profiles of the six women.

643. Gumpert, David E. "Wanted: Women Entrepreneurs for High-Tech Opportunities." *Working Woman* 10 (December 1985): 37-39.

Wendy Vittori majored in philosophy at Radcliffe, but later discovered she had a talent for computer programming. Now, at thirty-three, she is president and CEO of Computers in Medicine Inc., a two-year-old company with $3 to $5 million in sales. Gumpert offers three strategies for women interested in high technology fields: get the necessary technical background and experience; build up credibility; and get a solid business foundation.

644. Hellwig, Basia. "How Working Women Have Changed America: Entrepreneurship." *Working Woman* 11 (November 1986): 150-51.

The almost three million United States' businesses owned by women earn an impressive $98 million in sales annually. Many women become entrepreneurs because they want flexible schedules to accommodate family needs.

645. Hellwig, Basia. "1986: Year of the Woman Entrepreneur." *Working Woman* 11 (January 1986): 35, 37, 39-40.

There are 3 million women-owned businesses, 40 percent of them in the service sector. Women are starting new businesses at twice the rate of men. Small business consultant Geoffrey Kessler describes ten areas of business opportunity. Inserts profile three women entrepreneurs.

646. Hisrich, Robert D. "The Woman Entrepreneur in the United States and Puerto Rico: A Comparative Study." *Leadership and Organization Development Journal* 5 (1984): 3-8.

Hisrich reviews previous research on women entrepreneurs, then describes his study of 468 United States women entrepreneurs and thirty Puerto Rican women entrepreneurs. He analyzes the findings by demographics, business venture, management skills, and personality characteristics. Includes tables and reference.

647. Hisrich, Robert D., and Brush, Candida. "The Woman Entrepreneur: Management Skills and Business Problems." *Journal of Small Business Management* 22 (January 1984): 30-37.

The authors review the research on women entrepreneurs, then report on the findings of their survey of almost 500 women entrepreneurs. The results are categorized by demographics, composition and background, the nature of women entrepreneurs' businesses, their skills, and problems they encountered.

648. Jakobson, Cathryn. "The Entrepreneurial Spirit." *Savvy* 6 (March 1985): 52-55, 68-70, 72-73.

Jakobson lists entrepreneurial tendencies: strong need for independence, outspoken or opinionated, unhappiness with bureaucracy, slow pace or limited opportunities. Corporate misfits and troublemakers may exhibit traits that will make them successful entrepreneurs, often described as "intuitives" or people who "display a charming capacity to ignore the standard, the traditional, and the authoritative." *Savvy* profiles six female entrepreneurs.

649. Joyce, Nicky. "From Executive to Entrepreneur—A World of Difference." *Women in Management Review* 2 (Summer 1986): 100-02.

Joyce, the immediate past president of the British Association of Women Entrepreneurs and Secretary-General of Les Femmes Chefs d'Entreprises Mondiales, reviews the history of the association and claims networking is one of the association's strengths.

650. Klein, Julia M. "Life after the Corporation." *Savvy* 4 (March 1983): 21, 23.

According to 1980 data from the Internal Revenue Service, 25 percent of all sole proprietorships, 2.8 million, are owned by women, and more women are leaving corporate middle-management jobs to join the growing number of women entrepreneurs. New women business owners frequently make two mistakes—undercapitalizing and failing to develop an adequate business plan. Other common problems are working without a support staff, time management, and the necessity to constantly market and promote yourself and your service or product. The rewards of entrepreneurship are a sense of achievement and independence.

651. Morris, Michele. "The 1986 Harriet Alger Award." *Working Woman* 11 (November 1986): 61.

Women now own 2.88 million or one-quarter of the nation's businesses. *Working Woman* presents the first Harriet Alger Award to Frieda Caplan, founder of a $13 million-a-year wholesale produce company. Walecia Konrad tells Frieda Caplan's tale of success in the accompanying article.

652. "Quick Advice for Women Entrepreneurs." *Training and Development Journal* 39 (May 1985): 8.

With a $25,000 grant from Citicorp/Citibank, the American Woman's Economic Development Corp. (AWED) will offer toll-free business advice to United States women business owners. The "hotline" counseling lasts ten minutes, and the woman entrepreneur pays only $5.00. AWED offers a second service—intensive sixty- to ninety-minute business counseling sessions for $25.00. Contact the American Woman's Economic Development Corporation, The Lincoln Building, 60 E. 42nd St., New York, NY 10165 or call 1-800-222-AWED; in New York State, call 1-800-442-AWED; in New York City, Alaska, and Hawaii, call 212-692-9100.

653. Solis, Dianna. "Family Practices." *Wall Street Journal* (March 24, 1986): 22D.

Barrios Technology is owned by sixty-year-old Emrye Barrios Robinson. The aerospace consulting firm employs 325 and has annual revenues of $11.5 million. Barrios' company is one of the fastest-growing Hispanic companies, and *Texas Business* magazine called her one of the best of Texas's women entrepreneurs.

654. Stains, Laurence, et al. "Have You Dreamed about Running Your Own Business?" *Glamour* 83 (February 1985): 124.

After answering a ten-point quiz to help determine your entrepreneurial bent, read the comments on each question by Joseph Mancuso, CEM (Center for Entrepreneurial Management) president and compare your responses to those of 2,500 entrepreneurs surveyed by CEM. To take the unabridged version of the quiz (twenty-six questions), send 50 cents to CEM, 83 Spring St., New York, NY 10012.

655. Stechert, Kathryn B. "The Millionaires." *Savvy* 5 (April 1984): 62-65, 68.

Stechert interviewed four women entrepreneurs. None of the four women holds business degrees, and all are under thirty-five years of age. Includes photographs.

656. Stevens, Mark. "Seven Common Mistakes Small Businesses Make—How to Avoid Them." *Working Woman* 11 (January 1986): 44, 46, 48.

Stevens, author of *The 10-Minute Entrepreneur*, discusses seven common mistakes entrepreneurs make: (1) mistaking a hobby for a business, (2) trying to make a business appeal to everyone, (3) starting out with too little cash, (4) failing to detect bad credit risks early, (5) setting the wrong price, (6) bleeding the business, and (7) the fortress complex.

657. "Three Wishes for Women Entrepreneurs." *Savvy* 4 (December 1983): 17.

The Reagan administration supports women entrepreneurs in a "multi-faceted national initiative." National conferences will be held in twenty-four cities by the Small Business Association's Office of Women's Business Ownership; the Presidential Interagency Committee on Women's Business Enterprise (ICWBE) will formulate a plan to assure women entrepreneurs equal financial and technical assistance; and the Presidential Advisory Committee will seek help for women business owners from the private sector.

658. White, Jerry. "The Rise of Female Capitalism—Women as Entrepreneurs." *Business Quarterly* 49 (Spring 1984): 133-35.

White cites a 1984 U.S. Small Business Administration study that reports women are starting small businesses at five times the rate of men. He notes that while statistics for Canadian small businesswomen are not as high, a similar phenomenon is occurring there. In a 1982 study of 275 Ontario women, the women listed these reasons for starting their own businesses: challenge, being one's own boss, and inability to penetrate the executive job market.

Beauty and Health

659. "An Attractive Woman Is Judged Less Capable than Her Plainer Peers." *Wall Street Journal* (May 21, 1985): p. 1, col. 5.
Two New York University professors surveyed 113 people and found that attractiveness can have "negative consequences" for executive women. They concluded that a woman's attractiveness may affect her credibility and her legitimacy as a leader and that attractive males and females alike were perceived to use political savvy and social connections to advance.

660. "Blond Bombshell." *Wall Street Journal* (May 14, 1985): p. 28, col. 1.
The editor comments on implications of the findings of a recent *Journal of Applied Psychology* article by a psychologist and a doctoral student. The researchers concluded that "being attractive can have negative consequences for women managers," but attractiveness is a benefit for a man.

661. "Catering to Corporate Woman." *Advertising Age* 56 (February 21, 1985): 22.
Beauty salons attract a new customer in the 1980s—the corporate woman. The salons often give makeup and hairstyling seminars in corporate offices. Cosmetologist Marie Nunoz of Adrien Arpel cites the importance of good skin care when traveling frequently.

662. Cooper, Cary L. "Coping with the Stress of Being a Woman Executive." *Leadership and Organization Development Journal* 4 (1983): 15-26.
A study of the health of 135 women executives shows that over 40 percent complained of excessive tension, 55 percent from anxiety, and 70 percent from excessive fatigue. In a second study of 800 women executives, tiredness was the most common stress symptom listed. Researchers also learned that women managers were more likely to exhibit higher Type A coronary prone behavior than male managers. Cardiologists offer women executives nine tips for managing Type A behavior.

663. Cooper, Cary L., and Davidson, Marilyn J. "The Female Manager—The Pressures and the Problems." *Long Range Planning* 16 (February 1983): 10-14.

Although more women have become lower-level managers, it is still difficult for women to reach middle- and upper-level management. This barrier, in addition to the difficulty of balancing career and family, creates enormous stess that, in turn, results in these symptoms of strain: fatigue, anxiety attacks, migraine headaches, excessive drinking and/or smoking; neck or back tension, sleeplessness, and frustration or dissatisfaction. To help alleviate these stresses, organizations need to institute flexible work weeks, grant paternity and maternity leaves, offer day care, and revise relocation policies. Includes tables and references.

664. Cooper, Cary L., and Davidson, Marilyn J. "The High Cost of Stress on Women Managers." *Organizational Dynamics* 10 (Spring 1982): 44-53.

The authors summarize the research by Cooper and Melhuish on female managers' health, then review the research on stress and the physical, mental, and behavioral effects on women executives. Although some women managers show evidence of stress by becoming ill, others react with behavioral changes—increased smoking or use of drugs or alcohol and marital breakdowns. Bobbie Jacobson, author of *The Ladykillers: Why Smoking Is a Feminist Issue* (1981), found that United States' women executives smoke more than their male counterparts. Includes figures and bibliography.

665. Davidson, Marilyn J., and Cooper, Cary L. "Occupational Stress in Female Managers: A Comparative Study." *Journal of Management Studies* 21 (April 1984): 185-205.

Researchers at the University of Manchester Institute of Science and Technology explore occupational stress and stress manifestations for female managers compared to male managers. They divide the model of occupational stress into four areas: the work arena, the home/social arena, the individual arena, and the stress manifestation arena. In their in-depth interviews of sixty female managers and 185 male managers, Cooper and Davidson learned women in lower- and middle-management positions experienced the highest occupational stress. They recommend the following organizational and corporate policy changes: flexible work arrangements, reasonable maternity and paternity leave, opportunities for work at home, retraining for women reentering the workforce, adequate day care, changes in relocation policies, affirmative action activities, and changes in attitudes. Incudes figures and references.

666. Davidson, Marilyn J., and Cooper, Cary L. "She Needs a Wife: Problems of Women Managers." *Leadership and Organization Development Journal* 5 (1984): 3-30.

Davidson and Cooper present the findings of their research study on the problems and pressures of female managers, the final report of a research project, "The Problems of Women Managers," conducted for the Manpower Services Commission from 1980 to 1982. They describe the method of the study, the sample, evaluation measures, and stressors and stress outcomes for female and male managers. The authors conclude with suggestions for organizational and policy changes and management training implications. Includes tables and references.

667. Deutsch, Claudia H. "Stress Takes Toll on Women Who Succeed." *Des Moines (Iowa) Register* (September 12, 1986): 1.
The stress of corporate life leads some women executives to eating disorders, smoking, or drugs. Although they have fewer fatal heart attacks than executive males, a growing number of executive women have become cocaine users. The women cite powerlessness and lack of time as the factors that cause them the greatest stress.

668. "Distress Signal? Job Strains May Bother Managerial Women More Than Men." *Wall Street Journal* (August 4, 1981): 1.
Recent studies of female MBA graduates and female executives indicate that women managers exhibit more signs of stress than their male counterparts. The women seek counseling four times as often as men, and more frequently experience depression, nightmares, and stomach problems.

669. Dullea, Georgia. "On Corporate Ladder, Beauty Can Hurt." *New York Times* (June 3, 1985): sec. C, p. 13.
In a recent issue of the *Journal of Applied Psychology*, Dr. Madeline Heilman cites research showing that good looks can be a detriment to a woman's management advancement. Dr. Heilman's studies indicate that people have difficulty seeing attractive women in traditionally male occupations. Political researchers find the same phenomenon in political campaigns—voters prefer attractive male candidates and unattractive female candidates.

670. Epstein, Rachel S. "Stuck in Neutral." *Harper's Bazaar* 118 (March 1985): 106, 136, 144.
Epstein lists the warning signs of a dead-end job: boredom, destructive stress, chronic exhaustion, poor sleeping or eating patterns, and someone younger or less experienced getting the promotion you wanted. She reviews case histories of women who found themselves "stuck in neutral," and quotes advice from others who have made opportunities out of career roadblocks.

671. Etzion, Dalia. "Moderating Effect of Social Support on the Stress-Burnout Relationship." *Journal of Applied Psychology* 69 (November 1984): 615-22.
Six-hundred fifty-seven male and female Israeli managers and human service professionals answered a self-report questionnaire about life and work stresses, the social support in their lives and work, and their experience of burnout. Results indicate women experience more stress and burnout in life than men, but there was no difference for stress in work. Includes tables and references.

672. "Good Looks, Bad Image." *New York Times* (May 14, 1985): sec. 3, p. 4, col. 5.
The *Journal of Applied Psychology* reports on a study of 113 working men and women in New York City. Attractiveness is an asset for business men, but a liability for women. The psychologists who con-

ducted the study concluded that "being attractive can have negative consequences for women managers. . .," but that attractive men are believed to be hard workers, successful, and have integrity.

673. Halcomb, Ruth. "Do Pretty Women Get Ahead?" *Mademoiselle* 87 (October 1981): 170-71.
The author of *Women Making It, Patterns and Profiles of Success* (Ballantine, 1981) discusses the issue of attractiveness as a career liability or asset. Studies on attractive women achievers indicate that "To be pretty is a plus, to be too pretty can be disastrous." Beauty can be a source of power, but attractive and successful women are also frequently the subject of unfounded rumors about how they achieved success.

674. Horton, Elizabeth. "No Beauties in the Executive Suite." *Science Digest* 93 (October 1985): 24.
Psychologists Madeline Heilman and Melanie Stopeck surveyed workers in New York City and found that attractive male managers were perceived to have more integrity than plainer men, but attractive female executives were viewed as having less integrity than unattractive women managers. Researcher Heilman concludes, "Good looks are a benefit to a man, but often present problems for women in their climb to the top."

675. "How Female Execs Exercise." *Vogue* 175 (March 1985): 213.
A survey of 300 United States women executives indicates that many of the women exercise as hard as they work. Forty-four percent agree that physical activity increased their spirit of competition and most of the women engage in sports activities with clients or co-workers. Physical activities and the order of preference: aerobics, swimming, running, racquetball.

676. Kellogg, Mary Alice. "Upbeat Stress: Your Shortcut to the Top." *Harper's Bazaar* (September 1985): 248, 254.
Kellogg differentiates between "eustress" (healthy pressure) and "distress," claiming that stress is necessary, it is the way we respond to it that determines our health and success. People who seek change, adapt quickly to stressful situations, and feel a sense of control over their lives, are called "stress-resistant." The director for Stress and Pain-Related Disorders at Columbia-Presbyterian Medical Center, New York City, Dr. Kenneth Greenspan advises readers to build stress resistance by adopting these six techniques: be flexible about plans or results, ask for feedback, seek a smooth-running work situation, do relaxation exercises, make time for pleasurable pursuits, and do physical exercises you like.

677. Kiechel, Walter III. "Beauty and the Managerial Beast." *Fortune* 114 (November 10, 1986): 202-03.
Studies show that attractive men and women may be favored in hiring, determining initial pay, and in performance appraisals. Other research indicates, however, that less attractive women are more likely to be perceived as good managers. The author claims the studies may be questionable, because the respondents are generally college students who do not represent the corporate world.

678. Machlowitz, Marilyn. "How Businesswomen Can Husband Their Energies." *Wall Street Journal* (August 22, 1983): p. 14, col. 3.
Like the traditional corporate wife, corporate husbands can provide moral support, household help, and schedule flexibility to aid their spouses who also have demanding careers. Some working wives have difficulty relinquishing overall responsibility for home and family to their husbands.

679. Marquardt, Deborah. "Are You Too Tired to Read This?" *Savvy* 7 (April 1986): 88-90.
According to a recent study in *Organizational Dynamics*, 70 percent of women managers say chronic fatigue is their major problem. Stress, depression, and a feeling of lack of control are causes of fatigue, and according to experts, women must first understand why they are tired and determine the change of lifestyle that will cure their fatigue.

680. Ramsey, Nancy. "Are You Overworked and Undersexed?" *Harper's Bazaar* (September 1984): 244, 348.
The author describes a typical day in the life of a young woman manager—overworked, underloved, undersexed—the same path many men have taken for years. As women managers commit more time to their careers, social lives suffer. Ramsey states, "Success breeds success, not necessarily happiness." She poses a number of questions to help determine your satisfaction with your job and relationships.

681. Seligman, Daniel. "Beautyism." *Fortune* 112 (August 19, 1985): 219, 222.
A recent article in the *Journal of Applied Psychology* described the theory about attractiveness and success. Researchers found that beautiful women were thought to be less competent or to have less managerial ability than their plainer sisters. The opposite was true for males—attractive men were seen as better managers.

682. Shore, Elsie R. "Alcohol Consumpton Rates among Managers and Professionals." *Journal of Studies on Alcohol* 46 (March 1985): 153-56.
Almost 250 men and women managers and professionals participated in a study which included questions on the use of alcohol. The women in the sample reported a higher proportion of drinkers than previous studies, and Shore found that over 18 percent of never married, divorced or separated women were heavy drinkers, while only 6.5 percent of married women were heavy drinkers. Includes tables and references.

683. Weir, June. "Scents and Success." *New York Times Magazine* (June 2, 1985): 58.
Of 486 women executives surveyed by the Fragrance Foundation, over 50 percent wore perfume to work daily. Twenty-five career women who were interviewed at New York stores commented on fragrance and career relationships and their fragrance preference and usage habits.

684. Wheeler, Elizabeth. "Perils of Pretty: In Business, It Isn't Always Better to be Beautiful." *Working Woman* 6 (May 1981): 98-101.

Wheeler quotes several executive women who talk about the difficulty of being taken seriously if you are too attractive. A University of Rochester graduate student wrote her dissertation on sex-role stereotypes and attractiveness in hiring practices and found that pretty women were offered higher starting salaries, but only in "female" or sex-neutral occupations. Faye Wattleton, president of Planned Parenthood, says "I'm not ashamed of using my physical assets—I see that kind of attention as one more thing that can help the cause."

685. "Women Executives Drink Less Than Their Male Counterparts." *Wall Street Journal* (December 18, 1984): p. 1, col. 5.

A Johns Hopkins School of Public Health survey of 1,100 Baltimore women shows that as women move into traditional male executive jobs, they do not adopt their male colleagues' heavier drinking patterns. Twenty-one percent of top-level male executives are classified as heavy drinkers, while only 8 percent of executive females fall in that category. Other finding: women in professional, clerical, and service jobs display similar drinking habits.

686. "Women Executives' Luncheon Habits Are Putting Males in a Bad Light." *Wall Street Journal* (April 2, 1981): p. 1.

A Venet Advertising survey shows that women executives spend less than an hour at lunch, seldom drink alcoholic beverages at their noonday meal, and prefer to lunch with male executives. The women choose salads over steak, and 99 percent leave a 15 percent tip every time.

Sex and Romance

687. Auerbach, Stuart. "Love in the Executive Suite." *Washington Post* (August 25, 1983): p. C1, col. 2.

Auerbach comments on Eliza Collins' article, "Managers and Lovers," which appeared in the September/October issue of the *Harvard Business Review*. Collins cited four case histories of interoffice romances and advised executives to fire the company's least valuable manager, almost always the woman.

688. Brophy, Beth; Linnon, Nancy; and Moore, Marilyn A. "Sexual Dilemmas of the Modern Office." *U.S. News and World Report* (December 8, 1986): 55-58.

Along with an increase in the number of women in the workplace, companies must address the issue of romance in the office. The problem is especially difficult when the relationship is between a boss and a subordinate or when a person supervises his or her spouse. When companies discipline employees who are engaging in an office romance, the double standard still dictates that the woman is likely to suffer the most career damage. In a 1985 survey of 100 white-collar employees, a University of San Diego professor found that 90 percent thought they knew of a romance in their organization, but only one in four thought office affairs were positive.

689. "Business Problem Seen in Executive Romances." *New York Times* (August 26, 1983): sec. 1, p. 10, col. 6.

Eliza Collins, editor for the *Harvard Business Review*, wrote an article for the September/October issue called "Managers and Lovers." She is of the opinion that romance between executives is disruptive to organizations and should be treated as a conflict of interest. Her advice is that the less valuable employee—generally the woman—be asked to leave the company.

690. Collins, Eliza G. C. "Managers and Lovers." *Harvard Business Review* (September/October 1983): 142-53.

Collins concludes that love between two managers is harmful to the organization, to the lovers themselves, and to their careers. One study found that 90 percent of employees believe office romances impact negatively on an organization. Collins offers these guidelines to help companies handle these relationships: treat the relationship as a conflict of interest, advise the couple to get outside help, persuade the couple that either the person least essential to the company or both have to go, and help the ousted executive find a new and perhaps better job. Includes charts.

691. Dullea, Georgia. "The Issue of Office Romances." *New York Times* (May 17, 1982): sec. 2, p. 10, col. 1.

Mary Cunningham, who left Bendix after rumors of a romance with chairman William Agee, says that while some male/female office relationships are "counterproductive," it is possible that the men and women who work as a team may be more intellectually creative. However, a professor of organization management at the State University of New York at Albany claims that in a study of 130 office romances, job performance and productivity are negatively affected in 90 percent of the cases.

692. Graham, Ellen. "My Lover, My Colleague." *Wall Street Journal* (March 24, 1986): 23D, 26D.

Corporations have difficulty dealing with men and women managers involved in office romances. Barbara Gutek explores the issue in her book, *Sex and the Workplace.* Most employees agree that office romances are risky, particularly when one partner in the relationship has greater power or status in the organization.

693. Kaufman, Lois, and Wolf, John B. "Avoiding Unwanted Advances." *Supervisory Management* 29 (September 1984): 40-43.

Because women are such a small percent of all managers, they face "special scrutiny" which may take the form of harassment or discrimination. To avoid unwanted advances, Kaufman and Wolf advise women to exchange their "female talk" for a more direct way of speaking, to learn to say "no" verbally and nonverbally, and to take preventive security measures when traveling.

694. "No Place for Love." *New York Times* (September 4, 1983): sec. 4, p. 14.

The editor comments on Eliza Collins' article on office romance that appeared in the *Harvard Business Review* and agrees with Collins' arguments: emotional relationships affect decision making, office romance causes problems with peers and subordinates, often one of the lovers is asked to resign—usually it's the woman.

695. Powell, Gary N. "What Do Tomorrow's Managers Think about Sexual Intimacy in the Workplace?" *Business Horizons* 29 (July/August 1986): 30-33.

The author of *Women and Men in Management* discusses the results of a study of undergraduate business students and part-time MBA students to determine their beliefs regarding sexual intimacy in the workplace. Although most of the students felt that management should not be concerned with employees' personal lives and sexual habits, they did not believe sexual intimacy between supervisors and subordinates or between co-workers enhanced the work environment or productivity. Powell reports differences in attitudes between the groups: women and graduate students expressed more negative attitudes toward sexual intimacy at work than did male and undergraduate students. Incudes tables and references.

696. Schultz, Terri. "In Defense of the Office Romance." *Savvy* 3 (May 1982): 54-57, 61-62, 64.

Male and female managers and professionals learn romance can flourish in the work environment—"organizations are natural environments for the emergence of romantic relationships." A love affair can be stimulating and result in increased productivity by one or both partners. Executives and academics take both sides of the issue—some believing that romance is a personal issue and not necessarily deleterious to corporations, others claiming that romance is strictly taboo in the workplace. If corporations take the second view, frequently the woman is asked to leave.

697. "Sex and Success: A *Savvy* Survey." *Savvy* 6 (October 1985): 29-34.

Over 1,000 executive women answered sixty questions about their sex lives, their work, and how they feel about themselves. Srully Blotnick, a research psychologist and author of *Otherwise Engaged: The Private Lives of Successful Career Women*, analyzed the results. See page thirty-three for information about the women in the sample and page thirty-four for a reader survey, "Sex on the Job."

698. Spruell, Geraldine Romano. "Love in the Office." *Training and Development Journal* (February 1985): 2023.

Spruell discusses the inevitability of sexual attraction in the office as more powerful women and men work together. She reviews the benefits and disadvantages to the organization and tells about Kaleel Jamison's "touch spectrum" appropriate for five levels of a relationship. Spruell concludes with suggestions to management for dealing with office romances.

699. Westoff, Leslie Aldridge. "Mentor or Lover?" *Working Woman* 11 (October 1986): 116-19.

The author of *Corporate Romance* shares an excerpt on mentor/protégé relationships. A 1982 Korn/Ferry International study found that 42 percent of the senior executive women polled said "who you know, not what you know" was a true statement. Seventy-eight percent of the women indicated they mentored lower-level women.

700. "When Love Goes to Work." *Savvy* 4 (October 1983): 18.

Eliza Collins, editor at the *Harvard Business Review*, authored an article "Managers and Lovers" that was three years in the writing. Her concluson, that when high-level executives fall in love, the solution is for the "less effective" (usually female) partner to leave the company, may not be popular with women readers.

General Literature

JOURNAL ARTICLES

701. Allison, Mary Ann, and Allison, Eric. "Picking the Right Style." *Working Woman* 9 (October 1984): 31, 34, 38.
Sometimes a management style that was effective in one job will not be appropriate in a new job. The authors of *Managing Up, Managing Down* discuss four management styles—telling, selling, consulting, and joining—and give examples of when to use each style. They conclude with a list of eight things to consider when selecting the appropriate style: your authority, your predecessors, senior managers' styles, employees' attitudes, time, experience, extenuating circumstances, and your preferred style.

702. Barrett, Katherine, and Greene, Richard. "Success and Betrayal." *Savvy* 7 (December 1986): 22.
Sarah Hardesty and Nehama Jacobs, the authors of *Success and Betrayal: The Crisis of Women in Corporate America*, claim that media attention focusing on super-successful women creates disillusionment for many corporate women. The reviewers warn readers to take the book with a grain of salt, reminding them that the book is not a scientific survey.

703. Caraganis, Lynn L. "The Cosmetics Executive: How Does She Do It and Still Remain Cute?" *Atlantic* 249 (April 1982): 99-100.
Caraganis entertains readers with a fictional interview with Josephine Darnell, owner of Princess Josephine Industries. She parodies the popular press articles about women executives, their lifestyles, and families. Josephine hands the interviewer new company brochures—"Womanhood," "Make-Up," and "The Danger of Sports."

704. Evans, Heather. "The Plight of the Corporate Nun." *Working Woman* 9 (November 1984): 63-64.
According to an American Management Association survey, 60 percent of the women managers responding said they got the most satisfaction in life from their careers. Evans, an investment banker, warns that achievement and success may not necessarily bring fulfillment. She suggests following the advice of Herbert Freudenberger, author of *Burn-Out: The High Cost of High Achievement*.

705. Hymowitz, Carol. "Distaff Sequel to a Bestseller Offers Colorful Outlook on Executive Life." *Wall Street Journal* (December 12, 1984): p. 33, col. 1.

The *Executive Women's Coloring Book* jibes male chauvinists' attitudes toward women in the business world and also uses humor to poke fun at corporate women and subjects ranging from "dress for success" to sexual harassment. The $3.95 paperback stars a woman vice president of a Fortune 500 company who was first in her Wharton Business School class. The book was written by Martin Cohen and Mary McDonald Horowitz and is a sequel to Martin Cohen's *Executive Coloring Book* written in 1961.

706. Ferretti, Fred. "Poll Shows Cost of Success." *New York Times* (June 1, 1982): sec. 3, p. 8, col. 2.

One-hundred seven women corporate vice presidents of Fortune 500 companies participated in a survey by the Scotch Whiskey Information Center. The findings, published in "A Survey of Women Officers of America's Largest Corporations," show that 77 percent of the respondents were thirty to forty-nine years old, 64 percent earned $40,000 to $100,000, less than half were married, and 70 percent had no children. Most of the women felt that being female had made it more difficult to achieve success and that they were more competent than men in similar positions.

707. Foxworth, Jo. "Hal, Lee and Me." *Working Woman* 10 (October 1985): 122-24.

The author of *Boss Lady* and the president of her own advertising agency, Foxworth compares a woman's management style to those of Hal Geneen of ITT and Lee Iacocca of Chrysler Corp. It is her opinion that women managers can be strong but not overbearing, decisive but respectful of others' opinions.

708. Garen, Margo E. "A Management Model for the '80s." *Training and Development Journal* 36 (March 1982): 41-49.

Garen calls for a new management style for the 1980s, a male/female or androgynous style. She lists skills that major corporations use in assessing potential management candidates—oral communications, written communications, leadership, flexibility, decision-making ability, inner work standards, organization and planning, performance stability—and discusses women's strengths and weaknesses with regard to each skill. Includes bibliography.

709. Goldstein, Marilyn. "Women Executives—Speaking Up When There's Something to Lose." *Ms.* (March 1982): 100.

Goldstein laments the failure of women executives to speak up about women's issues. She fears that women executives are silent about the Women's Movement because they are afraid of losing their own positions.

710. Gordon, Suzanne. "The New Corporate Feminism." *The Nation* 236 (February 5, 1983): 129, 143, 146-47.

Gordon regrets that women have left their radical feminism for corporate feminism, an individual rather than a collective approach. She claims that the feminist promise to balance love, friendship, and work has become, instead, an attempt to make one's personal life serve professional goals. The networks designed to form alliances between women are only a "vehicle for the advancement of an elite."

711. Gray, Julie. "Are Women Executives Really Superwomen? The Latest Study Says No—They Have Made Trade-Offs." *Working Woman* 8 (March 1983): 38, 42.

The recent Korn/Ferry survey of executive women found that over half are vice presidents, work over fifty hours a week, and spend more than thirty days a year traveling on business. Seventy-five percent of the women want to advance further, and almost 70 percent work in the service sector. For a copy of the survey, send $10.00 to: Jacqueline Davis, Korn/Ferry International, 1900 Avenue of the Stars, Los Angeles, CA 90067.

712. Hacker, Randi. "Who Just Wants to Have Fun?" *Savvy* 6 (December 1985): 68-69.

Hacker takes a humorous jab at the executive woman as she charts her progress through Execuland, the theme park for executive women. She describes the Unfairway, the Managerial Loop, the Flow Chart Flume Ride, and the Day of Doom Horror House.

713. Helgesen, Sally. "Who Gets Ahead and Why? Strategies from Top Working Women." *Glamour* 83 (February 1985): 188-89, 191-92, 248-50.

The Center for Creative Leadership (Greensboro, NC) studied thirty-eight male executives, nineteen of whom succeeded and nineteen of whom derailed. Researchers describe similarities in the two groups, but noted that those who succeeded were more flexible and had fewer personality flaws. The center is working on a similar study of seventy-five female executives.

714. Henderson, C. Nell. "For These Bodyguards, Roses and Revolvers." *New York Times* (June 6, 1982): sec. 3, p. 19, col. 1.

Women executives, particularly those who work for controversial corporations, are hiring female bodyguards for protection. One Los Angeles security agency added three women to its ten-man full-time staff within a six-month period. Female bodyguards, including thirty women who work for the U.S. Secret Service, protect both male and female clients.

715. Hildebrandt, Herbert W. "Learning from Top Women Executives: Their Perceptions on Business Communication; Careers; and Education." Manuscript, basis of a speech given at the Association for Business Communication Convention, 1985.

Based on two questionnaires developed by Hildebrandt and other researchers at the University of Michigan, this paper profiles the top woman executive, her feelings about the importance of business communication, her pattern of career advancement, education, and personal life.

Executives at the president and vice president level felt that business communication courses were the most helpful in preparation for general management, personal challenge is the most important reason for changing jobs, and marketing/sales and finance/accounting are the best areas for specialization. Includes tables and reference.

716. Hildebrandt, Herbert W.; Miller, Edwin L.; and LaCivita, Stephen J. "A Managerial Profile: The Woman Manager." The Division of Research, the Graduate School of Business Administration, The University of Michigan, 1985.

Researchers report on the findings of a study of women managers who attended management education programs at the University of Michigan's Graduate School of Business in number 4 in the series, Michigan Management and Executive Development Studies. The results are organized by education, personal, career patterns, and career development. Includes several tables and Appendix: Research Program on Executives (Questionnaire).

717. Hughey, Ann, and Gelman, Eric. "Managing the Woman's Way." *Newsweek* (March 17, 1986): 46-47.

"Female" management skills will be especially valuable to corporations as the United States changes from an industrial to a service economy. Marilyn Loden, author of *Feminine Leadership: Or How to Succeed in Business without Being One of the Boys*, agrees that typically feminine traits such as sympathy, sensitivity, and intuition are the skills corporations will find most useful if the anticipated labor shortage occurs in the "baby bust" generation. Motherhood is also seen as an advantage when compromise, conciliation, listening, and crisis management skills are required. Many women managers who have decided not to adopt the male management style found in most corporations have joined the growing ranks of female entrepreneurs.

718. Jack, Sasha. "Career Crisis: Battling the Baby Boom Bulge." *Glamour* 83 (June 1985): 144, 146, 148, 152.

Many baby boomers, women in their twenties and thirties, are reaching career plateaus because of the intense competition for middle-management positions. Career counselors tell how to identify the signs of "career doldrums." Skills that will help advance a stalled career include an advanced degree, specialized job skills or expertise, functional skills (supervisory or communication), and political savvy. One solution may be a job change.

719. Kanter, Rosabeth Moss. "Confident Managing." *Harper's Bazaar* 117 (March 1984): 272, 164.

Kanter cites Tandem Computer, Citicorp, and Hewlett Packard as examples of companies that practice a participative, innovative management style—a new flexible style that grew out of economic necessity. The new managers, dubbed "change masters" by Kanter, are entrepreneurial and have five skills in common: expanding their thinking, communicating a clear vision, building coalitions, working through teams, and sharing credit and glory.

720. Keown, Ada Lewis, and Keown, Charles F. "Factors of Success for Women in Business." *International Journal of Women's Studies* 8 (May/June 1995): 278-85.

The authors interviewed twenty-one women executives about their career goals, work motivation, use of the informal organizational structure, mentors, and perceptions of factors for success. They conclude with a list of seven findings, including over half of the women never articulated a career goal, two-thirds had mentors at some point in their careers, and they believed that being female was an asset. Includes references.

721. Landers, Ann. "How Men Feel When Women Wear the Pants." *Woman's Day* 49 (April 27, 1982): 72, 74, 114.

Advice columnist Landers asked successful women how men feel about their success. They first answered "threatened," then qualified that response with comments on the man's success, age, and self-confidence. Landers shares details of her own thirty-six-year marriage and subsequent divorce because of her husband's loss of identity. She cites examples of successful marriages where the female superachiever is in a very visible position: Sandra Day O'Connor, Hanna Gray, Erma Bombeck, and Dianne Feinstein.

722. Levinson, William. "Memoirs of an Executive Woman." *Savvy* 2 (August 1981): 92-93.

A humorous jibe at the "memoirs" of executive women. Levinson's fictional heroine, named Iowa B. Cohen, overcomes obstacles and handicaps and tells how she achieves success in "I'm Earning as Fast as I Can: The Memoirs of an Executive Woman."

723. "Management Savvy: Do You Have What It Takes?" *Essence* 15 (March 1985): 71-72.

Catalyst, the New York-based nonprofit organization working to develop career and family options, offers a fifty-six-point checklist to help determine your management skills and weaknesses. The questions are adapted from Catalyst's 1981 publication "Upward Mobility" and are divided into eight sections: Are you a good problem solver? Are you a good decision maker? Are you a good planner? Are you a good organizer? Are you efficient? Are you a good delegator? Are you an effective manager? Are you a good communicator?

724. Murphy, Elizabeth R. "Don't Be This Kind of Manager." *Essence* 15 (March 1985): 78.

Murphy describes four management styles women will want to avoid: Heavy-Handed Hanna, Keep It-to-Herself Kitty, Mother Martha, and Just-the-Facts-Jessica. Hanna communicates by telling, never listening. Kitty works alone, not delegating to her staff. Martha takes care of her staff by nurturing. Jessica goes by rules and regulations and does not know how to motivate people.

725. Nordberg, Olivia Schieffelin. "In a Class by Ourselves." *Savvy* 3 (March 1982): 43-47, 50-51.

Almost 10,000 women responded to the *Savvy* Survey of Executive Behavior published in the August 1981 issue. Most of the women were professional managers, worked seven to nine hours a day, and earned

$15,000 to $40,000 per year. Although 96 percent rate their job performance as excellent or good, only 51 percent see opportunities for advancement in their present positions.

726. O'Toole, Patricia. "Corporate Meritocracies: The *Savvy* Sixteen." *Savvy* 3 (May 1982): 38-44.
The staff of *Savvy* name sixteen companies where growth means a good environment for women and where executive women are found throughout the company. The best opportunities for managerial women can be found in these companies: American Express Company, Atlantic Richfield, AT & T, Chemical New York Corporation, Connecticut General Corporation, Continental Illinois Corporation, Control Data Corporation, Digital Equipment Corporation, the Equitable Life Assurance Society of the United States, General Mills, Hewlett-Packard Company, Honeywell, IBM, Johnson & Johnson, Quaker Oats Company, and Security Pacific Corporation.

727. Rogan, Helen. "Achievement and Ambition Typify Younger Executives." *Wall Street Journal* (October 25, 1984): p. 35, col. 5.
A *Wall Street Journal* /Gallup Organization survey of executive women divided the women into six groups. The typical woman in the "young achievers" group is less than forty, has less than fifteen years of management experience, and earns $60,000 or more. Sixty-five percent of the young achievers earn more than their husbands and frequently cite lack of time for self as concern.

728. Rogan, Helen. "Top Women Executives Find Path to Power Is Strewn with Hurdles." *Wall Street Journal* (October 25, 1984): sec. 2, p. 35.
A survey of 722 female executives discovered that one-half of the women were the first women to reach management level in their companies, over 60 percent of the women had been mistaken for a secretary at a business meeting, and 82 percent said that a man had been the most helpful person in their careers. Eighty percent of the women executives believe that females are at a disadvantage in the business world, and 70 percent believe they are paid less than men of equal ability.

729. Rivers, Caryl. "Reaching for the Top." *Working Woman* 8 (September 1983): 137-38.
The authors of *The Managerial Woman* and deans of the School of Management at Simmons College, Anne Jardim and Margaret Hennig are at work on a new book on women managers. Their research identified three major issues: the large number of women now in middle management, resistance to women in senior management, and the productivity crisis in American management. They agree that men and women managers approach problems differently and take different approaches to decision making.

730. Salmans, Sandra. "Mentors, Managers and Mary Cunningham." *New York Times* (June 24, 1984): sec. 3, p. 15, col. 1.
Salmans reviews three books: *Powerplay* by Mary Cunningham, *Inside Moves* by Marilyn Machlowitz, and *The Manager's Adviser* by David M. Brownstone and Irene M. Franck with Rosemary Guiley. She says that

Cunningham's and Brownstone's books take a more pessimistic view of women's chances in the business world, while Machlowitz is more positive.

731. "The *Savvy* Survey of Executive Behavior." *Savvy* 2 (August 1981): 57-60.
Forty-three questions about the professional and personal demands of the lives of *Savvy* readers are listed.

732. Schwartzman, Sharon. "Reading for Fun and Profit." *Working Woman* 8 (July 1983): 46, 48.
Working Woman queried top women executives about their reading habits and choices. The respondents indicated they read trade journals and newspapers, popular management books, and a wide variety of books for pleasure, ranging from nonfiction to spy novels.

733. Stimpson, David V., and Revel, Lisa K. "Management Style: Modeling or Balancing?" *Journal of Psychology* 11 (March 1984) 169-73.
Male and female university students assumed the roles of middle manager, subordinate, or executive (boss) in a study of management styles. The researchers found that managers generally model the style of their boss (executive), female managers more so than males. Male managers become more democratic when working for a female executive, but female managers become more authoritarian when working for a female boss. Includes references.

734. "Success: On Our Own Terms." *Vogue* 175 (June 1985): 311, 315-19.
Vogue interviewed several well-known figures about the meaning of success, marriage, and job stress. The interviewees agreed that success is getting what you want. Panelists were Jean Baker Miller, Rosabeth Moss Kanter, Louise J. Kaplan, Barbara Ehrenreich, Nannerl Overholzer, Niki Sauvage Tsongas, Virginia L. Ernster, Trudy Berkowitz, and Ann Bedford Ulanor.

735. Trost, Cathy. "The Checkoff." *Wall Street Journal* (October 1, 1985): p. 1, col. 5.
"Some leaders are born women," reads a billboard advertising Seton Hill College, a women's school in Greensburg, PA.

736. "What It Takes." *Working Woman* 8 (November 1983): 87-88.
The four women named outstanding corporate leaders by Catalyst share their views on the qualities essential to corporate leadership. The women are Camron Cooper, vice president at Atlantic Richfield; Elaine Bond, senior vice president and director of corporate systems at Chase Manhattan Bank; Anne-Lee Verville, controller of the national accounts division, IBM; and Ruth Block, chief of the local accounts complex and chair and CEO of the Equitable Variable Life Insurance Company.

737. "Who Is That Masked Woman?" *Savvy* 4 (January 1983): 14.
Executive search firm Korn/Ferry International and UCLA's Graduate
School of Management describe the "typical" executive woman: she is
forty-six, unmarried, and has no children. Her salary is over $92,000,
and she is a senior vice president. A November 9, 1982 issue of the *Wall
Street Journal* indicates more women managers than men managers are
out of work as a result of the recession.

738. "Women Are Job Risk-Takers." *Wall Street Journal* (July 16,
1985): p. 1, col. 5.
So says a poll by the National Association for Female Executives. Sixty-
four percent of women under thirty-five who earn $40,000 or more have
changed careers.

739. "Would You Make a Good Manager?" *Glamour* 81 (September
1983): 56.
Columnist Marilyn Moats Kennedy suggests asking yourself these questions as a gauge of your "management mentality": Are you comfortable
being evaluated on what you can motivate, educate, or persuade others
to do? How do you feel when someone who works for you does something well? Do you try to sell people on an idea, or do you simply argue
about the right way to implement the idea? Are you confident enough in
your decisions to withstand the disapproval of your co-workers, or to be
publicly wrong?

740. Youdin, Beth Greer. "Test Your Executive Quotient: Do You
Have the E.Q. to Be an Executive Woman?" *Savvy* 2 (January 1981):
31.
Answer these eleven questions to determine how well you have been
reading the *Wall Street Journal*. At the end of the quiz, find a joke about
the executive woman.

BOOKS

741. Apter, Terri. *Why Women Don't Have Wives: Professional Success
and Motherhood*. London: Macmillan, 1985.
The author examines the phenomenon of the growth in the number of
working women who also choose to be mothers. Chapter 9 "Dressed for
Success" addresses the managerial woman versus the "new" managerial
women as mothers, the effect their careers have on their children, and
contrasts British women managers/mothers with their American counterparts. Includes notes, references, bibliography, and index.

742. Blotnick, Srully. *Otherwise Engaged: The Private Lives of Successful Career Women*. New York: Facts on File Publications, 1985.
The careers and personal lives of almost 3,500 women were studied for
over twenty-five years. Blotnick determined that social and economic
trends in the United States from 1958 to 1985 have resulted in two top
priorities for workers: to become "highly competent in a specialized
sphere of occupational activity" and to become "renowned for it as
well." Because of this emphasis on career and success, many women have

sacrificed their personal lives. Blotnick's findings indicate that "intimacy plus ambition," i.e., a satisfying personal life plus hard work, is the most successful combination for women.

743. Brownstone, David M., and Franck, Irene M. *The Manager's Advisor.* New York: Wiley, 1983.

This comprehensive handbook on all aspects of management includes a chapter on "Women and Minorities in Management." Although the chapter is directed toward the women and minorities themselves, it is also explained that the contents will be useful to other managers who wish to manage and organizations "free of discrimination." Establishing authority is viewed as the most critical skill for women and minority managers. Other areas covered are handling hostile subordinates, hiring and firing, entertaining and traveling, the office romance, handling prejudice and chauvinism, and moving up.

744. Carr-Ruffino, Norma. *The Promotable Woman: Becoming a Successful Manager.* Belmont, CA: Wadsworth, 1982.

Carr-Ruffino outlines the personal and management skills the promotable woman should master. In Part I, Developing Personal Skills that Promote Managerial Effectiveness, she discusses goal clarification, stress management, assertiveness, and effective communications. In Part II, Developing Management Skills, she offers advice on employee motivation, time management, problem-solving and decision making, organizing, financial planning, and team-building.

745. Collins, Eliza G. C. *Dearest Amanda: An Executive's Advice to Her Daughter.* New York: Harper & Row, 1984.

Collins, a senior editor of the *Harvard Business Review*, gives advice to women in business in the form of letters from an executive mother to her daughter. Topics covered include relationships with employees, colleagues, and bosses; self-confidence; organizational politics; male and female management styles; sexual harassment; power; working for a woman; and handling success and failure. Some parts of the book appeared first in *Working Woman* magazine.

746. Collins, Nancy W. *Professional Women and Their Mentors: A Practical Guide to Mentoring for the Woman Who Wants to Get Ahead.* Englewood Cliffs, NJ: Prentice-Hall, 1983.

The author analyzes the results of a questionnaire on mentoring that she mailed to 600 executive women. Four hundred women from the Peninsula Professional Women's Network (San Francisco, San Jose), the Bay Area Executive Women's Forum, and several major United States cities responded. Collins notes that almost all of the respondents had male mentors, and every woman who replied considered the mentor relationship to be positive. Includes appendices, bibliography, and index.

747. Colwill, Nina L. *The New Partnership: Women and Men in Organizations.* Palo Alto, CA: Mayfield Publishing, 1982.

The author explores the issues of sex-role problems in organizations: attitudes and behavior, sex-roles, traits and abilities, achievement and fear of success, power, and communication. She lists the six bases of power in Chapter 6: reward power, punishment power, legitimate power, expert power, referent power, and information power.

748. Cooper, Cary L., and Davidson, Marilyn J. *High Pressure.* Great Britain: Fontana Paperbacks, 1982.
Cooper and Davidson report the results of their year-long interview study of sixty British female managers. They conclude that female managers are faced with stress caused by work and home/social environment factors that their male counterparts do not experience. These stress factors may keep women from accepting or remaining in management positions and adversely affect their health and behavior. Includes index and a lengthy bibliography.

749. Copeland, Lennie, and Griggs, Lewis. *Going International: How to Make Friends and Deal Effectively in the Global Marketplace.* New York: Random House, 1985.
See Appendix 1: Women in International Business. Women account for only 3 percent of expatriate managers, and one-third of that number are employed by banks. Professor Nancy Adler lists three reasons employers give for the low figure: women do not want to go, companies will not send them, and foreigners are prejudiced against women. The authors conclude with five rules for managers and five rules for women in international business.

750. Cunningham, Mary. *Powerplay: What Really Happened at Bendix.* New York: Simon and Schuster, 1984.
At twenty-nine and fresh out of Harvard Business School, Mary Cunningham went to work as executive assistant to Bill Agee, chairman of Bendix. Within a year, Cunningham was promoted to the position of vice president for corporate and public affairs. Amid rumors of an affair with Agee, Cunningham resigned in October 1980 and went to work as corporate vice president of strategic planning and project development at Joseph Seagram & Sons. In *Powerplay* Cunningham tells her story of the year-and-a-half at Bendix, of Agee's unsuccessful takeover bid for Martin Marietta, and the personal story of their friendship, courtship, and marriage.

751. Davidson, Marilyn. *Reach for the Top: A Woman's Guide to Success in Business and Management.* London: Piatkus, 1985.
Davidson advises women to develop short-term, long-term, and life action plans and provides career-planning exercises. She tells how to combat isolation, start networks, and develop confidence and assertiveness. Two chapters deal with ways of handling stress and managing the home/work conflict. Includes Useful Addresses, Suggested Readings, and Index.

752. Davidson, Marilyn, and Cooper, Cary. *Stress and the Woman Manager.* Oxford: Martin Robertson, 1983.
This book, based on a survey of female managers in the United Kingdom and sponsored by the British Government's Manpower Services Commission, highlights the problems of men and women managers. The authors found that women managers experience more stress from work/home conflicts and thus more psychosomatic symptoms and as a

result have a poorer work performance than male managers. Includes index, extensive bibliography, and appendix, Survey Questionnaire.

753. Davidson, Marilyn J., and Cooper, Cary L., eds. *Working Women—An International Survey.* Chichester, England: Wiley, 1984.
Cooper and Davidson, researchers at the University of Manchester, edit this collection of eleven essays on the employment of women. The book is divided into three parts: Women at Work in Six EEC Countries, Women at Work in Three European Countries, and Women at Work: The Two Superpowers. See pages 58, 163, and 195 for discussions of women managers.

754. Devanna, Mary Anne. *Male/Female Careers: The First Decade: A Study of MBAs.* New York: Columbia University Graduate School of Business, 1984.
Devanna reports on a study to determine the effects of socioeconmic background, education, and family on forty-five male and forty-five female MBAs from Columbia University from 1969 to 1972. Findings showed no significant differences in men and women in regard to intrinsic or extrinsic rewards, but important findings were opportunity to learn new skills was most important to MBAs on the first job; after ten years responsibility was the most important job factor; promotion was more highly valued than pay and job title; job security was not as important as believed. Researchers concluded that motivation does not account for pay differences between male and female MBAs, but rather the difference is because of societal and organizational conditions. Includes lengthy bibliography.

755. Dight, Janet. *Breaking the Secretary Barrier: How to Get out from behind the Typewriter and into a Management Job.* New York: McGraw-Hill, 1986.
Dight, herself a former secretary, offers strategies for advancing from a secretarial to a management position. Her advice ranges from education, image, and telephone techniques to responsibility, risk, promotions, and office alliances. Includes recommended readings and subject index.

756. Douglass, Donna N. *Choice and Compromise: A Woman's Guide to Balancing Family and Career.* New York: Amacom, 1983.
Douglass' aim is to identify sources of conflict for women at home and on the job and suggest ways of being effective in both worlds. The last chapter, "Looking Ahead," includes "Keeping Your Balance While Juggling Choices." The author advocates the triangle approach—mind, spirit, body. Includes selected readings and index.

757. Farley, Jennie. *The Woman in Management: Career and Family Issues.* Ithaca, NY: State School of Industrial and Labor Relations, Cornell University, 1983.
"Papers and discussion from a conference on Women in Management sponsored by the New York State School of Industrial and Labor Relations at Cornell University, April 1982." Includes selections by Juanita Kreps, Betty Lehan Harragan, and Rosabeth Moss Kanter and essays by eight other women from panel presentations. Chapter 5 is an essay on

"Recommended Readings" and is followed by an annotated bibliography of recommended readings. Includes author, title, and subject indexes.

758. Feldon, Leah. *Traveling Light: Every Woman's Guide to Getting There in Style.* New York: G.P. Putnam's Sons, 1985.
A former photo-stylist and television fashion consultant, Feldon advises women on travel wardrobes, luggage, packing, traveling abroad, and shopping. The final chapter is an annotated list of personal care items, beauty products, medications, tools, and small appliances that should be considered when planning for business or personal trips.

759. Fields, Daisy. *Woman's Guide to Moving up in Business and Government.* Englewood Cliffs, NJ: Prentice-Hall, 1983.
President of her own human resources development firm and part-time executive director of the Women's Institute at the American University, Daisy Fields tells women how to get a Civil Service job, how to understand the system, and how to climb the career ladder. Fields directs her comments to businesswomen as well in chapter 7, "Conversations with Corporate Women" and chapter 8, "Climbing the Management Ladder." See pages 108 to 116 for highlights of major federal laws on sex discrimination in employment and Facts on Women Workers. Includes bibliography and index.

760. Foxworth, Jo. *Boss Lady's Arrival and Survival Plan.* New York: Warner Books, 1986.
The president of her own advertising agency, Foxworth directs her advice on making it in today's corporate world to young women on the way up, executive women who have already arrived, and employees who work for a "boss lady." Topics covered include etiquette, housework, cooking, children, aging, career planning, sales, clothes and cosmetics, confidence, living alone, travel, exclusive clubs, and enterpreneurship.

761. Fucini, Joseph J., and Fucini, Suzy. *Entrepreneurs: The Men and Women behind Famous Brand Names, and How They Made It.* Boston: G. K. Hall, 1985.
The Fucinis present in-depth biographies of fifty men and women entrepreneurs and cameo sketches of 175 others. The women include such notables as Mary Kay Ash, Coco Chanel, Elizabeth Arden, Olive Ann Beech, Fannie Farmer, Sara Lee Lubin, Gloria Vanderbilt, and Diane von Furstenberg. Includes index and extensive bibliography.

762. Gallese, Liz Roman. *Women like Us.* New York: Morrow, 1985.
Gallese talked to over eighty women of the class of 1975 from the Harvard Business School, the first class where women constituted 10 percent of the enrollment. She interviewed six of the women in depth. Some of the findings of her study and patterns she discovered are that few women appear to plan careers the same way men do; many were ambivalent about their roles as career women, wives, mothers, lovers; and a lack of control exists over their work environment and the direction of their lives.

763. Gillis, Phyllis. *Entrepreneurial Mothers: The Best Way in the World for Mothers to Earn Money without Being Tied to a 9-to-5 Job.* New York: Rawson Associates, 1984.

Gillis states that six times as many women as men are starting their own businesses as a means of integrating family and work life. Entrepreneurial mothers are seeking greater flexibility in work styles, more control over their time, and the opportunity for personal growth and greater financial rewards. The author advises women on determining what you are best at, drawing up a business plan, choosing the best place to work, how to raise money, ways to work with other entrepreneurial mothers, developing your market and involving your family in your work. Appendix lists sample business proposals, associations, reference directories, periodicals, resources, and small business development centers. Includes index.

764. Goffee, Robert, and Scase, Richard. *Women in Charge: The Experiences of Female Entrepreneurs.* London: Allen Unwin, 1985.

The authors state that there is a need for more study of women business owners, because there is a trend toward increased number of women-owned businesses. There are more female entrepreneurs for three reasons: high unemployment, job dissatisfaction, and the development of new technology. Goffee and Scase explore the benefits and difficulties these women face. Includes extensive bibliography and index.

765. Gruber, May. *Pandora's Pride.* Secaucus, NJ: Lyle Stuart, 1984.

In this biography, May Gruber tells the story of Pandora, the sweater and sportswear company she fought to keep after the death of her husband in 1964. When she resigned the presidency to become chair of the board of directors, she took pride in the fact that she had guided Pandora from $8 million to $30 million in volume in twelve years.

766. Gutek, Barbara A. *Sex and the Workplace: The Impact of Sexual Behavior and Harassment on Women, Men, and Organizations.* San Francisco, CA: Jossey-Bass, 1985.

Associate professor of psychology, business administration, and executive management at the Claremont Graduate School and author of five other books on women at work, Barbara Gutek based *Sex and the Workplace* on studies of almost 1,300 working men and women. She gives a historical overview, explores the general issues of men's and women's work, reviews the nature and frequency of sexual harassment, and discusses men's and women's attitudes regarding sexuality in the workplace. Includes Appendix A: Background for the Study; Appendix B: Sampling Strategy; and Appendix C: Main Questionnaire, extensive references, and index.

767. Harragan, Betty Lehan. *Knowing the Score: Play-by-Play Directions for Women on the Job.* New York: St. Martin, 1983.

This is a collection of Harragan's advice columns that have appeared in *Savvy* and *Working Woman.* She begins with "Basic Rules of the Working Game" and continues with "Problems with Bosses," "Troubles with Co-Workers," "Promotion Predicaments," "Sex Is a Business Problem," and "Painful Leavings." Includes subject index.

768. Harriman, Ann. *Women/Men/Management.* New York: Praeger, 1985.

Harriman, professor of human resource management at California State University and teacher of a course on Women/Men/Management, examines personal, social, and organizational influences on sexual behavior and identity and the ways sexual behavior affects organizational behavior. The final chapters analyze men's and women's careers and training and development. Also forecasts a future where electronic technology eliminates sex-based employment, redefines work, reduces family/work conflicts, and supports the integration of women into the power structure of the organization. Includes extensive bibliography and author and subject indexes.

769. Hart, Lois B., and Dalke, J. David. *The Sexes at Work: Improving Work Relationships between Men and Women.* Englewood Cliffs, NJ: Prentice-Hall, 1983.

Researchers surveyed men and women in professional, supervisory or management positions regarding male-female relationships in the workplace. The authors interpret the findings of the survey and make recommendations for eliminating gender-based work conflicts. Appendices: men's and women's versions of the questionnaire and explanation of survey methodology. Includes index.

770. Henry, Fran Worden. *Toughing It out at Harvard: The Making of a Woman MBA.* New York: G.P. Putnam, 1983.

This journal/biography of a woman's first year at Harvard Business School covers classes, study groups, pressures, and sex-role stereotypes. The last two chapters discuss recruiting/interviewing and graduation.

771. Highman, Edith L. *The Organization Woman: Building a Career—An Inside Report.* New York: Human Science Press, 1985.

Highman reports the results of surveys of almost 700 executive and managerial men and women in large corporations. She includes chapters on career/managerial traits; dealing with peers, bosses, spouses, and subordinates; understanding your boss and the organization; career and marriage; and sex and personal problems. She concludes with Chapter 12, "Your Legal Rights," and questionnaire, tables, references, bibliography, and index.

772. Hisrich, Robert D., and Brush, Candida G. *The Woman Entrepreneur: Starting, Financing, and Managing a Successful Business.* Lexington: D.C. Heath, 1985.

The authors give the results of a mail questionnaire to 1,000 United States women entrepreneurs and the investigation of demographic, sociological, and psychological characteristics of entrepreneurial women. Appendix I: Networks and Trade Associations; Appendix II: Bibliography; Appendix III: Pro Forma Statements. Notes and glossary.

773. Horn, Patricia D., and Horn, Jack C. *Sex in the Office.* Reading, MA: Addison-Wesley, 1982.

The Horns, editors of *Psychology Today,* address the issue of sex in the modern corporation. They discuss sex between equals, exploitive sex, and sexual harassment in the context of the business environment. They conclude that as American companies learn to deal "maturely" with this issue, there will be more romance and less sexual harassment in the workplace. Although the Horns are of the opinion that "Sexual relationships between two consenting adults are none of the company's business," they point out the political and economic consequences of the office romance.

774. Israel, Lee. *Estée Lauder: Beyond the Magic.* New York: Macmillan, 1985.

This unauthorized biography related the story of Estée Lauder, now almost eighty, and the billion-dollar-a-year cosmetics company she founded in 1947. Includes anecdotes about Estée's husband Joe and sons, Ronald and Leonard, and their participation in the Lauder business empire. Includes black and white photographs, notes, and index.

775. Jacobson, Aileen. *Women in Charge: Dilemmas of Women in Authority.* New York: Van Nostrand Reinhold, 1985.

Jacobson studies the problems women experience as authority figures and offers solutions based on the personal stories of women managers in a number of fields. She describes four management styles—authoritarian, democratic, collaborative or team approach, and laissez-faire. Includes references and index.

776. Jensen, Marlene. *Women Who Want to Be Boss: Business Revelations and Success Strategies from America's Top Female Executives.* New York: Doubleday, 1987.

Vice president of the magazine division of Springhouse Corporation, Jensen interviewed twenty-two top American female executives about the lessons they have learned in business. She covers these topics: traits of the successful woman executive, first day on the job, developing a success image, managing the boss, developing allies, how to pick winning employees, when and how to fire, women's management styles, creative selling techniques, employee incentives, sex, starting your own company, and others. Includes index.

777. Lauder, Estée. *Estée: A Success Story.* New York: Random House, 1985.

In a personal style, Estée Lauder tells how she established her successful cosmetics company. In chapter ten, she shares "What I Didn't Learn from Business Schools or Books" and includes what she calls "Lauderisms." The book is full of beauty hints, hostess tips, and personal advice.

778. Leavitt, Judith A. *American Women Managers and Administrators: A Selective Biographical Dictionary of Twentieth-Century Leaders in Business, Education, and Government.* Westport, CT: Greenwood Press, 1985.

The biographies of 226 American women managers, administrators, and leaders are arranged alphabetically and following the biographies are bibliographies by and about the women. Includes appendix, general bibliography, and index.

779. Lipman-Blumen, Jean. *Gender Roles and Power.* Englewood Cliffs, NJ: Prentice-Hall, 1984.
The author discusses "the sex-gender system as a blueprint for all other power relationships." Chapters include "Why the Powerless Do Not Revolt," "Socialization for Gender Roles," "Education and Gender Roles," "Gender Roles and Employment," and "Politics and Gender Roles." Lipman-Blumen concludes with "What Lies Ahead?" Includes name and subject index.

780. Loden, Marilyn. *Feminine Leadership or How to Succeed in Business without Being One of the Boys.* New York: Times Books, 1985.
Loden claims that to adapt to the fundamental changes in American industry, managers must adapt a new leadership style, the style most often employed by women. The flexible style includes concern for people, interpersonal skills, intuitive management, and creative problem-solving. Loden believes the Feminine Leadership Model will include cooperation, team structure, quality output, and an intuitive/rational problem-solving style. It will be characterized by lower control, empathy, collaboration, and high performance standards.

781. Machlowitz, Marilyn. *Inside Moves: Corporate Smarts for Women on the Way Up.* Boulder, CO: Careertrack Publications, 1984.
The author of *Whiz Kids* and *Workaholics,* Machlowitz originally wrote these articles for *Working Woman, Ladies Home Journal,* and *Family Circle* magazines. She starts by debunking ten of the most common career myths. Other topics covered include leadership; workaholism; work, marriage, and divorce; younger bosses; corporate husbands; job interviews; speaking and gaining visibility; managing conflict; corporate training; and leaving a job. Includes bibliography.

782. Marshall, Judi. *Women Managers: Travellers in a Male World.* New York: Wiley, 1984.
Marshall reports on a research study of women in management in the United Kingdom sponsored by the Equal Opportunities Commission. She is addressing women who are reassessing their position in the workplace. The last three chapters are directed to the future. Includes index and lengthy bibliography.

783. McBroom, Patricia A. *The Third Sex: The New Professional Woman.* New York: William Morrow, 1986.
Based on interviews with forty-four professional women in finance who work in New York and San Francisco, McBroom concludes that many women have consciously suppressed their "nurturing role" to achieve success in the masculine/hierarchical workplace. The author surveyed women with children, those who elected not to become mothers, and women who have not made a decision on motherhood. She concludes with a proposal to humanize the workplace by integrating women's values. Includes Questionnaire, extensive notes, bibliography, and index.

784. Missirian, Agnes K. *The Corporate Connection: Why Executive Women Need Mentors to Reach the Top.* Englewood Cliffs, NJ: Prentice-Hall, 1982.
Missirian surveyed 100 top businessmen and conducted fifteen in-depth interviews. She discovered that mentoring was a significant part of female managers' career development and describes the three phases of mentoring as initiation, development, and termination. The final chapter advises women on "What to Do until the Mentor Comes." Includes bibliography and index.

785. Mitchell, Charlene, and Burdick, Thomas. *The Extra Edge: Success Strategies for Women.* Washington, DC: Acropolis Books, 1983.
Mitchell interviewed women who graduated from Harvard Business School in the last fifteen years, asking them questions about their image, style of dress, physical condition, and requirements for success. Readers are asked to answer a forty-point IQ (image quotient) test, followed by advice on "power dressing," skin care, makeup, hairstyles, exercise, and speech. Other topics included in the book are interviewing, self-promotion, entertaining, travel, and executive pregnancy. Includes index.

786. Mitchell, Charlene, and Burdick, Thomas. *The Right Moves: Succeeding in a Man's World without a Harvard MBA.* New York: Macmillan, 1985.
Mitchell and Burdick, authors of *The Extra Edge*, tell executive women how to decipher their company's culture and codes. In Chapter Four they debunk the "seven most prevalent myths about business." The book is organized in three parts: The Corporate Environment, Basic Tactics and Advanced Strategies, and Corporate Brinksmanship. Chapter Fifteen, "Creating Visibility," offers nine strategies for developing positive visibility. Includes subject index.

787. Moore, Lynda L., ed. *Not as Far as You Think: The Realities of Working Women.* Lexington: D.C. Heath, 1986.
From her own research, teaching, training, consulting experiences, Moore concluded that "the barriers are still great for women in the workplace." The contributors to the eleven chapters of this book discuss several internal and external barriers facing women managers working to reach top management positions. Contributors include Rosabeth Moss Kanter and Natasha Josefowitz.

788. Moran, Peg. *Invest in Yourself: A Woman's Guide to Starting Her Own Business.* New York: Doubleday, 1983.
Moran wrote this book after running her own small business and teaching a "Starting a Business" class. The book is organized in five parts with a workbook format. Part V, Resources, lists books (fiction and nonfiction), magazines and newspapers, and organizations.

789. Nierenberg, Juliet, and Ross, Irene S. *Women and the Art of Negotiaton.* New York: Simon and Schuster, 1985.
Nierenberg and Ross present seminars on Women and the Art of Negotiating in the United States and abroad. In this book, they cover the elements of negotiation, negotiating skills, barriers to negotiating with

others, negotiating with difficult people, negotiating personal relationships, and negotiating in the workplace. Includes bibliography and index.

790. Rossman, Marge. *When the Headhunter Calls: A Guide for Women in Management.* Chicago: Contemporary Books, 1981.
The author is president of Women's Inc., a Chicago executive search firm which specializes in finding women for management, technical, and professional positions at salaries of $30,000. She uses stories from her experiences to illustrate points and describes how employment agencies, management recruitment firms, and executive career counselors work. Rossman ends the first several chapters with Checklists for Action. Includes index.

791. Rossman, Marlene L. *The International Businesswoman: A Guide to Success in the Global Marketplace.* New York: Praeger, 1986.
Rossman teaches international marketing at the Graduate School of Business of Iona College, leads seminars for women executives on doing business overseas, and writes and lectures on international trade and women in business. She tells business women how to prepare for careers overseas, claiming that international business is the field for the twenty-first century. She relates five stories of women who have had experience in international business and concludes with projections for women's status in the world marketplace in 2000 A.D. Includes bibliography.

792. Saisho, Yuriko. *Women Executives in Japan.* Tokyo: Yuri International, 1981.
Saisho states "I don't know why, but in Japan there is a prejudice against women in management." She further claims that there are two types of companies: companies that hold the traditional view that women do not possess the same managerial abilities as men and companies that seek to utilize capable women. Saisho advises women to concentrate less on working skills and more on these characteristics: originality; ability to judge, to plan, to manage; and sociability.

793. Scollard, Jeannette Reddish. *No-Nonsense Management Tips for Women.* New York: Simon and Schuster, 1983.
This is an "advice" book for women managers with rules about career planning, entertaining, travel, dress, health, families, job hunting, and working with peers, employees, bosses, and mentors. One chapter is devoted to executive language and explains commonly used financial and political terms. Includes index.

794. Scollard, Jeannette Reddish. *The Self-Employed Woman: How to Start Your Own Business and Gain Control of Your Life.* New York: Simon and Schuster, 1985.
The author of *No-Nonsense Management Tips for Women* counsels women contemplating leaving the corporate hierarchy to start their own businesses, thus joining the 3 to 4 million women business owners in the United States. Scollard offers advice on leaving the corporate job, raising money, hiring employees, forming a partnership, owning a franchise, structuring your company, going public, and selling out or retiring. Includes appendix and index.

795. Senter, Sylvia, with Howe, Marguerite, and Saco, Don. *Women at Work: A Psychologist's Secrets to Getting Ahead in Business.* New York: Putnam Publishing Group, 1982.
More women are qualified for executive and management positions, but their childhood conditioning may be a disadvantage. The authors focus on several problems and offer techniques for achieving self-confidence and the ability to work at your highest level. Take the Behavior Questionnaire on pages forty-nine to sixty to determine your attitudes regarding sexuality, nurturing, organization, passivity, perfectionism, teamwork, risk-taking, competitiveness, assertiveness, giving orders, criticism, rejection, public speaking, and authority figures. Includes subject index.

796. Silver, A. David. *Entrepreneurial Megabucks: The 100 Greatest Entrepreneurs of the Last Twenty-Five Years.* New York: Wiley, 1985.
The author's intent is to explain the process of entrepreneurship by example. His sample of 100 includes eight women. Chapter Four outlines the entrepreneurial process. Includes index.

797. Smith, Mike, et al. *A Development Programme for Women in Management.* Hampshire, England: Gower Publishing Company, 1984.
Smith and colleagues present the University of Manchester Institute of Science and Technology (UMIST) Development Programme for Potential Women Managers. The programme is in six modules. Each module is divided into sessions which are further divided into phases. Each session includes a tutor's text and a participant's text.

798. Stead, Bette A. *Women in Management.* 2d ed. Englewood Cliffs, NJ: Prentice-Hall, 1985.
Stead, professor of business administration at the University of Houston, has updated her 1978 text which is used in colleges and universities in forty-four states and eight countries. This collection of thirty-one articles covers the corporate woman, dual-career families, barriers to job mobility, sexual harassment, networking, moving from secretarial to career positions, and a review of articles from the first edition. Appendices include cases, annotated bibliography, glossary, research tools and laws. Most chapters include notes and/or discussion questions.

799. Van Hulsteyn, Peggy. *What Every Businesswoman Needs to Know to Get Ahead.* New York: Dodd, Mead, 1984.
Business consultant and former owner of an advertising agency, Van Hulsteyn gives businesswomen straightforward and often humorous advice on personal issues, promotions, packaging and power, time management, and "sex and sexism at the office." The final chapter is subtitled "Survival Tips for the Dual-Career Couple." Includes bibliography, notes, and index.

800. Weingand, Darlene E., ed. *Women and Library Management: Theories, Skills, and Values.* Ann Arbor, MI: Pierian Press, 1982.
This collection of twelve essays is a result of a two-day seminar on women in library management held at the University of Wisconsin-Madison campus in September 1981. Major topics of discussion were administrative characteristics, leadership, management development, mentors, planning, sex discrimination, sex-role socialization, supervision,

and the history of women managers. Includes bibliography on women in library management, subject index, and biographical information about contributors.

801. Wilson, Sandi. *Be the Boss: Start and Run Your Own Service Business.* New York: Avon Books, 1985.
Wilson offers succinct advice on running your own business. The 145 tips cover clients, vendors, employees, taxes, money, and "getting more business." Wilson and her partner started their own business in 1980 and earned $350,000 by the third year.

802. Winfield, Fairlee E. *Commuter Marriage: Living Together, Apart.* New York: Columbia University Press, 1985.
The author presents information on dual-career commuter marriages obtained from in-depth interviews with almost sixty spouses in commuter marriages, from 100 questionnaires, from business organizations, and from numerous secondary sources published between 1977 and 1984. Includes bibliograpy and index.

803. Wyse, Lois. *The Six Figure Woman and How to Be One.* New York: Simon and Schuster, 1983.
Lois Wyse, president of Wyse Advertising and winner of several advertising awards, offers women succinct advice on succeeding in a business career. She divides her book into three sections: advice to those women earning $25,000 or less; "the middle ground," or those earning $25,000 to $75,000; and those women earning six-figure salaries.

DISSERTATIONS

804. Azimi Anaraki, Sharareh. "Female Managers: Satisfaction, Motivations and Problems." 1980. 188 p. *Dissertation Abstracts International* 42 (December 1981): 2903-A.

805. Bertrand, Ursula Skarvan. "Personal and Organizational Correlates of Role Stress and Job Satisfaction in Female Managers." 1981. 133 p. *Dissertation Abstracts International* 42 (September 1981): 1051-A.

806. Chusmir, Leonard H. "Sex Differences in the Motivation of Managers: A Look at Need Achievement, Need Affiliation, and Need Power." 1981. 156 p. *Dissertation Abstracts International* 42 (October 1981): 1767-A.

807. Crenshaw, Donna Carole. "Attributions Leading to Career Success and Problems Leading to Career Difficulty as Perceived by Women Managers or Administrators." 1983. 225 p. *Dissertation Abstracts International* 44 (October 1984): 2952-A.

808. Dotlitch, David Landreth. "Worlds Apart: Perception of Opposite Sex Managers in Three Modern Organizations." 1981. 294 p. *Dissertation Abstracts International* 42 (December 1981) 2362-A.

809. Enriquez-White, Celia. "Attitudes of Hispanic and Anglo Women Managers toward Women in Management." 1982. 103 p. *Dissertation Abstracts International* 43 (February 1983): 2512-A.

810. Garrett, Lydia Bahnij. "A Comparison of Personality Characteristics and Coping Strategies between Nurse Managers and Business Women Managers." *Dissertation Abstracts International* 44 (October 1983): 1028-A.

811. Hick, Randall B. "The Effects of Management Styles Assimilating Three Degrees of Client-Centered Counseling on the Description and Evaluation of Male versus Female Managers." *Dissertation Abstracts International* 42 (January 1982): 3073-A.

812. Mack, Renee Vernice Mildred Berry. "Role Conflicts and Coping Strategies of Black Female Corporate Managers and Supervisors." 1983. 295 p. *Dissertation Abstracts International* 44 (February 1984): 2607-A.

813. Miles, Kathleen S. "A Naturalistic Inquiry into the Administrative Behavior of a Top-Level Woman Executive in a Two-Year College." 1985. 269 p. *Dissertation Abstracts International* 46 (April 1986): 2942-A.

814. Moore, Lydia Loftis. "An Analysis of the Internal Career Concepts of Female Middle Managers in the Banking Industry." *Dissertation Abstracts International* 44 (October 1983): 1185-A.

815. Napierkowski, Carol Maria. "Perceptions of Individual Interpersonal Power: A Study of Female Managers." 1983. 245 p. *Dissertation Abstracts International* 44 (October 1983): 991-A.

816. Payne, Mary Martha. "Critical Incidents of Women Managers with a Secretarial Orientation." 1985. 189 p. *Dissertation Abstracts International* 46 (February 1986): 2170-A.

817. Posey, Della Rose. "Skills Which Facilitate and Skills Which Inhibit Career Success for Women in Management as Perceived by Women Managers." 1984. 133 p. *Dissertation Abstracts International* 46 (December 1985): 1756-A.

818. Quinn, Rosemary. "An Examination of Competitiveness in Managers." 1986. 198 p. *Dissertation Abstracts International* 47 (December 1986): 2232-A.

819. Rankin, Jacqueline Annette. "A Description and Comparison of the Nonverbal Behavior of Men School Managers and Women School Managers in Work Settings." 1981. 175 p. *Dissertation Abstracts International* 42 (March 1982): 3831-A.

820. Samuelson, Jo Lynn. "The Relationship between Gender and the Interpersonal Communication Skills of Midlevel Managers in California Community Colleges." 1984. 164 p. *Dissertation Abstracts International* 45 (October 1984): 1008-A.

821. Schlesinger, Phyllis Fineman. "A Study of the Lives of Women Managers at Mid-Career." 1981. 209 p. *Dissertation Abstracts International* 42 (December 1981): 2424-A.

822. Shockley-Zalabak, Pamela Sue. "The Effects of Sex Differences on the Preference for Utilization of Conflict Styles of Managers in a Work Setting: An Exploratory Study." 1980. 213 p. *Dissertation Abstracts International* 42 (July 1981): 21-A.

823. Simpson, Richard E. "The Role of Personal Background and Locus of Control in Career Development and Aspirations of Women Managers." 1986. 187 p. *Dissertation Abstracts International* 47 (November 1986): 1810-A.

824. Vaudrin, Donna Marie. "Factors Contributing to the upward Mobility of Women Managers, and an Exploratory Study of Mentoring and Other Influential Relationships." 1983. 351 p. *Dissertation Abstracts International* 44 (February 1984): 2564-A.

825. Waldo, Karen Raines. "An Examination of Attitudes toward Women as Managers in Public Schools." 1982. 117 p. *Dissertation Abstracts International* 44 (July 1983): 40-A.

ERIC DOCUMENTS

826. Berryman-Fink, Cynthia. "Perceptions of Women's Communication Skills Related to Managerial Effectiveness." Paper presented at the Annual Meeting of the Communication, Language and Gender Conference, Athens, OH, October 1982. 16 p. (ED 227 519)
The author reviews the literature on women in management, followed by a description of a study of communication skills of 101 male and female managers. The respondents felt that women needed training in assertiveness, confidence-building, public speaking/making presentations, and dealing with males. They also felt that women already possess three communication skills necessary for managers: listening, verbal/writing skills, and nonverbal communication skills. Includes tables and references.

827. Eliason, Carol. "Entrepreneurship for Women: An Unfulfilled Agenda." Information Series, no. 221. Columbus, OH: Ohio State University, National Center for Research in Vocational Education. January 1981. 26 p. (ED 199 444) Available from National Center for Research in Vocational Education, Ohio State University, 1960 Kenny Rd, Columbus, OH 43210. $2.35.

Eliason reviews the characteristics and needs of entrepreneurs and the developments in entrepreneurship education, then describes federal programs that support women entrepreneurs and private sector initiatives. She discusses entrepreneurship training and vocational guidance and concludes with a call for additional research on women entrepreneurs. Includes references.

828. Iwao, Sumiko. "Skills and Life Strategies of Japanese Business Women." Paper from the Project on Human Potential, May 8, 1984. 37 p. (ED 254 465)

Iwao describes two successful Japanese businesswomen, one who follows the traditional model and one the modern model. However, both women, one a restaurant owner and one the operator of a veterinary pharmaceuticals firm, exhibit characteristics that are considered traditionally female in Japan: thrift, industriousness, avoidance of conflict, and empathy.

829. Kurchner-Hawkins, Ronnie. "Resources for Women in Management: A Guide to the Literature and an Annotated Bibliography." Southwest Educational Development Lab, Austin, TX. January 25, 1980. 21 p. (ED 190 869)

The author reviews the types of material available on women managers (self-help, factual information, psychology of women, and experimental and case study research), describes the three basic research orientations (research on sex differences, research on sex roles, and research on successful managerial behaviors). The materials included were selected because they were popular and well known, typical of the literature on women in organizations, offer a unique perspective on women in management, and are useful and informative. Lists fifteen books and eight articles.

830. Rossi, Ana, and Todd-Mancillas, William R. "A Comparison of Managerial Communication Strategies between Brazilian and American Women." Paper presented at the Annual Meeting of the International Communication Association, 35th, Honolulu, HI, May 23-27, 1985. May 26, 1985. 31 p. (ED 259 418)

Researchers compared communication strategies of forty Brazilian and American female managers. There were no differences in behavior toward men and women or toward disputes with employees or other managers. The Brazilian women managers were more likely to use power to solve challenges to their authority. Appendices A-D include scripts A-D, Appendices E-G include examples of communication, power, and a combination of the two as predominate response modes. Includes twelve tables and seven references.

831. Sohn, Ardyth B. "A Panel Study of Women Newspaper Managers: Their Goals and Achievement Orientation." Paper presented at the Annual Meeting of the Association for Education in Journalism and Mass Communication, 66th, Corvallis, OR, August 6-9, 1983. September 8, 1983. 23 p. (ED 232 180)

Sohn reports on a three-year longitudinal study of fifty-nine women newspaper managers. Low- to middle-level managers responded to questions about achievement, orientation, and goal-setting abilities. The author concludes that women are willing to "give almost total commitment to the job," and women managers set goals in a vacuum, i.e., they are not working on the requisite steps to reach their goals. Includes tables and references.

832. Stewart, Lea P. "Women in Management: Implications for Communication Researchers." Paper presented at the Annual Meeting of the Eastern Communication Association, Hartford, CT, May 6-9, 1982. 19 p. (ED 217 505)

Stewart addresses four issues regarding women in management: distinguishing highly mobile from less mobile managers; differentiating promotion from advancement; determining the effects of "velvet ghettos"; and determining how communication affects women's management advancement. She reviews the place of women managers in organizations and women's attitudes toward promotion.

833. Sylvan, Donna Landau. "When Manager Not Sex Is Salient: A Limitation to Sex Stereotypes as Barriers to Women in Management." Paper presented at the Annual Meeting of Southeastern Psychological Association, 29th, Atlanta, GA, March 23-26, 1983. 22 p. (ED 237 874)

One-hundred fifteen female and 110 male managers completed the ninety-two item adjective checklist known as the Descriptive Index in order to rate adult males, adult females, successful managers, unfamiliar managers (female or male), and familiar managers (female or male). The researcher concluded that categorization was based on manager not sex or degree of familiarity. Includes references and Appendix A: Adjectives used in the ratings scale. Appendix B: Questionnaire about contact with the manager described.

834. Zubin, Judie. "Developing Women's Management Programs: A Guide to Professional Job Reentry for Women." Available from WEAA Publishing Center, Educational Development Center, 55 Chapel Street, Newton, MA 02160, 1981. 249 p. (ED 217 805)

Zubin describes in detail the Women's Management Development Program (WMDP) at Goucher College to guide other colleges in organizing similar programs. The guide includes sections on project planning, staffing, internships, recruiting, selecting participants, the training course, counseling, time sharing, evaluation, and cost. Appendix: "Women in Management Development Project: A Course Syllabus" for the six-month, twenty-three week training course.

GOVERNMENT DOCUMENTS

835. "A Directory of Federal Government Business Assistance Programs for Women Business Owners: A Small Business Guide." Washington, DC: U.S. Department of Commerce, Economic Development Administration, 1980. 71 p. (C 1.8/3:Sm 1)

836. "Directory of Women-Owned Businesses in Energy-Related and Other Fields: Grouped by Key Words, SIC Codes." Washington, DC: The National Association of Women Federal Contractors, 1982. (268) p. (E 1.49:10108-2)

837. Ebner, Judy. "U.S. Department of Commerce Programs to Aid Women Business Owners." Washington, DC: U.S. Department of Commerce, Office of the Secretary, 1984. 42 p. (C 3.2:W 84/3)

838. "Focus on Survival: Leader's Guide." Washington, DC: U.S. Small Business Administration, Office of Women's Business Ownership, 1984? 73 p. (SBA 1.2:Su 7/2/guide)

839. "Focus on Survival: Workbook." Washington, DC: Office of Women's Business Ownership, 1984? 59 p. (SBA 1.2:Su 7/2/work)

840. "From Homemaking to Entrepreneurship/A Readiness Training Program." Washington, DC: U.S. Department of Labor, Office of the Secretary, Women's Bureau, 1985. 1 vol. various pagings. (L 36.102:H 75/2)

841. "A Guide to Doing Business with the Department of State." Washington, DC: U.S. Department of State, 1986. 1 vol. various pagings. (S 1.40/2:B 96/986)

842. Jones, Effie H. "Women and Minorities in School Administration: Strategies for Making a Difference." New York: ERIC Clearinghouse on Urban Education, 1983. 42 leaves. (ED 1.310/2:237607)

843. Mitchell, Linda S. "For Women, Managing Your Business: A Resource and Information Handbook." Washington, DC?: U.S. Small Business Administration, Office of Women's Business Ownership, 1983. 230 p. (SBA 1.2:W 84/3)

844. Murrell, Patricia H. "The Life Cycles and Career Stages of Senior-Level Administrative Women in Higher Education." Memphis, TN: Memphis State University, 1982. 159 leaves. (ED 1.310/2:219018)

845. "1977 Economic Censuses: Women-Owned Businesses." Washington, DC: U.S. Department of Commerce, Bureau of the Census, 1981. 6 microfiches. (C 3.250:77-1/ch. MF)

846. Norwood, Janet Lippe. "The Female-Male Earnings Gap: A Review of Employment and Earnings Issues." Washington, DC: U.S. Department of Labor, Bureau of Labor Statistics, 1982. 10 p. (L 2.71:673)

847. "Selected Characteristics of Women-Owned Businesses, 1977." Washington, DC?: U.S. Department of Commerce, Bureau of the Census, 1980. 59 p. (C 3.250:77-2)

848. "Surviving Business Crises: Workshop Materials." Washington, DC?: U.S. Small Business Administration, Office of Women's Business Ownership, 1984? 10 p. (SBA 1.2:C 85/3)

849. United States. Congress. House. Committee on Small Business. "National Commission on Women's Business Ownership. H.R. 3832." Washington: U.S. G.P.O., 1984. 73 p. (Y 4.?)

850. United States. Congress. House. Committee on Small Business. "Women's Small Business Ownership Act of 1984: Report." Washington, DC: U.S. G.P.O., 1984-. (Y 1.1/?)

851. United States. Congress. Senate. Committee on Foreign Relations. "Women in Development: Looking to the Future." Washington, DC: U.S. G.P.O., 1984-. (Y 4.F 76/2S.hrg.98-919/pt.2)

852. United States. Congress. Senate. Committee on Small Business. "Federal Contracting Opportunities for Minorities and Women-Owned Businesses." Washington: U.S. G.P.O., 1984. 253 p. (Y 4.Sm 1/2:S.hrg.98-570)

853. United States. Congress. Senate. Committee on Small Business. "Women Entrepreneurs: Their Success and Problems." Washington: U.S. G.P.O., 1984. 98 p. (Y 4.Sm 1/2:S.hrg.98-849)

854. United States. General Accounting Office. "Need to Determine Whether Existing Federal Programs Can Meet the Needs of Women Entrepreneurs." Washington, DC: U.S. General Accounting Office, 1981. 25 p. (GA 1.13:CED-81-90.)

855. "Women along Business Lines." Washington, DC: U.S. Small Business Administration, Women's Business Enterprise Division. Quarterly. (SBA 1.31/2:(date))

856. "Women and Business Ownership: An Annotated Bibliography." Washington, DC: U.S. Department of Commerce, 1986. 174 p. (C 1.54:W 84/corr.)

857. "Women Business Owners: Selling to the Federal Government." Washington, DC: U.S. Small Business Administration, Office of Women's Business Ownership, 1984. 65 p. (SBA 1.2:W 84/4)

858. "Women Business Owners: Selling to the Federal Government." Washington, DC: U.S. Small Business Administration, Interagency Committee on Women's Business Enterprise, 1985. 66 p. (SBA 1.2:W 84/4/985)

859. "Women Owned Business Directory: Iowa, Kansas, Missouri, Nebraska." Washington, DC: Supt. of Docs., U.S. G.P.O., distributor, 1980. 37 p. (GS 1.2:W 84/3)

860. "Women's Business Ownership." Washington, DC: U.S. Small Business Administration, 1986? 1 case (6 sheets) (SBA 1.2:W 84/5)

861. "Women's Handbook: How SBA Can Help You Go into Business." Washington, DC: U.S. Small Business Administration, Office of Management Assistance, 1983. 16 p. (SBA 1.19:W 84/983)

Core Library Collection

Fifty items have been selected for the core collection as most representative of the subjects covered in the extensive body of literature on women in management. The sources, dating from the early 1970s to the present, include books, bibliographies, articles, journals, and a database. Many of the books listed are especially valuable because they contain bibliographies, indices, appendices, and other sources of additional information on the topic of women managers.

BOOKS

862. Brown, Linda Keller. *The Woman Manager in the United States: A Research Analysis and Bibliography.* Washington, DC: Business and Professional Women's Foundation, 1981.

At the time this monograph was published, Brown was director of the Cross-National Project on Women as Corporate Managers at the Center for the Social Sciences at Columbia University in New York City. This excellent survey of the status of women managers in the United States up to 1981 is a must for every collection on women in management. In less than 100 pages, Brown covers the history, current status, stereotypes, and career development of women managers in the United States. In the last chapter she addresses the issue of the dual-career couple. Includes research notes, extensive bibliography, and tables.

863. Cannie, Joan K. *The Woman's Guide to Management Success: How to Win Power in the Real Organizational World.* Englewood Cliffs, NJ: Prentice-Hall, 1979.

Cannie, a high school graduate who started her own company at the age of twenty-four, offers advice on management skills and behavior. She covers leadership style, communication, negotiating, management by objectives, decision making, conflicts, and time management.

864. Carr-Ruffino, Norma. *The Promotable Woman: Becoming a Successful Manager.* Belmont, CA: Wadsworth, 1982.

Carr-Ruffino outlines the personal and management skills the promotable woman should master. In Part I, Developing Personal Skills that Promote Managerial Effectiveness, she discusses goal clarification, stress management, assertiveness, and effective communications; and in Part II, Developing Management Skills, she offers advice on employee motivation, time management, problem solving and decision making, organizing, financial planning, and team building. (See also entry 744.)

865. Collins, Nancy W. *Professional Women and Their Mentors: A Practical Guide to Mentoring for the Woman Who Wants to Get Ahead.* Englewood Cliffs, NJ: Prentice-Hall, 1983.

The author analyzes the results of a questionnaire on mentoring that she mailed to 600 executive women. Four hundred women from the Peninsula Professional Women's Network (San Francisco, San Jose), the Bay Area Executive Women's Forum, and several major United States' cities responded. Collins notes that almost all of the respondents had male mentors and every woman who replied considered the mentor relationship to be positive. Includes appendices, bibliography, and index. (See also entry 746.)

866. Davidson, Marilyn, and Cooper, Cary. *Stress and the Woman Manager.* Oxford: Martin Robertson, 1983.

This book, based on a survey of female managers in the United Kingdom and sponsored by the British Government's Manpower Services Commission, highlights the problems of men and women managers. The authors found that women managers experience more stress from work/home conflicts and thus more psychosomatic symptoms and as a result have a poorer work performance than male managers. Includes index, extensive bibliography, and appendix (Survey Questionnaire). (See also entry 752.)

867. Farley, Jennie, ed. *The Woman in Management: Career and Family Issues.* Ithaca, NY: New York State School of Industrial Relations, Cornell University, 1983.

"Papers and discussion from a conference on Women in Management sponsored by the New York State School of Industrial and Labor Relations at Cornell University, April 1982." Includes selections by Juanita Kreps, Betty Lehan Harragan, and Rosabeth Moss Kanter and essays by eight other women from panel presentations. Chapter 5 is an essay on "Recommended Readings" and is followed by an annotated bibliography of recommended readings. Includes author, title, and subject indexes. (See also entry 757.)

868. Fenn, Margaret. *In the Spotlight: Women Executives in a Changing Environment.* Englewood Cliffs, NJ: Prentice-Hall, 1980.

Fenn focuses on competence, confidence, and credibility as key assets for women managers. She discusses mentors, power, communication, negotiation, organizational conflict, management of change, and risk taking. Summaries of the main points conclude most chapters. Includes bibliography and index.

869. Foxworth, Jo. *Boss Lady: An Executive Woman Talks about Making It.* New York: Crowell, 1978.

Practical advice from an advertising executive on packaging yourself, hiring and firing, working for a woman, business clubs, dual careers, and the Equal Rights Amendment. Foxworth gives do's and don'ts at the end of each chapter. Includes index.

870. Gallese, Liz Roman. *Women like Us.* Morrow, 1985.
Gallese talked to over eighty women of the class of 1975 from the Harvard Business School, the first class where women constituted 10 percent of the enrollment. She interviewed six of the women in depth. Some of the findings of her study and patterns she discovered are that few women appear to plan careers the same way men do; many were ambivalent about their roles as career women, wives, mothers, lovers; and a lack of control exists over their work environment and the direction of their lives. (See also entry 762.)

871. Gerrard, Meg; Oliver, June; and Williams, Martha. *Women in Management.* Austin, TX: University of Texas, 1976.
The proceedings of a conference held at the University of Texas at Austin, May 16-17, 1975, this monograph includes the keynote address and the text of nine panel presentations. The work concludes with descriptions of six work sessions on assertion training, managerial and communication styles, role conflicts, legal rights, and superiors and subordinates.

872. Goffee, Robert, and Scase, Richard. *Women in Charge: The Experiences of Female Entrepreneurs.* London: Allen Unwin, 1985.
The authors state that there is a need for more study of women business owners, because there is a trend toward increased number of women-owned businesses. There are more female entrepreneurs for three reasons: high unemployment, job dissatisfaction, and the development of new technology. Goffee and Scase explore the benefits and difficulties these women face. Includes extensive bibliography and index. (See also entry 764.)

873. Gordon, Francine, and Strober, Myra H., eds. *Bringing Women into Management.* New York: McGraw-Hill, 1975.
This publication was the result of a conference on Women in Management held April 18, 1974, sponsored by the Stanford Graduate School of Business. The ten contributors wrote on institutional barriers, sex differences, law, strategies for bringing women into management, affirmative action, problems, and opportunities. Includes bibliographical references.

874. Harragan, Betty Lehan. *Games Mother Never Taught You: Corporate Gamesmanship for Women.* New York: Warner Books, 1978.
This "classic" advice book is still a best-seller. Harragan advises women managers how to play the game of "corporate politics." She describes and defines the jargon, the symbols, the players, the uniform, and the sex game in the corporate world.

875. Hennig, Margaret, and Jardim, Anne. *The Managerial Woman.* Garden City, NY: Anchor Press/Doubleday, 1977.
This seminal work on women in management is an absolute must for any collection on the topic. The authors analyze the differences between men and women managers and describe the patterns in the lives and careers of twenty-five top women managers. They conclude with suggestions for integrating more women into management. Includes bibliographical references and index.

876. Henry, Fran Worden. *Toughing It out at Harvard: The Making of a Woman MBA.* New York: G.P. Putnam, 1983.
This journal/biography of a woman's first year at Harvard Business School covers classes, study groups, pressures, and sex-role stereotypes. The last two chapters discuss recruiting/interviewing and graduation. (See also entry 770.)

877. Hisrich, Robert D., and Brush, Candida G. *The Woman Entrepreneur: Starting, Financing, and Managing a Successful Business.* Lexington, MA: D. C. Heath, 1985.
The authors give the results of a mail questionnaire to 1,000 United States' women entrepreneurs and the investigation of demographic, sociological, and psychological characteristics of entrepreneurial women. Appendix I: Networks and Trade Associations; Appendix II: Bibliography; Appendix III: Pro Forma Statements. Notes and glossary. (See also entry 772.)

878. Jewell, Donald, ed. *Women and Management: An Expanding Role.* Atlanta, GA: Georgia State University, School of Business Administration, 1977.
This collection of twenty-five addresses, essays, and lectures on women in management cover the changing roles of women in society, the current status of women in management, and suggestions and predictions for the future. Includes footnotes and bibliography.

879. Josefowitz, Natasha. *Paths to Power: A Woman's Guide from First Job to Top Executive.* Reading, MA: Addison-Wesley, 1980.
In her straightforward style, Josefowitz, professor of management at the College of Business Administration at San Diego State University, covers the progressive steps in women managers' careers: preparation, moving in, settling down, women as supervisors, middle-managers, leaders, and top executives. Includes appendices, general bibliography, and index.

880. Kanter, Rosabeth Moss. *Men and Women of the Corporation.* New York: Basic Books, 1977.
This early work by Kanter, chair of Goodmeasure, a management consulting firm, should go on the shelf right next to the works of Brown, Harragan, Hennig and Jardim, and Stead. In this study of the roles of women in corporations, she discusses power and opportunity, behavior in organizations, minorities, and affirmative action. Includes appendices, notes, bibliography, and index.

881. Larwood, Laurie, and Wood, Marion M. *Women in Management.* Lexington, MA: D.C. Heath, 1977.
Larwood and Wood present a statistical portrait of women's employment, salaries, and education. They examine the question of women's suitability for management and suggest way for women to enter management. Includes tables, bibliographies, appendices, and index.

882. Leavitt, Judith A. *American Women Managers and Administrators: A Selective Biographical Dictionary of Twentieth-Century Leaders in Business, Education, and Government.* Westport, CT: Greenwood Press, 1985.

The biographies of 226 American women managers, administrators, and leaders are arranged alphabetically, and following the biographies are bibliographies by and about the women. Includes appendix, general bibliography, and index. (See also entry 778.)

883. Leavitt, Judith A. *Women in Management: An Annotated Bibliography and Sourcelist.* Phoenix, AZ: Oryx Press, 1982.

This annotated bibliography covers the literature on women in management from 1970 to early 1981 and includes over 700 citations to books, papers, newspaper and journal articles, and dissertations. It is arranged in twenty subject categories and includes appendices which list films, periodicals, professional organizations, pamphlets, women's network directories, and other bibliographies. Excellent for research and for collection development.

884. Loden, Marilyn. *Feminine Leadership or How to Succeed in Business without Being One of the Boys.* New York: Times Books, 1985.

Loden claims that to adapt to the fundamental changes in American industry, managers must adapt a new leadership style, the style most often employed by women. The flexible style includes concern for people, interpersonal skills, intuitive management, and creative problem-solving. Loden believes the Feminine Leadership Model will include cooperation, team structure, quality output, an intuitive/rational problem solving style, and will be characterized by lower control, empathy, collaboration, and high performance standards. (See also entry 780.)

885. Lynch, Edith. *The Executive Suite: Feminine Style.* New York: AMACOM, 1973.

Lynch surveyed ninety-five middle- and upper-level management women for this review. She explores myths about women managers, legislation, and the women's movement, and gives advice to those on the way up. Includes appendices ("Quizzes for Women and Men," "Questionnaire Used in the Study," "Report on NOW's Accomplishments," and "Vignettes on the Women Who Participated in the Study") and bibliography.

886. Machlowitz, Marilyn. *Inside Moves: Corporate Smarts for Women on the Way Up.* Boulder, CO: Careertrack Publications, 1984.

The author of *Whiz Kids* and *Workaholics*, Machlowitz originally wrote these articles for *Working Woman, Ladies Home Journal,* and *Family Circle* magazines. She starts by debunking ten of the most common career myths. Other topics covered include leadership; workaholism, work, marriage, and divorce; younger bosses; corporate husbands, job interviews; speaking and gaining visibility; managing conflict; corporate training; and leaving a job. Includes bibliography. (See also entry 781.)

887. Marshall, Judi. *Women Managers: Travellers in a Male World.* New York: Wiley, 1984.
Marshall reports on a research study of women in management in the United Kingdom sponsored by the Equal Opportunities Commission. She is addressing women who are reassessing their position in the workplace. The last three chapters are directed to the future. Includes index and lengthy bibliography. (See also entry 782.)

888. McLane, Helen. *Selecting, Developing and Retaining Women Executives: A Corporate Strategy for the Eighties.* New York: Van Nostrand Reinhold, 1980.
McLane discusses affirmative action and awareness training for management and women and includes chapters on attracting, selecting, developing, and retaining women executives. Includes index, extensive bibliography, and appendices which list federal legislation dealing with sex discriminatin in employment, professional organizations offering assistance to employers, and seminars for and about women in management.

889. Missirian, Agnes K. *Corporate Connection: Why Executive Women Need Mentors to Reach the Top.* Englewood Cliffs, NJ: Prentice-Hall, 1982.
Missirian surveyed 100 top businessmen and conducted fifteen in-depth interviews. She discovered that mentoring was a significant part of female managers' career development and describes the three phases of mentoring as initiation, development, and termination. The final chapter advises women on "What to Do Until the Mentor Comes." Includes bibliography and index. (See also entry 784.)

890. Rossman, Marge. *When the Headhunter Calls: A Guide for Women in Management.* Chicago: Contemporary Books, 1981.
The author is president of Women's Inc., a Chicago executive search firm which specializes in finding women for management, technical, and professional positions at salaries of $30,000+. She uses her experiences to illustrate points and describes how employment agencies, management recruitment firms, and executive career counselors work. Rossman ends the first several chapters with checklists for action. Includes index. (See also entry 790.)

891. Scollard, Jeannette R. *No-Nonsense Management Tips for Women.* New York: Simon and Schuster, 1983.
This is an "advice" book for women managers with rules about career planning, entertaining, travel, dress, health, families, job hunting, and working with employees, bosses, and mentors. One chapter is devoted to executive language and explains commonly used financial and political terms. Includes index. (See also entry 793.)

892. Smith, Mike, et. al. *A Development Programme for Women in Management.* Hampshire, England: Gower Publishing Company, 1984.
Smith and colleagues present the University of Manchester Institute of Science and Technology (UMIST) Development Programme for Potential Women Managers. The program is in six modules. Each module is divided into sessions which are further divided into phases. Each session includes a tutor's text and a participant's text. (See also entry 797.)

893. Stead, Bette A. *Women in Management.* Englewood Cliffs, NJ: Prentice-Hall, 1978.

This is a textbook of articles on aspects of women managers written by leading authorities. Each article includes discussion questions. Appendices include cases, annotated bibliography, glossary, research tools, and laws.

894. Stead, Bette A. *Women in Management.* 2d ed. Englewood Cliffs, NJ: Prentice-Hall, 1985.

Stead, professor of business administration at the University of Houston, has updated her 1978 text which is used in colleges and universities in forty-four states and eight countries. This collection of thirty-one articles covers the corporate woman, dual-career families, barriers to job mobility, sexual harassment, networking, moving from secretarial to career positions, and a review of articles from the first edition. Appendices include cases, annotated bibliography, glossary, research tools and laws. Most chapters include notes and/or discussion questions. (See also entry 798.)

895. Stewart, Nathaniel. *The Effective Woman Manager: Seven Vital Skills for upward Mobility.* New York: Wiley, 1978.

In this early "advice" book, Stewart counsels women managers on planning, coordinating, delegating, evaluating, decision making, time allocating, and developing human resources. Includes appendix and bibliography.

896. Thompson, Ann McKay, and Wood, Marcia Donna. *Management Strategies for Women, or Now that I'm Boss, How Do I Run This Place?* New York: Simon and Schuster, 1981.

A guide for women moving into management, this work includes chapters on power, planning, economics, performance appraisals, effective meetings, and tokenism. Self-evaluation tests help women inventory career choices, identify professional fears, assess management skills, and evaluate financial knowledge. Includes glossary of communication terms.

897. Winston, Sandra. *The Entrepreneurial Woman.* New York: Newsweek Books, 1979.

One of the first authors to discuss women entrepreneurs, Winston describes the six traits that are essential for the potential woman entrepreneur and offers advice on starting your own business. Includes bibliography.

NETWORKING

Though these titles all date fom 1980, they are still useful to women wanting to establish or find networks that will help advance their careers in management.

898. Kleiman, Carol. *Women's Networks: The Complete Guide to Getting a Better Job, Advancing Your Career, and Feeling Great as a Woman through Networking.* New York: Lippincott & Crowell, 1980.
Kleiman defines networking and describes business and professional networks and a number of other types of networks. Chapter 9 provides a list of ten checkpoints to follow when setting up your own network. Chapter 10 lists more than 1,400 national, state, and local women's networks in the U.S.

899. Stern, Barbara S. *Is Networking for You? A Working Woman's Alternative to the Old Boy System.* Englewood Cliffs, NJ: Prentice-Hall, 1980.
This primer on networking defines networks and networking, tells how to organize a network, discusses the difficulties and advantages of publishing a membership directory, addresses questions of membership such as sexual segregation and elitism, and advises when, where, and whether to seek publicity.

900. Welch, Mary S. *Networking: The Great New Way for Women to Get Ahead.* New York: Harcourt, Brace, Jovanovich, 1980.
Welch defines networking and describes twenty-five network success stories. She lists fourteen questions a group should answer before organizing a network and lists thirty-two networking do's and don'ts. Includes appendices, a network directory arranged by state, a reading list, and index.
See also the National Alliance of Professional and Executive Women's Networks, for a list of networks.
See also Appendix I, Networks and Trade Associations, in (entry 772) *The Woman Entrepreneur: Starting, Financing, and Managing a Successful Business* for a list of almost 200 networks and trade associations arranged by state.

JOURNALS

901. *Equal Opportunities International.* Barmarick Publications, Enholmes Hall, Patrington Hull, HU 12 OPR, England, 1981–. (4/year) $165.00.

902. *Executive Female.* National Association for Female Executives. 1041 Third Ave., New York, NY 10021-8110 (212) 371-0740, 1978-. (Bimonthly) $24.00.
Indexed in *Business Periodicals Index, Business Index.*

903. *Savvy: the Magazine for Executive Women.* Family Media, 3 Park Avenue, New York, NY 10016 (212) 340-9200, 1980-. (Monthly) $18.00.
Indexed in *Abstrax, Access, Business Index, Popular Magazine Review.*

904. *Women in Management Review.* Equal Opportunities Commission, Anbar Publications, Ltd., P.O. Box 23, Wembley HA9 8DJ, England, 1985. £25.

905. *Working Woman.* Hal Publications, Inc., 342 Madison Ave., New York, NY 10173 (212) 309-9800, 1976-. (Monthly) $18.00.
Indexed in *Readers Guide, Business Index, Abstrax, Magazine Index, Popular Magazine Review.*

Special Issues of Magazines or Newspapers

906. Brown, Linda Keller. "Women and Business Management." *Signs* 5 (Winter 1979): 266-288.
This lengthy review article on women managers covers career choice, career development, and the availability of women for managerial positions. Includes a profile of the successful woman manager and reviews the current status of women managers.

907. "The Corporate Woman. A Special Report." *The Wall Street Journal.* March 24, 1986. Sec. 4. 1D-28D. The twenty articles in this special report on women managers cover the "glass ceiling," careers, attitudes, minorities, office romance, dual-career couples, advice books, women in industry, women entrepreneurs, and the workplace. Available for $2.00 from Special Publications Department, Dow Jones & Company, Inc., 200 Burnett Road, Chicopee, MA. 01021.

BIBLIOGRAPHIES

908. Bennett, Myrtle C. *Women in Management: A Selected Bibliography.* Monticello, IL: Vance Bibliographies, 1984.
Bennett compiled a list of books, articles, dissertations, and films on the topic of women in management. Most of the materials are from the 1970s, with only a few books and articles from the early 1980s. Available from Vance Bibliographies, P.O. Box 229, Monticello, IL $2.00.

909. Leavitt, Judith A. *Women in Management, 1970–79: A Bibliography. (CPL Bibliographies, No. 35)* Chicago: Council of Planning Librarians, 1980.
A forty-seven-page bibliography listing more than 500 books, newspaper and journal articles, papers, and dissertations on women in management published in the 1970s. Arranged in twenty subject categories. Available for $8.00 from Council of Planning Librarians, 1313 E. 60th St., Merriam Center, Chicago, IL 60637.

910. Pask, Judith M. *The Emerging Role of Women in Management: A Bibliography.* Lafayette, IN: Purdue University, Krannert Graduate School of Industrial Administration, 1976.
Compiled for a seminar held at Purdue in 1976, this 523-item bibliography is limited to women managers in business. Part I is organized by type of publication: bibliographies, dissertations, women's periodicals

and special issues, audiovisual materials, and historical and statistical background. Part II is organized by subject: the changing environment, equal employment opportunity, recruitment and training, the business world, and women managers. Includes author index. ED 132 490.

911. Williams, Martha; Oliver, June S.; and Gerrard, Meg. *Women in Management: A Selected Bibliography*. Austin, TX: University of Texas, Center for Social Work Research, 1977.

Lists over 600 books, articles, and papers arranged in seven categories: women in the work force, legal issues, internal factors, personal-work roles, women as leaders, organizational factors, and organizational and personal change strategies. Each category is introduced by a short essay on the topic. Available from The Center for Social Work Research, School of Social Work, University of Texas, Austin, TX 78712.

912. "Women in Business." Callahan, Geraldine, comp. 1986. Available from Newark Public Library, Business Library, 34 Commerce St., Newark, NJ 07102 $.30.

DATABASE

913. Catalyst Resource on the Workforce and Women. Catalyst Information Center, 250 Park Avenue, New York, NY 10003. Available on the BRS database system. Contact: Susan Barribeau, (212) 777-8900.

A computer database of journal articles, monographs, newspaper articles, pamphlets, papers, government reports and other materials on women's issues, in particular, issues relating to careers and the corporate world. Covers 1963 to the present.

Other Sources of Information

ASSOCIATIONS

Advertising Women of New York (AWNY). 153 E. 57th St., New York, NY 10022 (212) 593-1950.
"Women engaged in an executive or administrative capacity in advertising, publicity, marketing, research, or promotion."

Alliance of Female-Owned Businesses Involved in Construction (AFOBIC). 15195 Farmington Rd., Livonia, MI 48154 (323) 427-8731.
"To promote the acceptance of women-owned firms in the construction field."

American Association of Black Women Entrepreneurs (AABWE). 918 F St., N.W., Suite 312, Washington, DC 20004 (202) 882-5058.
"Black women who own businesses in industries including manufacturing, construction, service, finance, insurance, real estate, retail trade, wholesale trade, transportation, and public utilities."

American Business Women's Association (ABWA). P.O. Box 8728, Kansas City, MO 64114 (816) 361-6621.
"Women in business, including women owning or operating their own businesses, women in professions, and women employed in any level of government, education, retailing, manufacturing, or service companies."

American Entrepreneurs Association (AEA). 2311 Pontius Ave., Los Angeles, CA 90064 (213) 478-0437.
"People interested in business opportunities and in starting profitable businesses."

American Federation of Small Business (AFSB). 407 S. Dearborn St., Chicago, IL 60605 (312) 427-0207.
"Member firms include manufacturing, service, retail, construction, transportation, finance, and farming; individuals are professionals, property owners, resource developers, and self-employed."

American Society of Professional and Executive Women (ASPEW). 1511 Walnut St., Philadelphia, PA 19102 (215) 563-4415.
"To promote through practical information and benefits, a positive attitudinal environment for career women involved in all areas of American enterprise."

Note: Listings are from the *Encyclopedia of Associations*, 19th ed., 1985.

American Women's Economic Development Corporation (AWED). 60 E. 47th St., New York, NY 10165 (212) 692-9100.
"Nonmembership organization for women owning or planning to form small businesses."

Business and Professional Women's Foundation (BPW). 2012 Massachusetts Ave., N.W., Washington, DC 20036 (202) 293-1200.
"Dedicated to improving the economic status of working women through their integration into all occupations."

Canadian Association of Women Business Owners. 69 Sherbourne St., #222, Toronto, ON Canada (416) 364-1223.

Canadian Association of Women Executives. 121 Bloor St. E. Third Floor, Toronto, ON Canada M4W 3M5 (416) 920-1247.

Catalyst. 14 E. 60th St., New York, NY 10022 (212) 759-9700.
"To develop and expand career options for women and to increase corporate awareness of women as a resource."

Coalition of Women in National and International Business (CWNIB). P.O. Box 950, Boston, MA 02119 (617) 739-7388.
"Full members are businesses at least 51 percent female owned and controlled; associate members are businesses less than 51 percent owned and controlled; affiliate members are women interested in owning their own businesses; and general members are men and women supporting the idea of female-owned and controlled businesses."

Cosmetic Executive Women (CEW). 207 E. 85th St., Suite 214, New York, NY 10028 (212) 535-6177.
"Women who have served for more than three years in executive positions in the cosmetic and allied industries."

Executive Women International (EWI). Spring Run Office Plaza, 965 E. Van Winkle, Suite # 1, Salt Lake City, UT 84117 (801) 263-3296.
"Women employed as executive secretaries or in administrative positions."

The Fashion Group (TFG). Nine Rockefeller Plaza, New York, NY 10020 (212) 247-3940.
"Women executives in fashion and allied fields."

Federation or Organizations for Professional Women (FOPW). 1825 Connecticut Ave., #403, Washington, DC 20009 (202) 328-1415.
"Women's professional societies and women's groups concerned with economic, educational, and social equality for women."

Footwear and Accessories Council (FAC). P.O. Box 2337, Grand Central Station, New York, NY 10017 (212) 533-3111.
"Women executives in the footwear, accessories, and allied industries."

National Alliance of Homebased Businesswomen (NAHB). P.O. Box 306, Midland Park, NJ 07432.
"Women of all income levels, occupations, and ages who operate businesses from their homes."

National Alliance of Professional and Executive Women's Networks (TNA). One Faneuil Hall Marketplace, Boston, MA 02109 (617) 720-2874.
"Local networks comprising 4,500 professional and executive women."

National Association for Female Executives (NAFE). 120 E. 56th St., Suite 1440, New York, NY 10022 (212) 371-0740.
"Career women in all phases of business."

National Association of Black Women Entrepreneurs (NABWE). P.O. Box 1375, Detroit, MI 48231 (313) 963-8766.
"Black women who own and operate their own businesses; black women interested in starting businesses."

National Association of Business and Industrial Saleswomen. 90 Corona, Suite 1407, Denver, CO 80218 (303) 777-7257.
"Executive level saleswomen."

National Association of Negro Business and Professional Women's Clubs (NANBPWC). 1806 New Hampshire Ave., N.W., Washington, DC 20009 (202) 483-4206.
"Women actively engaged in a business or a profession who are committed individually, as club affiliates, and as a national organization to render service through club programs and activities."

National Association of Women Business Owners (NAWBO). 500 N. Michigan Ave., Suite 1400, Chicago, IL 60611 (312) 661-1700.
"Women who own and operate their own businesses."

National Business League (NBL). 4324 Georgia Ave., N.W., Washington, DC 20011 (202) 829-5900.
"Promotes the economic development of minorities."

National Federation of Business and Professional Women's Clubs (BPW/USA). 2012 Massachusetts Ave., N.W., Washington, DC 20036 (202) 293-1100.
"Business and professional women representing 300 occupations."

National Forum for Executive Women (NFEW). 1101 15th St., N.W., Washington, DC 20005 (202) 331-0270.
"Women from middle- and top-level management within the savings and loan industry."

Women Entrepreneurs (WE). 2030 Union St., Suite 310, San Francisco, CA 94123 (415) 929-0129.
"Women who actively own and operate a business."

Women Executives in Public Relations (WEPR). 200 Park Ave., Suite 303E, New York, NY 10017.
"Women executives in communications, primarily in public relations."

Women Executives International Tourism Association (WEXITA). 1790 Broadway, Suite 711, New York, NY 10019 (212) 265-7650.
"Female executives from the travel, transportation, tourism, recreation, and leisure industries, as well as travel-related and allied industries."

Women in Management (WIM). P. O. Box 11268, Chicago, IL 60611 (312) 963-0134.
"Support network of women in professional and management positions which facilitates the exchange of experience and ideas."

Women's Economic Round Table (WERT). 866 U.N. Plaza, Suite 4040, New York, NY 10017 (212) 688-9651.
"Businesswomen who question economic policymakers in a public forum; economists, business executives, and unionists."

DIRECTORIES

Albuquerque Women in Business
P.O. Box 6133
Albuquerque, NM 87197
(505) 884-6000
ASPA Women in Public
  Management Directory
  Committee on Women
American Society for Public
  Administration
1120 G. Street, N.W., No. 500
Washington, DC 20005
(202) 393-7878. $5.00
Atlanta Professional Women's
  Directory
250 Spring Street, N.W.
Atlanta, GA 30303
(404) 524-5121. $3.95
Business and Professional Women's
  Directory
12270 S.W. Center #48
Beaverton, OR 97005
(503) 644-7913
Business and Professional Women's
  Directory for Greater Grand
  Rapids
Millie Steketee
2604 Inverness Road, S.E.
Grand Rapids, MI 49506
(616) 949-2094
Business Women Unlimited &
  Riley-Jones, Inc. Directory
Rita Winter
315 E. Charles St.
Muncie, IN 47305
(317) 747-5762
Businesswomen's Directory
13131 Mill Stone Drive
Arlington, TX 78729
(512) 258-8872

Catalyst National Network of
  Career Resource Centers
Catalyst
14 E. 60th St.
New York, NY 10022
(212) 759-9700. Free.
Connecticut Women in Business
Connecticut Department of
  Economic Development
210 Washington Street
Hartford, CT 06106
(203) 566-2567. Free.
Directory of Lancaster County
  Business Women
1655 Manheim Pike
Lancaster, PA 17601
(717) 569-4900
Directory of Woman-Owned
  Construction Contractors and
  Truckers
San Francisco Redevelopment
  Agency
939 Ellis Street
San Francisco, CA 94109
(415) 771-8800. Free.
Directory of Women-Owned
  Businesses
National Association of Women
  Business Owners
500 N. Michigan Avenue, Suite
  1400
Chicago, IL 60611
(312) 661-1700. $10.00 each
  edition.

Directory of Women-Owned
Businesses in Energy-Related
and Other Fields
National Association of Women
Federal Contractors
Box 5543
Washington, DC 20016
(202) 638-3336. $22.00 paper,
$4.50 microfiche.
Indywomen: An Inventory of
Business Skills
Shepard Poorman
Communications
P.O. Box 68110
Indianapolis, IN 46268
(317) 293-1500
Maine Women's Business and
Resource Directory
Women's Development Program
University of Maine at Orono
Aubert Hall, Room 251
Orono, ME 04469
(207) 581-7957. Free.
Minority Business Directory
Black Economic Research Team
Box 13513
Baltimore, MD 21203
(301) 675-6600. $3.00.
National Alliance of Homebased
Businesswomen—Membership
Directory
Box 95
Norwood, NJ 07648
(201) 784-0229. Available to
members only.
National Association for Women
Deans, Administrators and
Counselors—Member
Handbook
1625 I Street, N.W., Suite 624-A
Washington, DC 20006
(202) 659-9330. Controlled
distribution.
National Directory of
Women-Owned Business
Firms
Business Research Services, Inc.
2 E. 22nd Street, Suite 308
Lombard, IL 60148
(312) 495-8787. $95.00

Ohio Women Entrepreneurs
Directory
Small Business Administration
Commerce Department
85 Marconi Boulevard
Columbus, OH 43215
(614) 469-5548. Apply.
Ohio Women in Business
518 E. 305th Street
Willowick, OH 44094
(216) 943-2471
Portland Women's Yellow Pages
14550 S.E. Fairoaks Lane
Milwaukie, OR 97222
(503) 659-9201. $3.95, plus $.60
shipping.
Professional Women's Groups
American Association of
University Women
2401 Virginia Avenue, N.W.
Washington, DC 20037
(202) 785-7772. $2.00, plus $1.00
shipping.
Who's Who of California Executive
Women
International Woman Center
P.O. Box 5293
Santa Cruz, CA 95063-5293.
$125.00 hardback.
Women and Business—A Women's
Business Directory for the
Rocky Mountain Region
Colorado Women and Business
Conference
c/o General Services
Administration
Building 41, Denver Federal
Center
Denver, CO 80225
(303) 236-7447. Free.
Women in Canadian Business and
Finance
Trans-Canada Press, Division
Cardamon Corporation
142-A Dupont Street
Toronto, Ontario M5R 1V2,
Canada
(416) 968-2714. $29.00 Canadian
dollars, plus $1.00 shipping.

Women-Owned Business Directory
for the State of North
Carolina
NC Dept. of Administration
116 W. Jones Street
Raleigh, NC 27611
(919) 733-7232
Women Working Home: The
Homebased Business Guide
and Directory
WWH Press
41 Hampton Road
Scarsdale, NY 10583
(914) 725-3632. $12.95 plus
$1.25 shipping.
Women's Business Enterprise
Directory
National Association of Women
in Construction
Box 181068
Fort Worth, TX 76118
(817) 284-7961. $1.75.

Women's Directory for Johnson
and Linn Counties
330 First Street S.E.
Cedar Rapids, IA 52401
(319) 362-5249
Women's Organizations: A New
York City Directory
New York City Commission on
the Status of Women
52 Chambers Street, Suite 207
New York, NY 10007
(212) 566-3830. $5.95.
Women's Organizations and
Leaders Directory
Triangle Press
National Press Building
Washington, DC 20045
(301) 622-5677. $85.00 (1984
edition)
Women's Work: A Directory of
Greater Boston Professional
Women
P.O. Box 399
Needham Heights, MA 02194
(617) 444-2623

Author Index

Numbers refer to citation numbers, not page numbers.

Title Index

Numbers refer to citation numbers, not page numbers.

Subject Index

Numbers in italic refer to page numbers. All other numbers refer to citation numbers.